## LAPLACE TRANSFORM

| $f(t)$ $\quad t \geq 0$ | $\mathscr{L}[f(t)] = F(s)$ |
|:---:|:---:|
| $A$ | $A/s$ |
| $A\epsilon^{at}$ | $A/(s-a)$ |
| $At^n$ | $An!/s^{n+1}$ |
| $A\cos\omega t$ | $As/(s^2 + \omega^2)$ |
| $A\delta(t)$ | $A$ |
| $2M\epsilon^{\alpha t}\cos(\omega t + \theta)$ | $\dfrac{M\epsilon^{j\theta}}{s - \alpha - j\omega} + \dfrac{M\epsilon^{-j\theta}}{s - \alpha + j\omega}$ |

$$\mathscr{L}\left[\frac{df(t)}{dt}\right] = sF(s) - f(0)$$

$$\mathscr{L}\left[\frac{d^n f}{dt^n}\right] = s^n F(s) - s^{n-1}f(0) - s^{n-2}df/dt\big|_0 - \cdots$$

$$\cdots - sd^{n-2}f/dt^{n-2}\big|_0 - d^{n-1}f/dt^{n-1}\big|_0$$

$$\mathscr{L}\left[\int_0^t f(t)\,dt\right] = F(s)/s$$

## INVERSE OF MATRIX

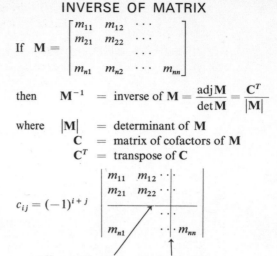

If $\mathbf{M} = \begin{bmatrix} m_{11} & m_{12} & \cdots \\ m_{21} & m_{22} & \cdots \\ & & \cdots \\ m_{n1} & m_{n2} & \cdots & m_{nn} \end{bmatrix}$

then $\quad \mathbf{M}^{-1} = $ inverse of $\mathbf{M} = \dfrac{\text{adj}\,\mathbf{M}}{\det \mathbf{M}} = \dfrac{\mathbf{C}^T}{|\mathbf{M}|}$

where $\quad |\mathbf{M}| = $ determinant of $\mathbf{M}$
$\qquad\quad \mathbf{C} = $ matrix of cofactors of $\mathbf{M}$
$\qquad\quad \mathbf{C}^T = $ transpose of $\mathbf{C}$

$$c_{ij} = (-1)^{i+j} \begin{vmatrix} m_{11} & m_{12} \cdots \vdots \\ m_{21} & m_{22} \cdots \vdots \\ \hline & \cdots \vdots \\ m_{n1} & \cdots \vdots\, m_{nn} \end{vmatrix}$$

strike out the $i$th row and $j$th column

## MASON GAIN RULE

$$T = \frac{\sum P_k \Delta_k}{\Delta}$$

where $\quad T = $ actual transmission gain from *an input node* to *an output node*.

$\qquad \Delta = $ graph determinant, formed by striking out terms containing *products* of touching loops from the expression:

$$(1 - L_1)(1 - L_2)(1 - L_3) \ldots (1 - L_j) \ldots$$
$$= 1 - \sum \text{loop gains}$$
$$+ \sum \text{products of the loop gains two at a time}$$
$$- \sum \text{products of the loop gains three at a time, and so on.}$$

$\quad L_j = $ gain around the $j$th loop

$\quad P_k = $ gain of the $k$th direct path from input to output

$\quad \Delta_k = $ cofactor of the $k$th path, formed by striking out from $\Delta$ all terms containing $L$'s which are touched by the $k$th path.

## SOLUTION OF THE
## TRANSFORMED STATE EQUATION

If $\dot{\mathbf{x}} = \mathbf{Ax} + \mathbf{Bu}$, then $\mathbf{X}(s) = (s\mathbf{I} - \mathbf{A})^{-1}\mathbf{x}(0) + (s\mathbf{I} - \mathbf{A})^{-1}\mathbf{B}\mathbf{U}(s)$
$$= \boldsymbol{\Phi}(s)\mathbf{x}(0) + \mathbf{H}(s)\mathbf{U}(s)$$
$$= \mathbf{X}_{\text{I.C.}}(s) + \mathbf{X}_F(s)$$

## TIME DOMAIN SOLUTION
## OF THE STATE EQUATION

If $\dot{\mathbf{x}} = \mathbf{Ax} + \mathbf{Bu}$, then $\mathbf{x}(t) = \epsilon^{\mathbf{A}t}\mathbf{x}(0) + \epsilon^{\mathbf{A}t}\int_0^t \epsilon^{-\mathbf{A}\tau}\mathbf{Bu}\,d\tau$

where $\epsilon^{\mathbf{A}t} = \mathbf{I} + \mathbf{A}t + \mathbf{A}^2\dfrac{t^2}{2!} + \cdots + \mathbf{A}^n\dfrac{t^n}{n!} + \cdots$

And, if $\mathbf{y}$ is the matrix of outputs,
$$\mathbf{y}(t) = \mathbf{Cx} + \mathbf{Du}$$

## ALGORITHM FOR COMPUTER SOLUTION

If $\dot{\mathbf{x}} = \mathbf{Ax} + \mathbf{Bu}$ and if $\mathbf{u}(t) = \mathbf{u}(kT)$ for $kT \leqslant t < \overline{k+1}T$

then $\quad \mathbf{x}(\overline{k+1}T) = \boldsymbol{\varphi}(T)\mathbf{x}(kT) + \boldsymbol{\Delta}(T)\mathbf{u}(kT)$

where $\quad \boldsymbol{\varphi}(T) = \epsilon^{\mathbf{A}T}$

$$= \mathbf{I} + \mathbf{A}T + \mathbf{A}^2\frac{T^2}{2!} + \cdots + \mathbf{A}^n\frac{T^n}{n!} + \cdots$$

and $\quad \boldsymbol{\Delta}(T) = \epsilon^{\mathbf{A}T}\int_0^T \epsilon^{-\mathbf{A}\tau}\,d\tau\,\mathbf{B}$

$$= \left[\mathbf{I}T + \mathbf{A}\frac{T^2}{2!} + \mathbf{A}^2\frac{T^3}{3!} + \cdots + \mathbf{A}^n\frac{T^{n+1}}{(n+1)!} + \cdots\right]\mathbf{B}$$

STATE VARIABLE ANALYSIS

A PROGRAMMED TEXT

# STATE VARIABLE ANALYSIS

JOHN R. WARD  /  ROBERT D. STRUM

*Department of Electrical Engineering*
*Naval Postgraduate School, Monterey, California*

PRENTICE-HALL, INC., ENGLEWOOD CLIFFS, N.J.

Prentice-Hall International, Inc., *London*
Prentice-Hall of Australia, Pty. Ltd., *Sydney*
Prentice-Hall of Canada, Ltd., *Toronto*
Prentice-Hall of India Private Limited, *New Delhi*
Prentice-Hall of Japan, Inc., *Tokyo*

Current printing (*last digit*):

10   9   8   7   6   5   4   3   2   1

13-843649-5

Library of Congress Catalog Card Number 70-127314

Printed in the United States of America

PREFACE

This program is an introduction to the methods of state variable analysis. It has been designed to lay down a firm foundation for the study of linear systems. To provide direction, and hence motivation, example problems have been drawn from various fields of engineering.

Emphasis has been placed on the manipulation of differential equations (and transfer functions) into state variable form and on the solution of the resulting state equation—utilizing matrix, signal flow graph, and digital computer methods. *The formulation of the state equation directly from the physical system has not been considered*—this can be approached from several points of view, and we feel that the instructor should be free to choose his own method. (One technique is treated briefly in Appendix 3.)

This program is intended for both class and individual self-study. It assumes competence in the application of Laplace transform and signal flow graph techniques. The time needed to complete the program will vary from about 15 to 25 hours—excluding the time taken to perform the digital computer work.

## PROGRAMMED INSTRUCTION

Programmed instruction has much to offer both instructor and student. This is not to say that whole courses should be programmed, but that the programming of certain key concepts and techniques can be mutually beneficial. To the student a program need not be impersonal, and it can offer a flexibility and a degree of interaction which approaches private tutoring. The instructor is provided with a virtual guarantee that all of his students who complete the program will demonstrate mastery of the material treated. He can then proceed to elaboration and application appropriate to the needs of his curriculum with the knowledge that he is building on strength. These benefits stem from the basic characteristics of programmed instruction:

1. The student is required to participate actively throughout. He "learns by doing."

2. The instruction is self-paced. A student progresses in carefully sequenced steps; he cannot start a new topic before he has developed a practiced competence in its prerequisites.

3. The student is provided with a continuous measure of his performance, and a source of assistance is always at hand.

This suggests, intuitively at least, why programmed instruction can be successful—it is geared to the needs and characteristics of the learner.*

At least as important is the fact that the preparation of a program lends itself to the engineering processes of specification, design, test, redesign, and evaluation.† A program is designed to meet given specifications or objectives on the basis of a knowledge of the learning process; it is tested in fine detail in the actual learning environment; shortcomings are corrected; and finally the program is evaluated by comparing student test (exam) results with the original specifications.

## TEACHING FORMAT

A glance at any page of this program will reveal a characteristic sequencing of "question" frames on the left with the corresponding "answers" on the right. The student responds to each frame, checks his answer, and goes to the next frame. A mask is used to conceal the answers until the corresponding responses have been made.

It is worth noting that one great advantage of programs in book format is that they are portable and always available to the student. This is not generally true of teaching machines, carrels, or instructional computer terminals. Further, the book can be retained by the student for later reference, and experience has shown that this is appreciated.

* For a more complete discussion, see B. F. Skinner, *The Technology of Teaching*, (New York: Appleton-Century-Crofts, 1968).

† Norman Balabanian, "The Educational Engineering called Programmed Instruction," *IEEE Trans. on Education* (June 1966).

## ACKNOWLEDGMENTS

The authors claim no originality for the technical content of the program. They are, however, glad to take the responsibility for their arrangement of the material in programmed format. We owe thanks to Professor Maynard Moe at the University of Denver and to several of our colleagues who have either worked through the program or used it in their classes. Their comments have always been helpful. We appreciate the patience of our students, particularly those who worked with the early versions of the program.

JOHN R. WARD / ROBERT D. STRUM
*Monterey* / *Carmel-by-the-Sea*

## TO THE INSTRUCTOR

The basic characteristics and *raison d'être* of programmed instruction have been outlined in the Preface.*  Here the technical aspects of this particular program will be described.

The Table of Contents defines the general scope and organization of the program, while a perusal of the frames referenced therein will establish rapport with the authors' detailed approach to the subject matter.  It has been our intention to introduce the basic techniques of the state variable, while providing suitable practice and insight.  Our long range aim is to prepare the ground for studies in advanced linear (and non-linear) dynamics.

Student prerequisites: Eighteen problems are provided at the beginning of the program to test the student's background.  No student having difficulty with any part of this test should be permitted to continue until the deficiency has been rectified.

Program objectives: A careful and complete specification of objectives is a characteristic of programmed instruction.†  In this sense the program has been designed to develop in

---

* For additional background see:

1. Robert Glaser, ed., *Teaching Machines and Programmed Learning Vol. II; Data & Directions* (Washington, D. C.; National Educational Association, 1965).
2. John P. Dececco, ed., *Educational Technology* (New York: Holt, Rinehart & Winston, Inc., 1965).
3. E. R. Hilgard and G. H. Bower, *Theories of Learning,* 3rd ed. (New York: Appleton-Century-Crofts, 1966).

† Robert F. Mager, *Preparing Instructional Objectives* (Palo Alto, Calif.: Fearon Publishers, 1962).

the student the ability to solve problems such as those in the sample examination at the end of the book. Notice that only linear, time-invariant systems are considered.

Program evaluation: Some two hundred students and a total of six instructors have used this program in a variety of classes and also for self-study review. Program revisions have been based on analyses of student responses (and comments) in the program itself, on exam performances, and on formal observations of student attitudes. The outcome is a program in which the student error rate will normally be well under 10% (excluding errors of algebraic carelessness). Further, at least 80% of a class can be expected to score 85% or more in a test such as the one at the end of the program, and the remaining 20% should score over 75%. This assumes, of course, that the students have performed acceptably in the test of prerequisites, have been given adequate time to complete the program, and have made an honest attempt to work through the program.

## SUGGESTIONS FOR CLASS USE

A safe procedure is simply to ask the students to work through the program. No special comments or instructions are needed, except possibly in relation to the use of the digital computer, as discussed below.

The authors suggest that about two weeks of class meetings be cancelled while the program is being worked. The students may require additional time to complete the digital computer assignments. *Their work will be greatly facilitated if you can arrange for your Computer Center to place SUBROUTINE FIDEL, together with its supporting subroutines, on their FORTRAN library file—see Appendix 1.*

It is recommended that a test be given as soon as possible after the program has been completed. This test may be along the lines of the sample included herein. In every case care must be taken to test *only* those skills developed by the program. Questions seeking, perhaps, to "separate the men from the boys" may easily destroy the whole spirit of programmed instruction. The students are told implicitly that they will *not* be asked to recall any result, identity, comment, or technique which they have not *practiced* in the program.

Finally, the students should be made aware of the following:

1. The class period by which the program is to be completed;

2. The times when the instructor will be available to answer questions; and

3. The class period during which they will be required to work the final test.

*Since the program does* not *discuss the writing of state equations directly from the corresponding physical systems, it is suggested that this topic be taken up as soon as the program—and exam— have been completed. Alternatively, this topic may be discussed when Section 12 of the program has been completed. Appendix 3 may be helpful in this regard.*

CONTENTS

```
┌─────────────────┐
│                 │
│  THE PROGRAM    │
│  STARTS HERE    │
│                 │
└─────────────────┘
```

## TO THE STUDENT

This programmed book has been designed to make your study as efficient and interesting as possible. It will certainly require concentrated effort on your part, but you *will* learn all that is expected of you *if* you play the game according to the rules. Because of the concentration demanded, we suggest that you do not work for more than an hour at a time. Good luck!

We will start out with a quick test of your prerequisites. This should not take you more than 25 to 50 minutes and it will help you get used to working in the program. *Don't* skip it, *please*.

First, TEAR OUT THE MASK (which is inside the front cover) AND SLIP IT UNDER THIS PAGE (with the Laplace transform data facing you).

Then, TURN THE PAGE.

The answers to the questions below are under the MASK opposite.

## PROBLEM 1

The equation $2\dfrac{d^2y(t)}{dt^2} + 6\dfrac{dy(t)}{dt} + 4y(t) = 10g(t)$ is of _____ order in $y(t)$.

SLIDE THE MASK DOWN LEVEL WITH THE LINE AND CHECK YOUR ANSWER.

## PROBLEM 2

The equation $2\dfrac{dy}{dt} + 6y + 4\displaystyle\int_0^t y\,dt = 5f(t)$ is of _____ order in $y$.

LAPLACE TRANSFORM the equation, using information on the MASK as needed.

SLIDE THE MASK DOWN AGAIN TO CHECK YOUR ANSWER.

## PROBLEM 3

SOLVE for $Y(s)$ in the above transformed equation, given that $y(0) = 0$.

second order in $y(t)$—the order of the highest derivative of $y$.

LEAVE THE MASK WHERE IT IS AND ANSWER PROBLEM 2.

---

second order in $y(t)$

(The given "integro-differential" equation must be differentiated to turn it into a differential equation:

$$2\frac{d^2y}{dt^2} + 6\frac{dy}{dt} + 4y = 5\frac{df(t)}{dt}$$

This is clearly second order in $y$.)

The initial condition—value of $y(t)$ when $t = 0$.

$$2\{sY(s) - y(0)\} + 6Y(s) + \frac{4Y(s)}{s} = 5F(s)$$

NOW, GO TO PROBLEM 3.

---

$$\left\{2s + 6 + \frac{4}{s}\right\}Y(s) = 5F(s)$$

$$(s^2 + 3s + 2)Y(s) = 2.5sF(s)$$

$$\text{or } Y(s) = \frac{2.5sF(s)}{s^2 + 3s + 2} \quad \text{or equivalent}$$

AGAIN, INSERT THE MASK BEHIND THIS PAGE.

THEN, TURN THE PAGE.

---

## PROBLEM 4

Given $Y(s) = \dfrac{2.5sF(s)}{s^2 + 3s + 2}$ and $f(t) = 2$, FIND $y(t)$.

## PROBLEM 5

Given $V(s) = \dfrac{-2(s + 4)}{(s + 1)^2(s + 2)}$, FIND $v(t)$.

## PROBLEM 6

If $\delta(t)$ represents a unit delta (impulse) function at $t = 0$, $\mathcal{L}[6\delta(t)] = $ _____

$$Y(s) = \frac{2.5s(2/s)}{s^2 + 3s + 2} = \frac{5}{(s+1)(s+2)} = \frac{A}{s+1} + \frac{B}{s+2}$$

$$A = \left.\frac{5\cancel{(s+1)}}{\cancel{(s+1)}(s+2)}\right|_{s=-1} = 5$$

$$B = \left.\frac{5\cancel{(s+2)}}{(s+1)\cancel{(s+2)}}\right|_{s=-2} = -5$$

$$\therefore \quad Y(s) = \frac{5}{s+1} - \frac{5}{s+2}$$

and $\underline{y(t) = 5\epsilon^{-t} - 5\epsilon^{-2t}} \qquad t \geq 0$

---

$$V(s) = \frac{A}{(s+1)^2} + \frac{B}{s+1} + \frac{C}{s+2}$$

$$A = \left.\frac{-2(s+4)\cancel{(s+1)^2}}{\cancel{(s+1)^2}(s+2)}\right|_{s=-1} = \frac{-2(3)}{1} = -6 \qquad \text{(we must find } A \text{ before solving for } B\text{)}.$$

$$B = \left\{\frac{-2(s+4)(s+1)}{(s+1)^2(s+2)} - \frac{A\cancel{(s+1)}}{(s+1)^{\cancel{2}}}\right\}\Bigg|_{s=-1} \qquad \text{(where } A \text{ is now known)}$$

$$= \left.\frac{-2s - 8 + 6s + 12}{(s+1)(s+2)}\right|_{s=-1} = \left.\frac{4\cancel{(s+1)}}{\cancel{(s+1)}(s+2)}\right|_{s=-1} = 4$$

and $\quad C = \left.\dfrac{-2(s+4)\cancel{(s+2)}}{(s+1)^2\cancel{(s+2)}}\right|_{s=-2} = \dfrac{-2(2)}{(-1)^2} = -4$

$$\therefore \quad \underline{v(t) = -6t\epsilon^{-t} + 4\epsilon^{-t} - 4\epsilon^{-2t}} \qquad t \geq 0$$

(Any legitimate method for finding partial fraction constants is acceptable.)

---

$\mathcal{L}[6\delta(t)] = \underline{6}$

KEEP MOVING THE MASK AHEAD AS YOU FINISH EACH PAGE.

## PROBLEM 7

If you solved a first order differential equation in $x(t)$ and found

$$X(s) = \frac{x(0)}{s + 4} + \frac{2U(s)}{s + 4}$$

Then the initial condition (I.C.) solution—due to $x(0)$—would be

$$x_{\text{I.C.}}(t) = \underline{\hspace{3cm}}$$

and the forced solution, due to the input $u(t) = 4$, would be

$$x_F(t) = \underline{\hspace{3cm}} \qquad \text{(you may need to do some calculation.)}$$

---

## PROBLEM 8

SOLVE $\left. \begin{array}{l} (s + 20)X(s) - 10Y(s) = \dfrac{100}{s} \\[2mm] - 10X(s) + (s + 20)Y(s) = 0 \end{array} \right\}$  for $X(s)$, using Cramer's rule

---

## PROBLEM 9

COMPLETE the signal flow graph corresponding to the equation:

$$0.5\{sI(s) - i(0)\} + 2I(s) = V(s)$$

$\circ\ i(0)$

$\underset{V(s)}{\circ} \qquad\qquad \underset{sI(s)}{\circ}\!\longrightarrow\!\underset{I(s)}{\circ}$

---

$$X(s) = X_{\text{I.C.}}(s) + X_F(s)$$

$$= \frac{x(0)}{s + 4} + \frac{8}{s(s + 4)}$$

$$x_{\text{I.C.}}(t) = \mathscr{L}^{-1}\left[\frac{x(0)}{s + 4}\right] = \underline{x(0)\epsilon^{-4t}} \qquad t \geqslant 0$$

$$x_F(t) = \mathscr{L}^{-1}\left[\frac{8}{s(s + 4)}\right] = \underline{2 - 2\epsilon^{-4t}} \qquad t \geqslant 0$$

$\llcorner$ forced (due to input)

---

$$X(s) = \frac{\begin{vmatrix} 100/s & -10 \\ 0 & s + 20 \end{vmatrix}}{\begin{vmatrix} s + 20 & -10 \\ -10 & s + 20 \end{vmatrix}} = \frac{100(s + 20)/s}{(s + 20)(s + 20) - 100}$$

$$= \frac{100(s + 20)}{s(s^2 + 40s + 300)} \qquad \text{or equivalent}$$

---

Rearranging,

$$sI(s) = i(0) - 4I(s) + 2V(s)$$

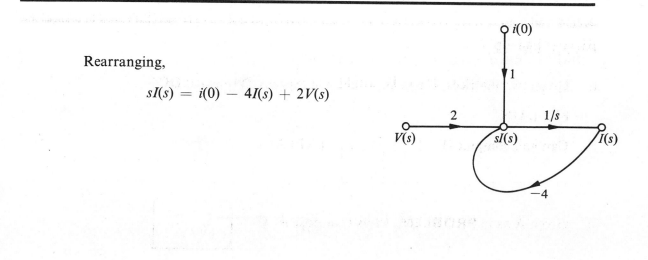

**PROBLEM 10**

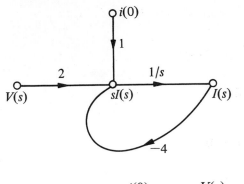

Use the Mason gain rule
(see MASK) to FIND $I(s)$.

*Answer:* $I(s) = \dfrac{i(0)}{\phantom{xxxx}} + \dfrac{V(s)}{\phantom{xxxx}}$

---

**PROBLEM 11**

Given $\mathbf{A} = \begin{bmatrix} 1 & 2 \\ 3 & 4 \end{bmatrix}$, $\mathbf{B} = \begin{bmatrix} 1 & 2 \\ 3 & 4 \end{bmatrix}$, and $\mathbf{X} = \begin{bmatrix} -2 & 1 \\ \frac{3}{2} & -\frac{1}{2} \end{bmatrix}$

$\mathbf{A} + \mathbf{B} = \begin{bmatrix} \phantom{xxxxx} \end{bmatrix}$, $\mathbf{A} - \mathbf{B} = \begin{bmatrix} \phantom{xxxxx} \end{bmatrix}$, and $\mathbf{AX} = \begin{bmatrix} \phantom{xxxxx} \end{bmatrix}$

(We will use boldface letters to represent matrices.)

---

**PROBLEM 12**

a.  Given two matrices, $\mathbf{C}$ and $\mathbf{D}$, would you expect $\mathbf{CD}$ to equal $\mathbf{DC}$?

   EXPLAIN.

b.  Can you compute $\begin{bmatrix} 1 & 2 & 3 \end{bmatrix} \begin{bmatrix} 1 & 2 \\ 3 & 4 \end{bmatrix}$? EXPLAIN.

c.  Given $\mathbf{A}$ as in **PROBLEM 11** its transpose is $\mathbf{A}^T = \begin{bmatrix} \phantom{xxxxx} \end{bmatrix}$

---

$$\Delta(\text{graph determinant}) = 1 - \frac{-4}{s} = \frac{s+4}{s}$$

from $i(0)$ to $I(s)$:

$$P_1 = \frac{1}{s} \text{ and } \Delta_1 = 1$$

$$T_1 = \frac{P_1\Delta_1}{\Delta} = \frac{(1/s)(1)}{(s+4)/s}$$

$$= \frac{1}{s+4}$$

from $V(s)$ to $I(s)$:

$$P_1 = \frac{2}{s} \text{ and } \Delta_1 = 1$$

$$T_1 = \frac{P_1\Delta_1}{\Delta} = \frac{(2/s)(1)}{(s+4)/s}$$

$$= \frac{2}{s+4}$$

$$\therefore \quad I(s) = \underline{\frac{i(0)}{s+4}} + \underline{\frac{2V(s)}{s+4}}$$

---

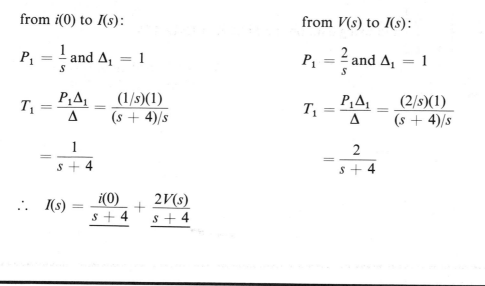

$$\mathbf{A} + \mathbf{B} = \begin{bmatrix} 1+1 & 2+2 \\ 3+3 & 4+4 \end{bmatrix} = \begin{bmatrix} 2 & 4 \\ 6 & 8 \end{bmatrix} \text{ and } \mathbf{A} - \mathbf{B} = \begin{bmatrix} 0 & 0 \\ 0 & 0 \end{bmatrix}$$

called the null matrix and written **O**

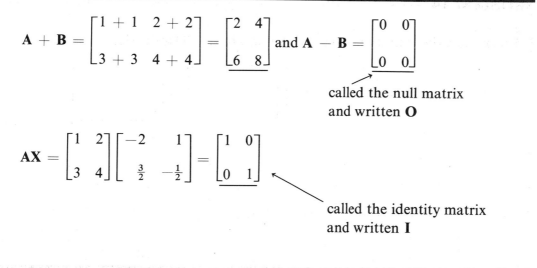

$$\mathbf{AX} = \begin{bmatrix} 1 & 2 \\ 3 & 4 \end{bmatrix} \begin{bmatrix} -2 & 1 \\ \frac{3}{2} & -\frac{1}{2} \end{bmatrix} = \begin{bmatrix} 1 & 0 \\ 0 & 1 \end{bmatrix}$$

called the identity matrix and written **I**

---

a. No—the order of a matrix product must be preserved except in some very special cases.

b. No—the matrices must be conformable (i.e., the first matrix must have the same number of columns as the second has rows).

c. $\mathbf{A}^T = \begin{bmatrix} 1 & 3 \\ 2 & 4 \end{bmatrix}$

**PROBLEM 13**

Given $\mathbf{A} = \begin{bmatrix} 1 & 2 \\ 3 & 4 \end{bmatrix}$ and using data on the MASK, FIND $\mathbf{A}^{-1}$.

---

**PROBLEM 14**

If $\mathbf{I}$ represents the identity matrix, and $\mathbf{A}$ is as above, COMPUTE:

$$\mathbf{IA} = \begin{bmatrix} & \\ & \end{bmatrix}\begin{bmatrix} & \\ & \end{bmatrix} = \begin{bmatrix} \underline{\quad\quad} \\ \underline{\quad\quad} \end{bmatrix}$$

---

**PROBLEM 15**

WRITE the following equations in matrix form:

$$3x_1 + 2x_3 = 5$$
$$x_2 + 2x_3 = 2$$
$$x_1 - 2x_2 + 3x_3 = 4$$

*Answer:*

$$\begin{bmatrix} & \\ & \end{bmatrix}\begin{bmatrix} \\ \end{bmatrix} = \begin{bmatrix} \\ \end{bmatrix}$$

---

From the MASK

$$\mathbf{C} = \begin{bmatrix} 4 & -3 \\ -2 & 1 \end{bmatrix}$$

*Note:*
When *you* write a matrix, such as **C**, you should use a wavy underscore to show that it *is* a matrix. Thus: $\underset{\sim}{C}$

and $\mathbf{A}^{-1} = \dfrac{\text{adj } \mathbf{A}}{\det \mathbf{A}} = \dfrac{\mathbf{C}^T}{|\mathbf{A}|} = \dfrac{\begin{bmatrix} 4 & -2 \\ -3 & 1 \end{bmatrix}}{4-6} = \begin{bmatrix} -2 & 1 \\ \frac{3}{2} & -\frac{1}{2} \end{bmatrix}$

*Comment:*

As a check, you can easily show that $\mathbf{A}\mathbf{A}^{-1} = \mathbf{A}^{-1}\mathbf{A} = \begin{bmatrix} 1 & 0 \\ 0 & 1 \end{bmatrix} = \mathbf{I}.$

---

$$\mathbf{IA} = \begin{bmatrix} 1 & 0 \\ 0 & 1 \end{bmatrix} \begin{bmatrix} 1 & 2 \\ 3 & 4 \end{bmatrix} = \begin{bmatrix} 1 & 2 \\ 3 & 4 \end{bmatrix}$$

the identity matrix must be chosen so that **IA** is a conformable product

*Comment:*
In general $\mathbf{IA} = \mathbf{AI} = \mathbf{A}.$

---

$$\begin{bmatrix} 3 & 0 & 2 \\ 0 & 1 & 2 \\ 1 & -2 & 3 \end{bmatrix} \begin{bmatrix} x_1 \\ x_2 \\ x_3 \end{bmatrix} = \begin{bmatrix} 5 \\ 2 \\ 4 \end{bmatrix}$$

*Comment:*
This matrix equation is of the form $\mathbf{Ax} = \mathbf{B}.$

## PROBLEM 16

Given the matrix equation $\mathbf{Py} = \mathbf{Q}$, SOLVE for $\mathbf{y}$:

---

## PROBLEM 17

$$\text{Given } \mathbf{R} = \begin{bmatrix} t & \sin \omega t \\ 0 & t^2 \end{bmatrix}, \quad \frac{d\mathbf{R}}{dt} = \begin{bmatrix} & \\ & \end{bmatrix}$$

*Hint:*
Differentiate each element.

---

## PROBLEM 18

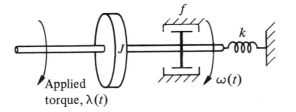

Applied torque, $\lambda(t)$

$\omega(t)$

In terms of the shaft's angular velocity, $\omega(t)$, the differential equation for this system is:

$$J\frac{d\omega}{dt} + f\omega + k\int_0^t \omega dt + T_0 = \lambda(t)$$

where $T_0$ is the initial spring torque, and $\omega(0)$ is the initial angular shaft velocity.

TRANSFORM the equation and then DETERMINE the transfer function
$H(s) = \Omega_F(s)/\Lambda(s)$
Here $\Omega_F(s)$ is the transform of the *forced* output—due to the input, $\lambda(t)$, alone.

Premultiplying by $\mathbf{P}^{-1}$

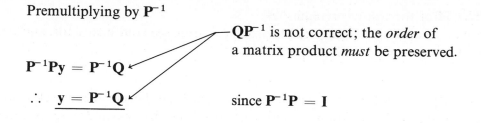

$\mathbf{QP}^{-1}$ is not correct; the *order* of a matrix product *must* be preserved.

$$\mathbf{P}^{-1}\mathbf{Py} = \mathbf{P}^{-1}\mathbf{Q}$$

$$\therefore \quad \underline{\mathbf{y} = \mathbf{P}^{-1}\mathbf{Q}} \qquad \text{since } \mathbf{P}^{-1}\mathbf{P} = \mathbf{I}$$

Don't forget to indicate matrices by a wavy underscore.

Differentiating each element in $\mathbf{R}$ with respect to time:

$$\frac{dR}{dt} = \begin{bmatrix} 1 & \omega\cos\omega t \\ 0 & 2t \end{bmatrix}$$

Set the I.C.'s to zero to find the *forced* response

$$J\{s\Omega(s) - \omega(0)\} + f\Omega(s) + \frac{k}{s}\Omega(s) + \frac{T_0}{s} = \Lambda(s)$$

$$\left(sJ + f + \frac{k}{s}\right)\Omega_F(s) = \Lambda(s)$$

$$\therefore \quad H(s) = \frac{\Omega_F(s)}{\Lambda(s)} = \frac{(1/J)s}{s^2 + \frac{f}{J}s + \frac{k}{J}} \quad \text{or equivalent}$$

*Comment:*
The transfer function is defined to be:

$$\frac{\text{transform of } \textit{forced} \text{ output}}{\text{transform of input}}$$

where the forced response is that due only to the input—with the initial conditions zero.

That is the end of the test of prerequisites.

If you have had trouble solving *any* of the problems, *stop*, see your instructor, and/or review the topic which caused your difficulty.

The rest of the program follows a similar pattern—work on the left, then check your results on the right. If many of the "frames" seem easy, don't use this as an excuse to skip ahead; the sequencing is critical. If, on the other hand, the frames seem difficult and you find yourself making a lot of errors, *stop*, and see your instructor. (Not counting errors due to carelessness, you should not make more than one error in every ten frames or so.)

If you work through the program in the prescribed manner, you *will* learn all that is expected of you. Trust the program; it will give you adequate practice in all the important techniques, and it will provide you with periodic review. In addition, you will have the opportunity to test yourself by completing a sample exam.

---

### GROUND RULES

1. Work sequentially, do *not* skip or browse.
   (You may refer *back* to earlier frames at any time.)
2. *Always write* down your answer *before* you look under the mask.
   (*If* you are *completely* "stuck," don't hesitate to look at the answer for help.)
3. If your answer is wrong, partially wrong, or incomplete, or if you needed help,
   (a) Mark the frame with an "X" in the box provided; and
   (b) Correct or complete your answer with a red pencil or the equivalent.
   (This will help you track down difficulties when you review your work.)

---

SLIP THE MASK UNDER THE PAGE OPPOSITE, AND CONTINUE TO READ.

## PREVIEW

The advent of the digital computer has stimulated a more systematic approach to problem solving in many fields. The study of dynamic systems, for example, is now based on a system's "state equations." These are of the form

$$\frac{dx_1}{dt} = f_1(x_1, x_2, \ldots, x_n, u_1, u_2, \ldots, u_m, t)$$

$$\frac{dx_2}{dt} = f_2(x_1, x_2, \ldots, x_n, u_1, u_2, \ldots, u_m, t)$$

and so on, for a total of $n$ equations, where $n$ is the order of the system. That is, the equations are always written in simultaneous *first order* form, which we will see later is well suited to computer solution. The $n$ variables, $x_1, x_2, \ldots, x_n$ are called the "state variables," since they completely define the state of a system at any instant. The $u$'s are inputs to the system, and $t$ is the independent variable.

The first section of this program is mostly a review of needed techniques. In Section 2 we will introduce the state variable concept, and at the end of that section, we will be in a better position to discuss the overall content and aim of the program.

You can expect to take from 20 to 40 minutes working through Section 1.

## A VIBRATING MACHINE

**1.1**

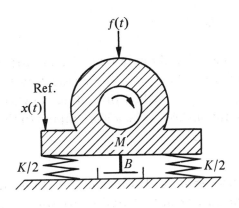

Here an unbalanced rotary machine will be subject to vertical vibration due to the vertical component, $f(t)$, of the out-of-balance force.

If we choose the reference so that the spring force is zero when $x(t) = 0$, then

$$M\frac{d^2x(t)}{dt^2} + B\frac{dx(t)}{dt} + Kx(t) = Mg + f(t)$$

The first move in state variable analysis is to put the system's equations into *simultaneous first order* form. The simplest way to do this here is to define a new—and obvious—variable, the velocity $v(t)$. That is:

$$\frac{dx(t)}{dt} = v(t) \tag{1}$$

Now, SUBSTITUTE for $d^2x(t)/dt^2$ and $dx(t)/dt$ in the system equation, and then REARRANGE to obtain $dv(t)/dt$ in terms of $x(t)$ and $v(t)$:

*Answer:* $\dfrac{dv(t)}{dt} =$ _____ (2)

*Comment:*

The derivation of a system's equation(s) from the physics of the situation is *not* a part of this program—although this topic is introduced in Appendix 3.

$$\frac{d^2x(t)}{dt^2} = \frac{dv(t)}{dt}$$

$$\therefore \quad M\frac{dv(t)}{dt} + Bv(t) + Kx(t) = Mg + f(t)$$

$$\text{or } \frac{dv(t)}{dt} = \frac{-B}{M}v(t) - \frac{K}{M}x(t) + \frac{1}{M}f(t) + g$$

**1.2**  We found that we could rewrite our system equations in the following first order form:

$$\frac{dx(t)}{dt} = v(t) \tag{1}$$

$$\frac{dv(t)}{dt} = -\frac{K}{M}x(t) - \frac{B}{M}v(t) + \frac{1}{M}f(t) + g \tag{2}$$

You should have no difficulty putting these equations into matrix form:

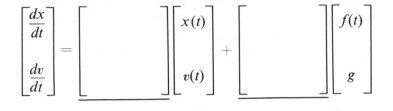

**1.3**  One way of solving the above equations is to use the normal techniques of the Laplace transform. First, TRANSFORM equations (1) and (2), taking the initial condition terms onto the right-hand side of the equations:

$sX(s) = $ _____ (1a)

$sV(s) = $ _____ (2a)

$$\begin{bmatrix} \dfrac{dx}{dt} \\[2ex] \dfrac{dv}{dt} \end{bmatrix} = \begin{bmatrix} 0 & 1 \\[2ex] \dfrac{-K}{M} & \dfrac{-B}{M} \end{bmatrix}\begin{bmatrix} x(t) \\[2ex] v(t) \end{bmatrix} + \begin{bmatrix} 0 & 0 \\[2ex] \dfrac{1}{M} & 1 \end{bmatrix}\begin{bmatrix} f(t) \\[2ex] g \end{bmatrix}$$

*Notes:*

1. These are "state equations"—being in simultaneous *first order* form.

2. Later in the program we will show how to solve these equations directly in the time domain. Here we will review Laplace transform methods of solution.

---

$$sX(s) = \underline{x(0) + V(s)}$$

transform of the
constant, $g$

$$sV(s) = v(0) - \frac{K}{M}X(s) - \frac{B}{M}V(s) + \frac{g}{s} + \frac{1}{M}F(s)$$

*Comment:*

Note that the equations are in an appropriate form for signal flow graph (S.F.G.) representation—see, for example, **PROBLEM 9** in the test of prerequisites.

---

**1.4**     The transformed equations were

$$sX(s) = x(0) + V(s)$$

$$sV(s) = v(0) - \frac{K}{M}X(s) - \frac{B}{M}V(s) + \frac{g}{s} + \frac{1}{M}F(s)$$

DRAW the corresponding signal flow graph (S.F.G.):

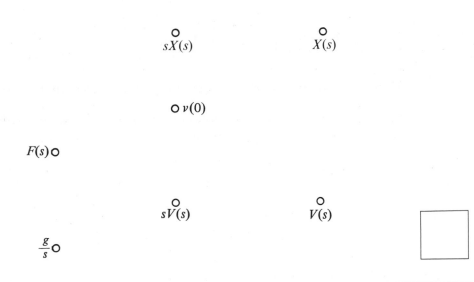

⊙ $x(0)$

⊙ $sX(s)$          ⊙ $X(s)$

⊙ $v(0)$

$F(s)$⊙

⊙ $sV(s)$          ⊙ $V(s)$

$\frac{g}{s}$⊙

---

**1.5**     We know that:

$$X(s) = T_1 x(0) + T_2 v(0) + T_3 F(s) + T_4 \frac{g}{s}$$

and     $$V(s) = T_5 x(0) + T_6 v(0) + T_7 F(s) + T_8 \frac{g}{s}$$

where, for example, $T_1$ is the transmission gain between the nodes ____ and ____ in the S.F.G.

---

**1.6**     Now WRITE these equations in matrix form:

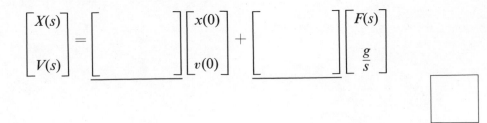

$$\begin{bmatrix} X(s) \\ V(s) \end{bmatrix} = \begin{bmatrix} \quad \\ \quad \end{bmatrix} \begin{bmatrix} x(0) \\ v(0) \end{bmatrix} + \begin{bmatrix} \quad \\ \quad \end{bmatrix} \begin{bmatrix} F(s) \\ \frac{g}{s} \end{bmatrix}$$

---

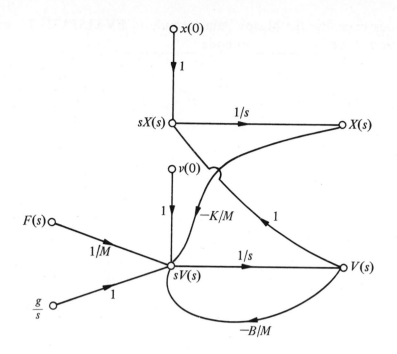

---

$T_1$ is the transmission gain between $\underline{x(0)}$ and $\underline{X(s)}$

---

$$\begin{bmatrix} X(s) \\ \\ V(s) \end{bmatrix} = \begin{bmatrix} T_1 & T_2 \\ \\ T_5 & T_6 \end{bmatrix} \begin{bmatrix} x(0) \\ \\ v(0) \end{bmatrix} + \begin{bmatrix} T_3 & T_4 \\ \\ T_7 & T_8 \end{bmatrix} \begin{bmatrix} F(s) \\ \\ \frac{g}{s} \end{bmatrix}$$

---

**1.7**  Referring to the previous page, use the Mason gain formula to EVALUATE $T_7$, which is the transmission gain from node _____ to node _____.

**1.8**  Similarly, FIND $T_2$:

$T_7$ is the transmission gain from $\underline{F(s)}$ to $\underline{V(s)}$.

$$\Delta = 1 - \left(-\frac{B}{Ms} - \frac{K}{Ms^2}\right) = 1 + \frac{B}{Ms} + \frac{K}{Ms^2}$$

$$= \frac{s^2 + \dfrac{B}{M}s + \dfrac{K}{M}}{s^2}$$

$$P_1 = \frac{1}{Ms} \quad \text{and} \quad \Delta_1 = 1$$

$$\therefore \quad T_7 = \frac{s/M}{s^2 + \dfrac{B}{M}s + \dfrac{K}{M}}$$

---

$T_2$ is the transmission gain from $v(0)$ to $X(s)$.

$$\Delta = \frac{s^2 + \dfrac{B}{M}s + \dfrac{K}{M}}{s^2} \quad \text{as above}$$

$$P_1 = \frac{1}{s^2} \quad \text{and} \quad \Delta_1 = 1$$

$$\therefore \quad T_2 = \frac{1}{s^2 + \dfrac{B}{M}s + \dfrac{K}{M}}$$

*Comment.*

We can similarly find the other $T$'s and hence $X(s)$ and $V(s)$, as in frame **1.5**.

Then $x(t) = \mathscr{L}^{-1}[X(s)]$ and $v(t) = \mathscr{L}^{-1}[V(s)]$.

**1.9**   Going back a step, we wrote the transformed system equations (frame **1.4**) in the form:

$$sX(s) = x(0) + V(s)$$

$$sV(s) = v(0) - \frac{K}{M}X(s) - \frac{B}{M}V(s) + \frac{1}{M}F(s) + \frac{g}{s}$$

As an alternative to solution by S.F.G., you can **REARRANGE** the above equations and then **SOLVE** for $X(s)$ by determinants (Cramer's rule):

$$(\underline{\phantom{xxxx}})X(s) + (\underline{\phantom{xxxx}})V(s) = \underline{\phantom{xxxxxxxx}}$$

$$(\underline{\phantom{xxxx}})X(s) + (\underline{\phantom{xxxx}})V(s) = \underline{\phantom{xxxxxxxx}}$$

The working time for Section 2 is from 20 to 30 minutes.

$$(s)X(s) + (-1)V(s) = x(0)$$

$$\left(\frac{K}{M}\right)X(s) + \left(s + \frac{B}{M}\right)V(s) = v(0) + \frac{1}{M}F(s) + \frac{g}{s}$$

Using Cramer's rule,

$$X(s) = \frac{\begin{vmatrix} x(0) & -1 \\ v(0) + \dfrac{1}{M}F(s) + \dfrac{g}{s} & s + \dfrac{B}{M} \end{vmatrix}}{\begin{vmatrix} s & -1 \\ \dfrac{K}{M} & s + \dfrac{B}{M} \end{vmatrix}}$$

$$= \frac{\left(s + \dfrac{B}{M}\right)x(0) + v(0) + \dfrac{1}{M}F(s) + \dfrac{g}{s}}{s^2 + \dfrac{B}{M}s + \dfrac{K}{M}}$$

*Comments:*

1. As before $X(s)$ may be written in the form

$$X(s) = T_1 x(0) + T_2 v(0) + T_3 F(s) + T_4 \frac{g}{s}$$

where, for example, you can see from the above solution that

$$T_2 = \frac{1}{s^2 + \dfrac{B}{M}s + \dfrac{K}{M}}$$

   $\dot{V}(s)$ could be similarly computed.

2. You obtained the *same* result by S.F.G. in frames **1.5** through **1.8** (Compare, for example, $T_2$ above, with $T_2$ as calculated in frame **1.8**)
   That is, the transformed system equations may be solved *either* by S.F.G. *or* by determinants. It is desirable to be familiar with both methods.

In the last section we took a second order differential equation in the variable $x(t)$ and rewrote it in the form of two simultaneous first order equations in $x(t)$ and the new variable $v(t)$. We then transformed the equations and indicated how one may solve for the unknowns $X(s)$ and $V(s)$ either by S.F.G. or by determinants. Let's now complicate the situation slightly.

## A VIBRATION ABSORBER

**2.1**

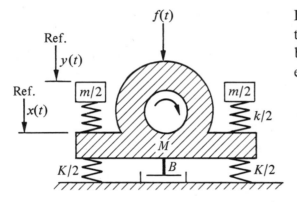

If the machine's speed is normally constant, the out-of-balance vibration can be "absorbed" by the sprung masses if $m$, $K$, and $k$ are properly chosen.

Here we are concerned with the system's equations of vertical motion:

$$M\frac{d^2x}{dt^2} + B\frac{dx}{dt} + Kx + k(x - y) = Mg + f(t)$$

$$m\frac{d^2y}{dt^2} + k(y - x) = mg$$

To put these into first order form, we first define two new variables:

$$\frac{dx}{dt} = v(t) \tag{1}$$

and
$$\frac{dy}{dt} = w(t) \tag{2}$$

Now, following the procedure of frame **1.1**,

$$\frac{dv}{dt} = \underline{\hspace{5cm}} \tag{3}$$

and
$$\frac{dw}{dt} = \underline{\hspace{5cm}} \tag{4}$$

12

*Comment:*

In this program we will often write $x$ instead of $x(t)$, $v$ instead of $v(t)$, $dx/dt$ instead of $dx(t)/dt$ etc.

$$\frac{d^2x}{dt^2} = \frac{dv}{dt}$$

$$\therefore \quad M\frac{dv}{dt} + Bv + Kx + kx - ky = Mg + f(t)$$

$$\text{or} \quad \frac{dv}{dt} = -\frac{K+k}{M}x - \frac{B}{M}v + \frac{k}{M}y + g + \frac{1}{M}f(t) \tag{3}$$

$$\frac{d^2y}{dt^2} = \frac{dw}{dt}$$

$$\text{and} \quad \frac{dw}{dt} = \frac{k}{m}x - \frac{k}{m}y + g \tag{4}$$

**2.2** We have:

$$\frac{dx}{dt} = v(t)$$

$$\frac{dv}{dt} = -\frac{K+k}{M}x - \frac{B}{M}v + \frac{k}{M}y + g + \frac{1}{M}f(t)$$

$$\frac{dy}{dt} = w(t)$$

$$\frac{dw}{dt} = \frac{k}{m}x - \frac{k}{m}y + g$$

In matrix form this becomes:

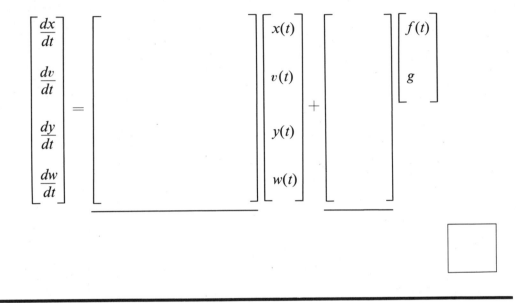

---

**2.3** This is a *very* important form of a system's equations. We started out in frame **2.1** with two second order equations in the two variables _____ and _____.

We then rewrote the system's equations as four _____ order equations in the variables _____ , _____ , _____ , and _____ .

It would seem logical to say that the *total system* order is _____ .

$$
\begin{bmatrix} \dfrac{dx}{dt} \\[2ex] \dfrac{dv}{dt} \\[2ex] \dfrac{dy}{dt} \\[2ex] \dfrac{dw}{dt} \end{bmatrix}
=
\begin{bmatrix}
0 & 1 & 0 & 0 \\[1.5ex]
-\dfrac{K+k}{M} & -\dfrac{B}{M} & \dfrac{k}{M} & 0 \\[1.5ex]
0 & 0 & 0 & 1 \\[1.5ex]
\dfrac{k}{m} & 0 & \dfrac{-k}{m} & 0
\end{bmatrix}
\begin{bmatrix} x \\[1.5ex] v \\[1.5ex] y \\[1.5ex] w \end{bmatrix}
+
\begin{bmatrix}
0 & 0 \\[1.5ex]
\dfrac{1}{M} & 1 \\[1.5ex]
0 & 0 \\[1.5ex]
0 & 1
\end{bmatrix}
\begin{bmatrix} f(t) \\[1.5ex] g \end{bmatrix}
$$

The two original variables were $x$ and $y$.
We then rewrote the original equations as four 1st order equations in the variables $x, v, y,$ and $w$.

The system is of 4th order.

> { 2 simultaneous 2nd order equations $\Longrightarrow$ total order $= 4$
> { 4 simultaneous 1st order equations $\Longrightarrow$ total order $= 4$

**2.4**   We have written the equations for the vibration absorber as:

$$
\begin{bmatrix} \dfrac{dx(t)}{dt} \\[2ex] \dfrac{dv(t)}{dt} \\[2ex] \dfrac{dy(t)}{dt} \\[2ex] \dfrac{dw(t)}{dt} \end{bmatrix}
=
\begin{bmatrix} 0 & 1 & 0 & 0 \\[1ex] -\dfrac{K+k}{M} & -\dfrac{B}{M} & \dfrac{k}{M} & 0 \\[1ex] 0 & 0 & 0 & 1 \\[1ex] \dfrac{k}{m} & 0 & -\dfrac{k}{m} & 0 \end{bmatrix}
\begin{bmatrix} x(t) \\[2ex] v(t) \\[2ex] y(t) \\[2ex] w(t) \end{bmatrix}
+
\begin{bmatrix} 0 & 0 \\[1ex] \dfrac{1}{M} & 1 \\[1ex] 0 & 0 \\[1ex] 0 & 1 \end{bmatrix}
\begin{bmatrix} f(t) \\[2ex] g \end{bmatrix}
$$

Such a set of $n$ first order differential equations is conventionally represented by:

$$\dot{\mathbf{x}}(t) = \mathbf{A}\mathbf{x}(t) + \mathbf{B}\mathbf{u}(t)$$

The variables in the $\mathbf{x}(t)$-matrix are called "state variables" since they describe the state or condition of the system at any time, $t$. In this problem:

$$\mathbf{x}(t) = \begin{bmatrix} \phantom{xx} \\ \phantom{xx} \\ \phantom{xx} \\ \phantom{xx} \end{bmatrix}$$

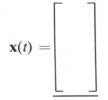

The $\mathbf{x}(t)$-matrix is called the "state matrix" and $\dot{\mathbf{x}}(t) = \mathbf{A}\mathbf{x}(t) + \mathbf{B}\mathbf{u}(t)$ is called the "state equation."

---

**2.5**   In the present problem:

$$\mathbf{A} = \begin{bmatrix} \phantom{xxxxxxxxx} \\ \phantom{xxxxxxxxx} \\ \phantom{xxxxxxxxx} \\ \phantom{xxxxxxxxx} \end{bmatrix}$$

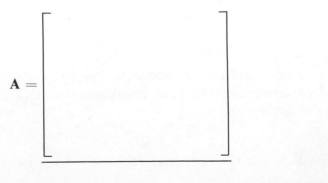

---

**2.6**   You will note that the elements of the system matrix, $\mathbf{A}$, depend upon the _____ of the system.

16

$$\mathbf{x}(t) = \begin{bmatrix} x(t) \\ v(t) \\ y(t) \\ w(t) \end{bmatrix}$$

*Comments:*

1. Column matrices, such as $\mathbf{x}(t)$, are often called vectors. Thus $\mathbf{x}(t)$ may also be called the state *vector*.
2. You should use a wavy underscore for *all* matrices, including vectors.

---

$$\mathbf{A} = \begin{bmatrix} 0 & 1 & 0 & 0 \\ -\dfrac{K+k}{M} & -\dfrac{B}{M} & \dfrac{k}{M} & 0 \\ 0 & 0 & 0 & 1 \\ \dfrac{k}{m} & 0 & -\dfrac{k}{m} & 0 \end{bmatrix}$$

*NOTE:*

$\mathbf{A}$ is a square matrix of constants. It is *not* a function of time.

---

constants or parameters or dynamics or physical characteristics

**2.7**    Referring to the previous page you will see that the input matrix $u(t)$ in the present problem is:

$$\mathbf{u}(t) = \begin{bmatrix} \phantom{xx} \\ \phantom{xx} \end{bmatrix}$$

---

**2.8**    Finally, the **B**-matrix, which describes how the inputs appear in the system's equations, is:

$$\mathbf{B} = \begin{bmatrix} \phantom{xx} \\ \phantom{xx} \end{bmatrix}$$

---

**2.9**    In this problem the *system* is of  _____  order, there are  _____  state variables, and  _____  inputs.

---

**2.10**    Thus the **A**-matrix in the state equation $\dot{\mathbf{x}} = \mathbf{A}\mathbf{x} + \mathbf{B}\mathbf{u}$ for the above system has  _____  rows and  _____  columns, and the **B**-matrix has  _____  rows and  _____  columns.

$$\mathbf{u}(t) = \begin{bmatrix} f(t) \\ g \end{bmatrix}$$

*Comment:*
As before this could also be called the input *vector*.

---

$$\mathbf{B} = \begin{bmatrix} 0 & 0 \\ \dfrac{1}{M} & 1 \\ 0 & 0 \\ 0 & 1 \end{bmatrix}$$   **B**, like **A**, is a matrix of constants

---

<u>4th</u> order

<u>4</u>   state variables

<u>2</u>   inputs

---

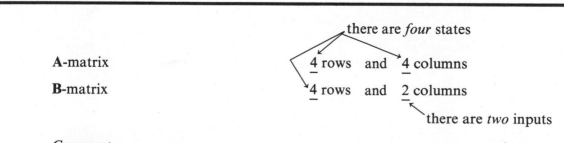

**A**-matrix

**B**-matrix

*Comment:*
**A** will always be square.
The "shape" of **B** depends on the system order and the number of inputs.

---

## 2.11 REVIEW AND INTRODUCTION

You have now had an opportunity to see that a system's equations can be rewritten in simultaneous first order form. Thus in matrix notation we can write the system's first order (state) equations as

$$\dot{\mathbf{x}}(t) = \mathbf{A}\mathbf{x}(t) + \mathbf{B}\mathbf{u}(t)$$

where $\mathbf{x}(t)$ is the matrix of state variables and $\mathbf{u}(t)$ is the matrix of system inputs.

This program has two basic aims:
1. To put a system's equations into the above form, and
2. To solve the resulting state equations.

We will find that there is more than one way to achieve each of these objectives. For example, you have already seen that one can transform the state equations and then solve them by S.F.G.'s *or* by determinants. Inverse transformation will then yield the time solution. Later we will find that the state equations can be solved entirely in the time domain.

All three methods of solution can become quite cumbersome if one does the necessary calculations by hand. However, all three methods are easily handled by standard computer techniques, and this is a major reason for using the state variable approach.

For the moment we will forego the process of solution and concentrate on the *formulation* of the state equations—item (1) above.

You can expect to spend an hour on the next section.

Try to avoid working sessions longer than an hour or so. It is desirable to take a break between sections—or perhaps after two sections, if they are short.

## AN INSTRUMENT SERVOMECHANISM

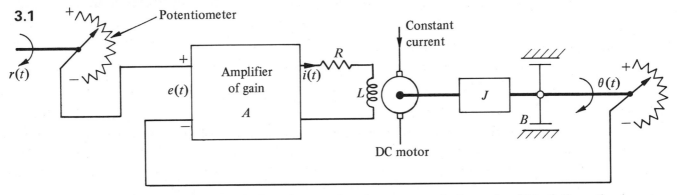

**3.1**

This servomechanism is designed to make the output shaft angle, $\theta(t)$, follow the input shaft angle, $r(t)$. The equations are:

$$e(t) = k_p\{r(t) - \theta(t)\} \qquad \text{where } k_p \text{ is the potentiometer "gain"}$$

$$L\frac{di(t)}{dt} + Ri(t) = Ae(t)$$

$$\lambda(t) = ki(t) = J\frac{d^2\theta(t)}{dt^2} + B\frac{d\theta(t)}{dt} \qquad \text{where } \lambda(t) \text{ is the electric torque.}$$

These three equations may be combined into one third order equation:

$$\frac{d^3\theta}{dt^3} + \left(\frac{R}{L} + \frac{B}{J}\right)\frac{d^2\theta}{dt^2} + \left(\frac{RB}{LJ}\right)\frac{d\theta}{dt} + \left(\frac{kk_pA}{LJ}\right)\theta = \left(\frac{kk_pA}{LJ}\right)r(t)$$

or, more simply,

$$\frac{d^3\theta}{dt^3} + k_1\frac{d^2\theta}{dt^2} + k_2\frac{d\theta}{dt} + k_3\theta = k_3 r(t)$$

We now define the angular velocity and acceleration of the output shaft

$$\frac{d\theta}{dt} = \omega(t) \qquad \text{(shaft velocity)}$$

and $\qquad \dfrac{d\omega}{dt} = \gamma(t) \qquad$ (shaft acceleration)

Now SUBSTITUTE into the third order system equation so that it can be written in first order form:

$$\frac{d\gamma}{dt} = \underline{\hspace{5cm}}$$

Substituting $\quad \omega(t) \quad$ for $\dfrac{d\theta}{dt}$

$$\gamma(t) \quad \text{for} \quad \frac{d^2\theta}{dt^2} \left( = \frac{d\omega}{dt} \right)$$

and $\quad \dfrac{d\gamma}{dt} \quad$ for $\dfrac{d^3\theta}{dt^3}$

it follows that:

$$\frac{d\gamma}{dt} = -k_3\theta - k_2\omega - k_1\gamma + k_3r(t)$$

**3.2**    Collecting our system equations:

$$\frac{d\theta}{dt} = \omega \tag{1}$$

$$\frac{d\omega}{dt} = \gamma \tag{2}$$

$$\frac{d\gamma}{dt} = -k_3\theta - k_2\omega - k_1\gamma + k_3 r(t) \tag{3}$$

Here the system is of _____ order, and with reference to the general matrix state equation $\dot{\mathbf{x}} = \mathbf{Ax} + \mathbf{Bu}$ we have:

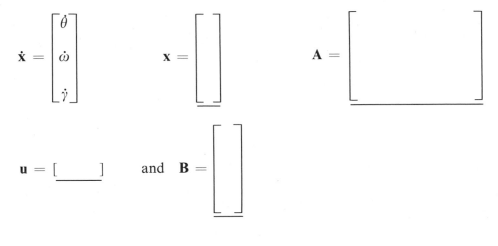

$$\dot{\mathbf{x}} = \begin{bmatrix} \dot{\theta} \\ \dot{\omega} \\ \dot{\gamma} \end{bmatrix} \qquad \mathbf{x} = \begin{bmatrix} \\ \\ \end{bmatrix} \qquad \mathbf{A} = \begin{bmatrix} \\ \\ \end{bmatrix}$$

$$\mathbf{u} = [\quad] \qquad \text{and} \quad \mathbf{B} = \begin{bmatrix} \\ \\ \end{bmatrix}$$

---

**3.3**    The three state variables in this example are all physical quantities.  NAME them (in words):

_____

_____

_____

The system is <u>3rd</u> order.

$$\dot{\mathbf{x}} = \begin{bmatrix} \dot{\theta} \\ \dot{\omega} \\ \dot{\gamma} \end{bmatrix} \qquad \mathbf{x} = \begin{bmatrix} \theta \\ \omega \\ \gamma \end{bmatrix} \qquad \mathbf{A} = \begin{bmatrix} 0 & 1 & 0 \\ 0 & 0 & 1 \\ -k_3 & -k_2 & -k_1 \end{bmatrix} = \begin{bmatrix} 0 & 1 & 0 \\ 0 & 0 & 1 \\ -\dfrac{kk_p A}{LJ} & -\dfrac{RB}{LJ} & -\left(\dfrac{R}{L} + \dfrac{B}{J}\right) \end{bmatrix}$$

$$\mathbf{u} = \begin{bmatrix} r(t) \end{bmatrix} \qquad \text{and} \qquad \mathbf{B} = \begin{bmatrix} 0 \\ 0 \\ k_3 \end{bmatrix}$$

*Comments:*

1. In this case $\mathbf{u}$ is a $1 \times 1$ matrix, often called a scalar, and often written without the brackets: $\mathbf{u} = r(t)$.

2. Remember that $\dot{\mathbf{x}}$, $\mathbf{x}$, and $\mathbf{u}$ are functions of time: $\dot{\mathbf{x}}(t)$, $\mathbf{x}(t)$, and $\mathbf{u}(t)$.

<hr>

output shaft position $(\theta)$

output shaft velocity $(\omega)$      or equivalent

output shaft acceleration $(\gamma)$

**3.4** An alternative approach to the previous problem is to write the system's equations in the form:

$$J\frac{d\omega}{dt} + B\omega = ki$$

$$\frac{d\theta}{dt} = \omega$$

and $L\frac{di}{dt} + Ri = Ak_p r(t) - Ak_p\theta$

where the variables are $\omega$, $\theta$, and $i$ and where $r(t)$ is the input. These equations can be put in state form by simple rearrangement. When you have done this, COMPLETE the matrix state equation below:

$$\begin{bmatrix} \dfrac{d\omega}{dt} \\[2mm] \dfrac{d\theta}{dt} \\[2mm] \dfrac{di}{dt} \end{bmatrix} = \begin{bmatrix} \phantom{xxx} \end{bmatrix}\begin{bmatrix} \omega \\ \theta \\ i \end{bmatrix} + \begin{bmatrix} \phantom{xxx} \end{bmatrix} r(t)$$

**3.5** NAME the three state variables (in words):

_____

_____

_____

(Refer to the diagram in frame **3.1**)

**3.6** COMPARE the **A** matrices in frames **3.2** and **3.4**. They are different, even though they relate to the same system. EXPLAIN.

$$\begin{bmatrix} \dfrac{d\omega}{dt} \\[2ex] \dfrac{d\theta}{dt} \\[2ex] \dfrac{di}{dt} \end{bmatrix} = \begin{bmatrix} -\dfrac{B}{J} & 0 & \dfrac{k}{J} \\[2ex] 1 & 0 & 0 \\[2ex] 0 & -\dfrac{Ak_p}{L} & -\dfrac{R}{L} \end{bmatrix} \begin{bmatrix} \omega \\[2ex] \theta \\[2ex] i \end{bmatrix} + \begin{bmatrix} 0 \\[2ex] 0 \\[2ex] \dfrac{Ak_p}{L} \end{bmatrix} r(t)$$

the input in this problem is a scalar

output shaft velocity ($\omega$)

output shaft position ($\theta$)     or equivalent

motor field current or current     ($i$)

*In your own words:*
Different choices have been made for the state variables. This will result in differing **A** (and **B**) matrices.

# A CIRCUIT EXAMPLE

**3.7**

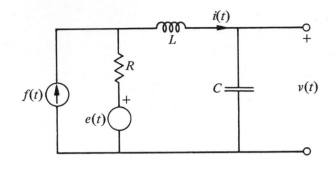

Here $f(t)$ is a current source, $e(t)$ is a voltage source, and

$$LC\frac{d^2v}{dt^2} + RC\frac{dv}{dt} + v = Rf(t) + e(t)$$

In this case a possible choice of variables would be $v$ and $w$, where $w$ is defined by:

$$\frac{dv}{dt} = w$$

Now COMPLETE the matrix state equation:

$$
\begin{bmatrix} \dfrac{dv}{dt} \\[2mm] \dfrac{dw}{dt} \end{bmatrix}
=
\begin{bmatrix} \phantom{XXXX} \end{bmatrix}
\begin{bmatrix} v \\ w \end{bmatrix}
+
\begin{bmatrix} \phantom{XXXX} \end{bmatrix}
\begin{bmatrix} f(t) \\ e(t) \end{bmatrix}
$$

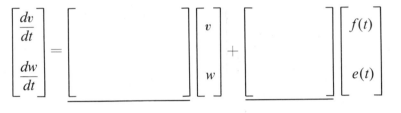

---

**3.8**    Alternatively, the system's equations can be written in the form:

$$C\frac{dv}{dt} = i$$

$$\text{and} \quad -e(t) + R\{i - f(t)\} + L\frac{di}{dt} + v = 0$$

These equations can be rearranged and written as:

$$
\begin{bmatrix} \dfrac{dv}{dt} \\[2mm] \dfrac{di}{dt} \end{bmatrix}
=
\begin{bmatrix} \phantom{XXXX} \end{bmatrix}
\begin{bmatrix} v \\ i \end{bmatrix}
+
\begin{bmatrix} \phantom{XXXX} \end{bmatrix}
\begin{bmatrix} f(t) \\ e(t) \end{bmatrix}
$$

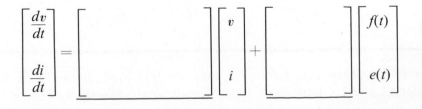

$$\frac{dv}{dt} = w$$

$$\frac{dw}{dt} = -\frac{1}{LC}v - \frac{R}{L}w + \frac{R}{LC}f(t) + \frac{1}{LC}e(t)$$

$$\begin{bmatrix} \dfrac{dv}{dt} \\[2ex] \dfrac{dw}{dt} \end{bmatrix} = \begin{bmatrix} 0 & 1 \\[2ex] -\dfrac{1}{LC} & -\dfrac{R}{L} \end{bmatrix} \begin{bmatrix} v \\[2ex] w \end{bmatrix} + \begin{bmatrix} 0 & 0 \\[2ex] \dfrac{R}{LC} & \dfrac{1}{LC} \end{bmatrix} \begin{bmatrix} f(t) \\[2ex] e(t) \end{bmatrix}$$

---

$$\frac{dv}{dt} = \frac{1}{C}i$$

$$\frac{di}{dt} = -\frac{1}{L}v - \frac{R}{L}i + \frac{R}{L}f(t) + \frac{1}{L}e(t)$$

$$\begin{bmatrix} \dfrac{dv}{dt} \\[2ex] \dfrac{di}{dt} \end{bmatrix} = \begin{bmatrix} 0 & \dfrac{1}{C} \\[2ex] -\dfrac{1}{L} & -\dfrac{R}{L} \end{bmatrix} \begin{bmatrix} v \\[2ex] i \end{bmatrix} + \begin{bmatrix} 0 & 0 \\[2ex] \dfrac{R}{L} & \dfrac{1}{L} \end{bmatrix} \begin{bmatrix} f(t) \\[2ex] e(t) \end{bmatrix}$$

*Comment:*
Again, the **A** and **B** matrices differ from those in the previous frame since the state variables are different.

**3.9**  Given: The system equation:

$$\frac{d^2z}{dt^2} + 3\frac{dz}{dt} + 2z = 4f(t) + 5g(t) + 6h(t)$$

where $f(t)$, $g(t)$, and $h(t)$ are *inputs*.
The number of state variables in this instance is _____ .

---

**3.10**  The logical choice of variables will be _____ and _____ .

(refer to frame **3.7** if you need help)

---

**3.11**  Thus, writing $w$ for $dz/dt$:

$$\begin{bmatrix} \ \\ \ \end{bmatrix} = \begin{bmatrix} \quad \\ \quad \end{bmatrix}\begin{bmatrix} \ \\ \ \end{bmatrix} + \begin{bmatrix} \quad \\ \quad \end{bmatrix}\begin{bmatrix} \ \\ \ \end{bmatrix}$$

---

**3.12**  And since $\dot{\mathbf{x}} = \mathbf{Ax} + \mathbf{Bu}$, it follows that:

$$\mathbf{x} = \begin{bmatrix} \ \\ \ \end{bmatrix} \qquad \dot{\mathbf{x}} = \begin{bmatrix} \ \\ \ \end{bmatrix} \qquad \mathbf{A} = \begin{bmatrix} \quad \\ \quad \end{bmatrix} \qquad \mathbf{B} = \begin{bmatrix} \quad \\ \quad \end{bmatrix} \qquad \text{and } \mathbf{u} = \begin{bmatrix} \ \\ \ \end{bmatrix}$$

---

**3.13**  Note that **A** is a $2 \times 2$ matrix since 2 is the _____ of the system.

Similarly **B** is a $2 \times 3$ matrix since 2 is the _____ and 3 is the _____

_____ .

---

— equal to the order of the system
equation

$\underline{2}$

---

$\underline{z}$ and $\dfrac{dz}{dt}$

If you represented $dz/dt$ by another symbol (such as $w$), you're on the ball. We will use $w$ to represent $dz/dt$ in the rest of this problem.

---

$$\underline{\begin{bmatrix} \dot{z} \\ \dot{w} \end{bmatrix} = \begin{bmatrix} 0 & 1 \\ -2 & -3 \end{bmatrix} \begin{bmatrix} z \\ w \end{bmatrix} + \begin{bmatrix} 0 & 0 & 0 \\ 4 & 5 & 6 \end{bmatrix} \begin{bmatrix} f(t) \\ g(t) \\ h(t) \end{bmatrix}}$$

---

$$\mathbf{x} = \begin{bmatrix} z \\ w \end{bmatrix} \quad \dot{\mathbf{x}} = \begin{bmatrix} \dot{z} \\ \dot{w} \end{bmatrix} \quad \mathbf{A} = \begin{bmatrix} 0 & 1 \\ -2 & -3 \end{bmatrix} \quad \mathbf{B} = \begin{bmatrix} 0 & 0 & 0 \\ 4 & 5 & 6 \end{bmatrix} \quad \mathbf{u} = \begin{bmatrix} f(t) \\ g(t) \\ h(t) \end{bmatrix}$$

---

2 is the order of the system

2 is the order of the system or number of state variables

3 is the number of inputs

**3.14**    Given:

$$\frac{d^3p}{dt^3} + 2\frac{d^2p}{dt^2} + 3\frac{dp}{dt} + 4p = 5\alpha(t) + 6\beta(t)$$

This is the equation of a _____ order system, and there will therefore be _____ state variables.  The logical choice of variables will be _____ .

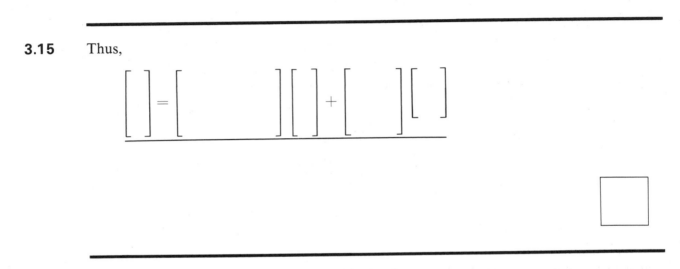

**3.15**    Thus,

**3.16**    *Note:*

Whenever you write an *n*th order equation ($n \geqslant 2$) in state variable form it is necessary to choose symbols for the derivatives of the basic variable. We chose $q$ and $r$ in the above example, but $a$ and $b$, or $\xi$ and $\zeta$ would be just as good.  It is a free choice!

More conveniently, we will choose $x_1$ to represent the basic variable, and $x_2$, $x_3$, . . . to represent its derivatives. We can also use the symbols $u_1$, $u_2$, . . . to represent the inputs. Thus the above equation can be written:

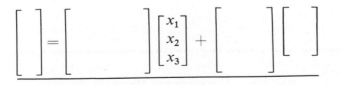

32

A 3rd order system has 3 state variables.

$p, dp/dt$, and $d^2p/dt^2$   or   $p, \dot{p}$, and $\ddot{p}$

For convenience, we will use $q$ for $\dot{p}$ and $r$ for $\ddot{p}$. Our state variables are then $p$, $q$, and $r$. *Please use this choice of symbols in the next frame.*

$$\begin{bmatrix} \dot{p} \\ \dot{q} \\ \dot{r} \end{bmatrix} = \begin{bmatrix} 0 & 1 & 0 \\ 0 & 0 & 1 \\ -4 & -3 & -2 \end{bmatrix} \begin{bmatrix} p \\ q \\ r \end{bmatrix} + \begin{bmatrix} 0 & 0 \\ 0 & 0 \\ 5 & 6 \end{bmatrix} \begin{bmatrix} \alpha(t) \\ \beta(t) \end{bmatrix}$$

representing $p$, $\dot{p}$, and $\ddot{p}$

representing $\alpha(t)$ and $\beta(t)$

$$\begin{bmatrix} \dot{x}_1 \\ \dot{x}_2 \\ \dot{x}_3 \end{bmatrix} = \begin{bmatrix} 0 & 1 & 0 \\ 0 & 0 & 1 \\ -4 & -3 & -2 \end{bmatrix} \begin{bmatrix} x_1 \\ x_2 \\ x_3 \end{bmatrix} + \begin{bmatrix} 0 & 0 \\ 0 & 0 \\ 5 & 6 \end{bmatrix} \begin{bmatrix} u_1 \\ u_2 \end{bmatrix}$$

We haven't changed *anything* other than the *names* of the state variables and system inputs.

## ONE MORE EXAMPLE

**3.17** Given:

$$\frac{d^3y}{dt^3} + a\frac{dy}{dt} + b\frac{dz}{dt} = c\alpha(t) + d\beta(t)$$

$$\text{and} \quad \frac{d^2z}{dt^2} + e\frac{dy}{dt} = f\beta(t) + g\gamma(t)$$

where $\alpha(t)$, $\beta(t)$, and $\gamma(t)$ are inputs.

These equations are _____ order in $y$, and _____ order in $z$. Thus the total system order will be _____, and there will be _____ state variables.

---

**3.18** The state variables corresponding to the above equations are

_____

---

**3.19** As in the NOTE on the previous page we will represent $y$ by $x_1$, $dy/dt$ by $x_2$ _____ by $x_3$, $z$ by $x_4$, and _____ by _____. Similarly we will represent $\alpha(t)$, $\beta(t)$, and $\gamma(t)$ by _____, _____, and _____.

---

**3.20** In these terms the equations may be written:

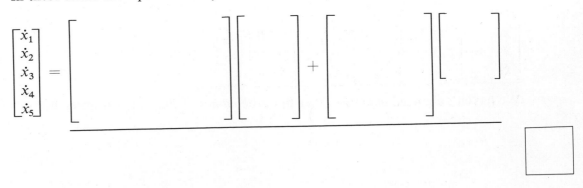

---

Section 4 will require about 30 minutes to complete.

The equations are <u>3rd</u> order in $y$, and <u>2nd</u> order in $z$.

The system is of <u>5th</u> order, and there will be <u>5</u> state variables.

---

<u>$y$, $dy/dt$, $d^2y/dt^2$, $z$, and $dz/dt$</u>

---

represent   <u>$d^2y/dt^2$</u> by $x_3$ and <u>$dz/dt$</u> by <u>$x_5$</u>.

and $\alpha$, $\beta$, and $\gamma$ by <u>$u_1$, $u_2$, and $u_3$</u>.

---

$$
\begin{bmatrix} \dot{x}_1 \\ \dot{x}_2 \\ \dot{x}_3 \\ \dot{x}_4 \\ \dot{x}_5 \end{bmatrix} = \begin{bmatrix} 0 & 1 & 0 & 0 & 0 \\ 0 & 0 & 1 & 0 & 0 \\ 0 & -a & 0 & 0 & -b \\ 0 & 0 & 0 & 0 & 1 \\ 0 & -e & 0 & 0 & 0 \end{bmatrix} \begin{bmatrix} x_1 \\ x_2 \\ x_3 \\ x_4 \\ x_5 \end{bmatrix} + \begin{bmatrix} 0 & 0 & 0 \\ 0 & 0 & 0 \\ c & d & 0 \\ 0 & 0 & 0 \\ 0 & f & g \end{bmatrix} \begin{bmatrix} u_1 \\ u_2 \\ u_3 \end{bmatrix}
$$

## THE SERVOMECHANISM AGAIN

**4.1**    In frame **3.1** you saw an instrument servo described by the equation

$$\frac{d^3\theta}{dt^3} + k_1 \frac{d^2\theta}{dt^2} + k_2 \frac{d\theta}{dt} + k_3\theta = k_3 r(t)$$

where $\theta(t)$ was the output shaft angle, and $r(t)$ was the input angle. You then observed (frame **3.2**) that this equation could be rewritten in state matrix form:

$$\begin{bmatrix} \dot{\theta} \\ \dot{\omega} \\ \dot{\gamma} \end{bmatrix} = \begin{bmatrix} 0 & 1 & 0 \\ 0 & 0 & 1 \\ -k_3 & -k_2 & -k_1 \end{bmatrix} \begin{bmatrix} \theta \\ \omega \\ \gamma \end{bmatrix} + \begin{bmatrix} 0 \\ 0 \\ k_3 \end{bmatrix} r(t)$$

where $\omega$ was the shaft velocity, and $\gamma$ its acceleration.

Take the Laplace transform of the three state equations and DRAW the corresponding S.F.G.   Notation:  $\mathscr{L}[\theta(t)] = \Theta(s)$, $\mathscr{L}[\omega(t)] = \Omega(s)$, and $\mathscr{L}[\gamma(t)] = \Gamma(s)$.

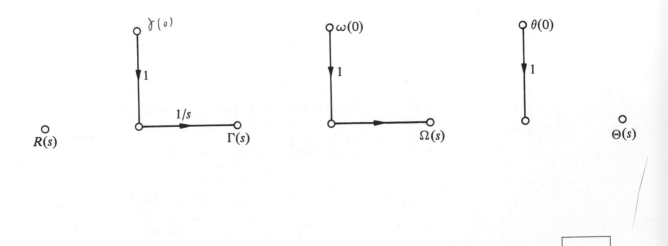

Although you probably transformed the three state equations separately, they can be kept in matrix form:

$$\begin{bmatrix} s\Theta(s) & - & \theta(0) \\ s\Omega(s) & - & \omega(0) \\ s\Gamma(s) & - & \gamma(0) \end{bmatrix} = \begin{bmatrix} 0 & 1 & 0 \\ 0 & 0 & 1 \\ -k_3 & -k_2 & -k_1 \end{bmatrix} \begin{bmatrix} \Theta(s) \\ \Omega(s) \\ \Gamma(s) \end{bmatrix} + \begin{bmatrix} 0 \\ 0 \\ k_3 \end{bmatrix} R(s)$$

or

$$\begin{bmatrix} s\Theta(s) \\ s\Omega(s) \\ s\Gamma(s) \end{bmatrix} = \begin{bmatrix} \theta(0) \\ \omega(0) \\ \gamma(0) \end{bmatrix} + \begin{bmatrix} 0 & 1 & 0 \\ 0 & 0 & 1 \\ -k_3 & -k_2 & -k_1 \end{bmatrix} \begin{bmatrix} \Theta(s) \\ \Omega(s) \\ \Gamma(s) \end{bmatrix} + \begin{bmatrix} 0 \\ 0 \\ k_3 \end{bmatrix} R(s)$$

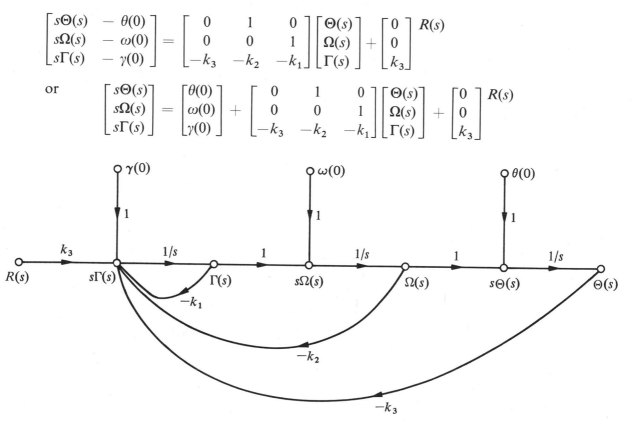

*Comment:*

If we want to find the transform of one of the states [say $\Theta(s)$], we can use the Mason gain rule to calculate the signal due to each of the inputs and initial conditions.
For example:

$$\Theta_F(s) = \frac{k_3 R(s)}{s^3 + k_1 s^2 + k_2 s + k_3} = \frac{\dfrac{kk_p A}{LJ} R(s)}{s^3 + \left(\dfrac{R}{L} + \dfrac{B}{J}\right)s^2 + \dfrac{RB}{LJ}s + \dfrac{kk_p A}{LJ}}$$

**4.2**    In frame **3.4** you saw that by deriving the servo's equations in terms of the variables $\omega$, $\theta$, and $i$, one obtains three first order equations which can be written in the form

$$\begin{bmatrix} \dot{\omega} \\ \dot{\theta} \\ \dot{i} \end{bmatrix} = \begin{bmatrix} -\dfrac{B}{J} & 0 & \dfrac{k}{J} \\ 1 & 0 & 0 \\ 0 & -\dfrac{Ak_p}{L} & -\dfrac{R}{L} \end{bmatrix} \begin{bmatrix} \omega \\ \theta \\ i \end{bmatrix} + \begin{bmatrix} 0 \\ 0 \\ \dfrac{Ak_p}{L} \end{bmatrix} r(t)$$

TRANSFORM, and COMPLETE the S.F.G.:

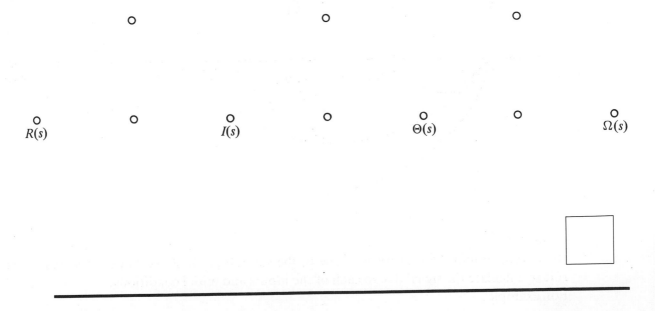

_____

*NOTE:*

**4.3**    COMPARE the comments opposite frames **4.1** and **4.2**.

Observe that if we choose different states ($\theta$, $\omega$, $\gamma$ in frame **4.1**, and $\omega$, $\theta$, and $i$ in frame **4.2**) the state equations will differ, as will the S.F.G.'s. *But* a given output, such as $\Theta_F(s)$, will necessarily be the same no matter which route we follow.

$$
\begin{bmatrix} s\Omega(s) \\ s\Theta(s) \\ sI(s) \end{bmatrix} = \begin{bmatrix} \omega(0) \\ \theta(0) \\ i(0) \end{bmatrix} + \begin{bmatrix} -\dfrac{B}{J} & 0 & \dfrac{k}{J} \\ 1 & 0 & 0 \\ 0 & -\dfrac{Ak_p}{L} & -\dfrac{R}{L} \end{bmatrix} \begin{bmatrix} \Omega(s) \\ \Theta(s) \\ I(s) \end{bmatrix} + \begin{bmatrix} 0 \\ 0 \\ \dfrac{Ak_p}{L} \end{bmatrix} R(s)
$$

From now on we will not bother to label nodes such as $sI(s)$, $s\Theta(s)$, and $s\Omega(s)$. This has the advantage of emphasizing the inputs, I.C.'s, and states.

*Comment:*

Calculating $\Theta_F(s)$ as in the previous frame,

$$
\Theta_F(s) = \frac{\dfrac{kk_p A}{LJ}\, R(s)}{s^3 + \left(\dfrac{R}{L} + \dfrac{B}{J}\right)s^2 + \dfrac{RB}{LJ}\,s + \dfrac{kk_p A}{LJ}}
$$

## SOME POINTS OF INTEREST

**4.4** We have seen that the state equations are automatically in the proper form for drawing an S.F.G. In turn, the S.F.G. is an s-domain representation of the analog computer set-up which could be used to solve the state equations, since $1/s$ represents the time-domain process of integration.

As a matter of interest, then, the S.F.G. in frame **4.1** could be used to generate the following analog computer wiring diagram.

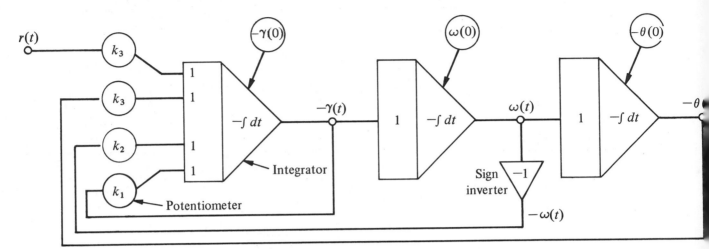

Further, most digital computer facilities have a routine for numerically integrating (solving) differential equations which have been written in state variable form.

As an example, the routine in use at the Naval Postgraduate School requires that the state equations (in frame **4.1**) be written

$$\dot{x}_1 = x_2$$
$$\dot{x}_2 = x_3$$
and $\quad \dot{x}_3 = -C_3 x_1 - C_2 x_2 - C_1 x_3 + C_3 \; \sin 3t$

Here we have simply re-named the variables and constants, and assumed that $r(t) = \sin 3t$ was the input given.

The corresponding FORTRAN statements are on the opposite page.

| T Y P E | STATEMENT NUMBER | C O N T. | FORTRAN STATEMENT |
|---|---|---|---|
| 1 | 2          5 | 6 | 7 |
| | | | XDØT (1) = X(2) |
| | | | XDØT (2) = X(3) |
| | | | XDØT (3) = − C(3)*X(1) − C(2)*X(2) − C(1)*X(3) |
| | | 1 | + C(3)*SIN (3.0*T) |
| | | | |

The above statements are imbedded in a standard program, and the appropriate values of the constants and initial conditions are punched on data cards.

In summary, state equations have immediate application in their relation to S.F.G.'s and to digital and analog computation.  Later we will look at this in more detail.

You will need 30 to 40 minutes to work the next Section.

**5.1**   So far you have always been given strong hints as to how to choose your state variables. One reason for this was that there are usually many ways of writing a system's equations in state form, depending upon one's choice of variables, and we wished to focus on one particular choice.

Here we will generalize on that choice of variables which leads one most easily to a set of state equations.

For example, suppose a system's equations have been derived in the form:

$$\frac{d^2v}{dt^2} + 7v + 6w = 5\alpha(t) - 4\beta(t)$$

$$\frac{dw}{dt} - 3v = 2\beta(t)$$

where $v(t)$ and $w(t)$ are the basic problem variables, and $\alpha(t)$ and $\beta(t)$ are the inputs.

The first step is to scan the equations and CIRCLE the highest order derivative of each of the problem variables.

**5.2**   Next, REARRANGE each equation so that the highest derivative (as circled above) appears on the left of the equation, with unity coefficient:

$$\underline{\hspace{4cm}} = \underline{\hspace{5cm}}$$

$$\underline{\hspace{4cm}} = \underline{\hspace{5cm}}$$

*Comment:*

It is, of course, possible for the highest derivative of a problem variable to appear in more than one equation. There would then be some question as to *where* one should circle each highest derivative. We will, for the moment, avoid this difficulty.

$$\frac{d^2v}{dt^2} = -7v - 6w + 5\alpha(t) - 4\beta(t)$$

$$\frac{dw}{dt} = 3v + 2\beta(t)$$

**5.3**    We have rearranged our example equations into the form:

$$\frac{d^2v}{dt^2} = -7v - 6w + 5\alpha(t) - 4\beta(t)$$

$$\frac{dw}{dt} = 3v + 2\beta(t)$$

For state variables we choose *the basic problem variables and all of their derivatives up to, but NOT including, the derivatives on the left of the above equations.*

Here the choice of state variables will be:

———————————————

---

**5.4**    Representing the above state variables by $x_1$, $x_2$, ..., and maintaining the same order as above-right,

$x_1 = $ ————— , $x_2 = $ ————— , and $x_3 = $ —————

We will also write $u_1$ for $\alpha(t)$ and $u_2$ for $\beta(t)$.

---

**5.5**    Finally, we can write the state equation $\dot{\mathbf{x}} = \mathbf{A}\mathbf{x} + \mathbf{B}\mathbf{u}$ in the form:

$$\begin{bmatrix} \dot{x}_1 \\ \dot{x}_2 \\ \dot{x}_3 \end{bmatrix} = \begin{bmatrix} \phantom{xxxxx} \end{bmatrix} \begin{bmatrix} x_1 \\ x_2 \\ x_3 \end{bmatrix} + \begin{bmatrix} \phantom{xxxxx} \end{bmatrix} \begin{bmatrix} u_1 \\ u_2 \end{bmatrix}$$

$$v, \frac{dv}{dt}, w \qquad \text{(in any order)}$$

---

$$x_1 = \underline{v}, \ x_2 = \frac{dv}{dt}, \text{ and } x_3 = \underline{w}$$

---

$$\begin{bmatrix} \dot{x}_1 \\ \dot{x}_2 \\ \dot{x}_3 \end{bmatrix} = \begin{bmatrix} 0 & 1 & 0 \\ -7 & 0 & -6 \\ 3 & 0 & 0 \end{bmatrix} \begin{bmatrix} x_1 \\ x_2 \\ x_3 \end{bmatrix} + \begin{bmatrix} 0 & 0 \\ 5 & -4 \\ 0 & 2 \end{bmatrix} \begin{bmatrix} u_1 \\ u_2 \end{bmatrix}$$

## ANOTHER EXAMPLE

**5.6**  Given: A system's equations:

$$\frac{d^3p}{dt^3} + 2\frac{dp}{dt} + 3q - 4\frac{dr}{dt} = 5\alpha(t)$$

$$p + 8\frac{dq}{dt} + 9q = 10\alpha(t) - 11\beta(t)$$

$$\frac{d^2p}{dt^2} - 6\frac{d^2r}{dt^2} + 7r = 0$$

where $p(t)$, $q(t)$, $r(t)$ are the basic problem variables, and $\alpha(t)$ and $\beta(t)$ are the inputs.

CIRCLE the highest order derivatives above and REARRANGE each equation to bring that derivative to the left-hand side:

$$= \rule{4in}{0.4pt}$$

$$= \rule{4in}{0.4pt}$$

$$= \rule{4in}{0.4pt}$$

---

**5.7**  The state variables are:

_____

---

**5.8**  Keeping the variables in the same order as in the answer to the previous frame, we can represent them as follows:

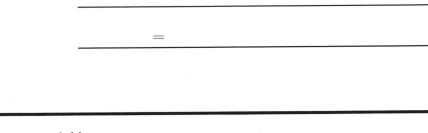

$$x_1 = \rule{1in}{0.4pt}, \; x_2 = \rule{1in}{0.4pt}, \; x_3 = \rule{1in}{0.4pt}$$

$$x_4 = \rule{1in}{0.4pt}, \; x_5 = \rule{1in}{0.4pt}, \; x_6 = \rule{1in}{0.4pt}$$

---

**5.9**  Additionally, the *inputs* are:

$$u_1 = \rule{1in}{0.4pt} \quad \text{and } u_2 = \rule{1in}{0.4pt}$$

---

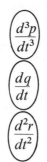

$$\frac{d^3p}{dt^3} = -2\frac{dp}{dt} - 3q + 4\frac{dr}{dt} + 5\alpha(t)$$

$$\frac{dq}{dt} = -\frac{1}{8}p - \frac{9}{8}q + \frac{10}{8}\alpha(t) - \frac{11}{8}\beta(t)$$

$$\frac{d^2r}{dt^2} = \frac{1}{6}\frac{d^2p}{dt^2} + \frac{7}{6}r$$

As defined in frame **5.3**, the state variables are:

$$p, \quad \frac{dp}{dt}, \quad \frac{d^2p}{dt^2}, \quad q, \quad r, \quad \frac{dr}{dt} \qquad \text{(in any order)}$$

$$x_1 = \underline{p}, \quad x_2 = \frac{dp}{dt}, \quad x_3 = \frac{d^2p}{dt^2}$$

$$x_4 = \underline{q}, \quad x_5 = \underline{r}, \quad x_6 = \frac{dr}{dt}$$

$$u_1 = \underline{\alpha(t)} \text{ and } u_2 = \underline{\beta(t)}$$

**5.10**  Summarizing, we have:

$$\frac{d^3p}{dt^3} = -2\frac{dp}{dt} - 3q + 4\frac{dr}{dt} + 5\alpha(t)$$

$$\frac{dq}{dt} = -\frac{1}{8}p - \frac{9}{8}q + \frac{10}{8}\alpha(t) - \frac{11}{8}\beta(t)$$

$$\frac{d^2r}{dt^2} = \frac{1}{6}\frac{d^2p}{dt^2} + \frac{7}{6}r$$

and we have agreed to represent:

$$p \text{ by } x_1, \frac{dp}{dt} \text{ by } x_2, \frac{d^2p}{dt^2} \text{ by } x_3$$

$$q \text{ by } x_4, r \text{ by } x_5, \frac{dr}{dt} \text{ by } x_6$$

$\alpha(t)$ by $u_1$, and $\beta(t)$ by $u_2$.

Now WRITE the appropriate state equation, in terms of the variables **x** and the inputs **u**:

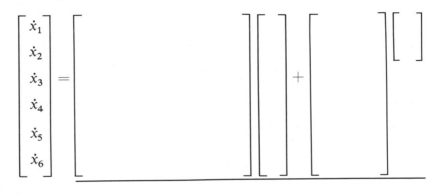

$$
\begin{bmatrix} \dot{x}_1 \\ \dot{x}_2 \\ \dot{x}_3 \\ \dot{x}_4 \\ \dot{x}_5 \\ \dot{x}_6 \end{bmatrix} = \begin{bmatrix} 0 & 1 & 0 & 0 & 0 & 0 \\ 0 & 0 & 1 & 0 & 0 & 0 \\ 0 & -2 & 0 & -3 & 0 & 4 \\ -\dfrac{1}{8} & 0 & 0 & -\dfrac{9}{8} & 0 & 0 \\ 0 & 0 & 0 & 0 & 0 & 1 \\ 0 & 0 & \dfrac{1}{6} & 0 & \dfrac{7}{6} & 0 \end{bmatrix} \begin{bmatrix} x_1 \\ x_2 \\ x_3 \\ x_4 \\ x_5 \\ x_6 \end{bmatrix} + \begin{bmatrix} 0 & 0 \\ 0 & 0 \\ 5 & 0 \\ \dfrac{10}{8} & -\dfrac{11}{8} \\ 0 & 0 \\ 0 & 0 \end{bmatrix} \begin{bmatrix} u_1 \\ u_2 \end{bmatrix}
$$

## AN EARLIER CIRCUIT REVISITED

**5.11**

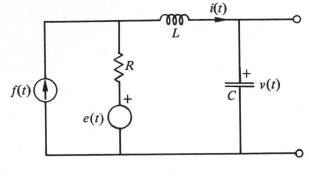

Earlier we wrote the equations for this circuit in terms of $v$ (Frame **3.7**), and again in terms of $v$ and $i$ (Frame **3.8**).

Alternatively, in terms of $i$ alone:

$$L\frac{di}{dt} + R\{i - f(t)\} + \frac{1}{C}\int_0^t i\,dt + v(0) = e(t)$$

As in PROBLEM 2 in the test of prerequisites, this integro-differential equation is *second* order in the basic variable, $i$. We must therefore choose *two* state variables.

In this situation the integral itself will be one of the state variables. That is:

$$x_1 = \underline{\hspace{2cm}} \quad \text{and} \quad x_2 = i$$

---

**5.12**    Here there are three "inputs," which we write as:

$$u_1 = f(t), \quad u_2 = \underline{\hspace{2cm}}, \quad \text{and} \quad u_3 = \underline{\hspace{1cm}}$$

---

**5.13**    Using our choice of $x$'s and $u$'s the state equations are:

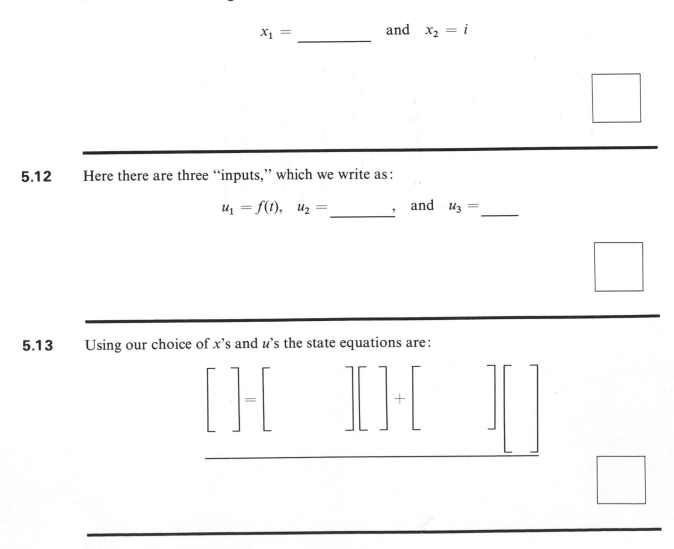

---

Allow about 50 minutes for the next Section.

$$x_1 = \int_0^t i\,dt$$

---

$u_1 = f(t)$, $u_2 = e(t)$, and $u_3 = v(0)$ in any order

*Comment:*

Whenever one of the states is an integral of a problem variable, you must expect an initial value to show up as an "input."

---

$$\begin{bmatrix} \dot{x}_1 \\ \dot{x}_2 \end{bmatrix} = \begin{bmatrix} 0 & 1 \\ -\dfrac{1}{LC} & -\dfrac{R}{L} \end{bmatrix} \begin{bmatrix} x_1 \\ x_2 \end{bmatrix} + \begin{bmatrix} 0 & 0 & 0 \\ \dfrac{R}{L} & \dfrac{1}{L} & -\dfrac{1}{L} \end{bmatrix} \begin{bmatrix} u_1 \\ u_2 \\ u_3 \end{bmatrix}$$

GO BACK and REREAD frame **2.11**. We have reached the first objective—that of putting a system's equations in state variable form. Now we are ready to consider various methods for solving these equations. First we will use the S.F.G. to solve the transformed state equation.

**6.1**    As a simple illustrative example, suppose we try to solve the equation:

$$\begin{bmatrix} \dot{x}_1 \\ \dot{x}_2 \end{bmatrix} = \begin{bmatrix} 0 & 1 \\ 0 & 0 \end{bmatrix} \begin{bmatrix} x_1 \\ x_2 \end{bmatrix} + \begin{bmatrix} 0 \\ k \end{bmatrix} u_1(t)$$

The first step is to TRANSFORM and REARRANGE into the form:

$$\begin{bmatrix} sX_1(s) \\ sX_2(s) \end{bmatrix} = \begin{bmatrix} x_1(0) \\ x_2(0) \end{bmatrix} + \begin{bmatrix} \quad\quad\quad \end{bmatrix} \begin{bmatrix} X_1(s) \\ X_2(s) \end{bmatrix} + \begin{bmatrix} \quad \end{bmatrix}$$

**6.2**    DRAW the corresponding S.F.G.:

**6.3**    Use the Mason gain rule to SOLVE for $X_1(s)$:

*Answer:*  $X_1(s) = ($_____$)x_1(0) + ($_____$)x_2(0) + ($_____$)U_1(s)$

$$\begin{bmatrix} sX_1(s)-x_1(0) \\ sX_2(s)-x_2(0) \end{bmatrix} = \begin{bmatrix} 0 & 1 \\ 0 & 0 \end{bmatrix} \begin{bmatrix} X_1(s) \\ X_2(s) \end{bmatrix} + \begin{bmatrix} 0 \\ k \end{bmatrix} U_1(s)$$

Rearranging,

$$\begin{bmatrix} sX_1(s) \\ sX_2(s) \end{bmatrix} = \begin{bmatrix} x_1(0) \\ x_2(0) \end{bmatrix} + \begin{bmatrix} 0 & 1 \\ 0 & 0 \end{bmatrix} \begin{bmatrix} X_1(s) \\ X_2(s) \end{bmatrix} + \begin{bmatrix} 0 \\ k \end{bmatrix} U_1(s)$$

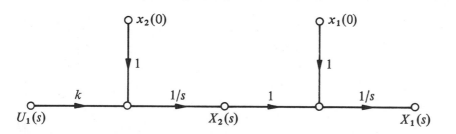

Again we have not labeled the nodes $sX_1(s)$ and $sX_2(s)$.

$\Delta = 1 \quad - \quad$ there are no loops!

The transmission gains $T_1$, $T_2$, and $T_3$, from $x_1(0)$, $x_2(0)$, and $U_1(s)$ to $X_1(s)$ are:

$$T_1 = \frac{P_1\Delta_1}{\Delta} = \frac{1}{s}, \quad T_2 = \frac{1}{s^2}, \quad \text{and} \quad T_3 = \frac{k}{s^2}$$

Therefore, by superposition:

$$X_1(s) = \left(\frac{1}{s}\right)x_1(0) + \left(\frac{1}{s^2}\right)x_2(0) + \left(\frac{k}{s^2}\right)U_1(s)$$

**6.4**     FIND $X_2(s)$ in the same way:

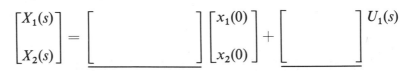

---

**6.5**     Therefore the transformed solution of the original equation can be written:

$$\begin{bmatrix} X_1(s) \\ X_2(s) \end{bmatrix} = \begin{bmatrix} \quad\quad\quad \end{bmatrix} \begin{bmatrix} x_1(0) \\ x_2(0) \end{bmatrix} + \begin{bmatrix} \quad\quad\quad \end{bmatrix} U_1(s)$$

Note that this equation is of the form:

$$X(s) = \Phi(s)x(0) + H(s)U(s)$$

---

**6.6**     Given $k = 1$, $u_1(t) = 10$, $x_1(0) = 2$, and $x_2(0) = -3$, take the inverse transform to FIND $x_1(t)$ *and* $x_2(t)$.
*Hint:*
Treat each equation separately; *don't* work in matrix form.

$$X_2(s) = (0)x_1(0) + \left(\frac{1}{s}\right)x_2(0) + \left(\frac{k}{s}\right)U_1(s)$$

$$\begin{bmatrix} X_1(s) \\ X_2(s) \end{bmatrix} = \begin{bmatrix} \dfrac{1}{s} & \dfrac{1}{s^2} \\ 0 & \dfrac{1}{s} \end{bmatrix} \begin{bmatrix} x_1(0) \\ x_2(0) \end{bmatrix} + \begin{bmatrix} \dfrac{k}{s^2} \\ \dfrac{k}{s} \end{bmatrix} U_1(s)$$

Substituting data,

$$X_1(s) = \frac{2}{s} - \frac{3}{s^2} + \frac{10}{s^3}$$

$$\therefore \quad x_1(t) = 2 - 3t + 5t^2 \qquad t \geqslant 0$$

Similarly,

$$X_2(s) = \frac{-3}{s} + \frac{10}{s^2}$$

and $\quad x_2(t) = -3 + 10t \quad t \geqslant 0$

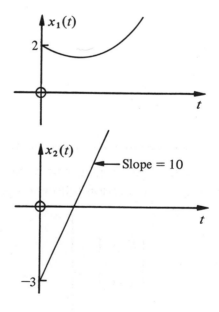

## A SECOND EXAMPLE

**6.7**    Here we want to solve the equation:

$$\dot{\mathbf{x}} = \begin{bmatrix} -1 & 1 \\ 0 & -2 \end{bmatrix} \mathbf{x} + \begin{bmatrix} 0 & 1 \\ 1 & 0 \end{bmatrix} \mathbf{u}$$

TRANSFORM this equation, putting your result in the following form, and then DRAW the S.F.G.:

$$\begin{bmatrix} sX_1(s) \\ sX_2(s) \end{bmatrix} = \begin{bmatrix} \quad \end{bmatrix} + \begin{bmatrix} \quad \end{bmatrix}\begin{bmatrix} \quad \end{bmatrix} + \begin{bmatrix} \quad \end{bmatrix}\begin{bmatrix} \quad \end{bmatrix}$$

**6.8**    Use the Mason gain rule to SOLVE for $X_1(s)$ *and* $X_2(s)$. You may work on the opposite page—our solution follows on page 58.

$$\textit{Answer:}\quad \begin{bmatrix} X_1(s) \\ X_2(s) \end{bmatrix} = \begin{bmatrix} \quad \end{bmatrix}\begin{bmatrix} x_1(0) \\ x_2(0) \end{bmatrix} + \begin{bmatrix} \quad \end{bmatrix}\begin{bmatrix} U_1(s) \\ U_2(s) \end{bmatrix}$$

$$\begin{bmatrix} sX_1(s) \\ sX_2(s) \end{bmatrix} = \begin{bmatrix} x_1(0) \\ x_2(0) \end{bmatrix} + \begin{bmatrix} -1 & 1 \\ 0 & -2 \end{bmatrix} \begin{bmatrix} X_1(s) \\ X_2(s) \end{bmatrix} + \begin{bmatrix} 0 & 1 \\ 1 & 0 \end{bmatrix} \begin{bmatrix} U_1(s) \\ U_2(s) \end{bmatrix}$$

conformability of the matrix product
requires that there be two inputs

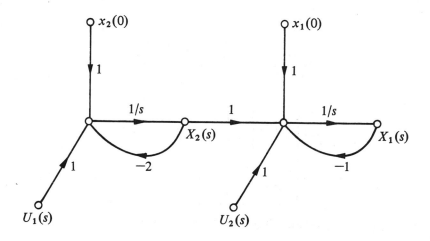

**6.8**    (Solution) From the S.F.G., $\Delta = 1 + \dfrac{2}{s} + \dfrac{1}{s} + \dfrac{2}{s^2} = \dfrac{s^2 + 3s + 2}{s^2}$

Then $X_1(s) = \dfrac{1/s\,(1 + 2/s)}{\Delta}\, x_1(0) + \dfrac{(1/s^2)\,(1)}{\Delta}\, x_2(0) + \dfrac{(1/s^2)(1)}{\Delta}\, U_1(s) + \dfrac{1/s(1 + 2/s)}{\Delta}\, U_2(s)$

$$= \dfrac{1}{s + 1}\, x_1(0) + \dfrac{1}{(s + 1)(s + 2)}\, x_2(0) + \dfrac{1}{(s + 1)(s + 2)}\, U_1(s)$$

$$+ \dfrac{1}{s + 1}\, U_2(s)$$

Similarly,

$$X_2(s) = \dfrac{1}{s + 2}\, x_2(0) + \dfrac{1}{s + 2}\, U_1(s)$$

Therefore,

$$
\begin{bmatrix} X_1(s) \\ \\ X_2(s) \end{bmatrix}
=
\begin{bmatrix} \dfrac{1}{s + 1} & \dfrac{1}{(s + 1)(s + 2)} \\ \\ 0 & \dfrac{1}{s + 2} \end{bmatrix}
\begin{bmatrix} x_1(0) \\ \\ x_2(0) \end{bmatrix}
+
\begin{bmatrix} \dfrac{1}{(s + 1)(s + 2)} & \dfrac{1}{s + 1} \\ \\ \dfrac{1}{s + 2} & 0 \end{bmatrix}
\begin{bmatrix} U_1(s) \\ \\ U_2(s) \end{bmatrix}
$$

This is the answer to the previous frame. Note that the solution takes the form:

$$\mathbf{X}(s) = \mathbf{\Phi}(s)\, \mathbf{x}(0) + \mathbf{H}(s)\, \mathbf{U}(s)$$

or,    $$\mathbf{X}(s) = \mathbf{X}_{\text{I.C.}}(s) + \mathbf{X}_F(s)$$

this relationship is
provided on the MASK
for reference

---

**6.9**    Now FIND $x_{1_{\text{I.C.}}}(t)$ *and* $x_{2_{\text{I.C.}}}(t)$ in terms of $x_1(0)$ and $x_2(0)$:

$$X_{1_{\text{I.C.}}}(s) = \frac{1}{s+1} x_1(0) + \frac{1}{(s+1)(s+2)} x_2(0)$$

$$\therefore \quad \underline{x_{1_{\text{I.C.}}}(t) = \epsilon^{-t} x_1(0) + \{\epsilon^{-t} - \epsilon^{-2t}\} x_2(0)} \qquad t \geqslant 0$$

and $\quad \underline{x_{2_{\text{I.C.}}}(t) = \epsilon^{-2t} x_2(0)} \qquad t \geqslant 0$

*Comment:*
In matrix form

$$\mathbf{x}_{\text{I.C.}}(t) = \begin{bmatrix} \epsilon^{-t} & \epsilon^{-t} - \epsilon^{-2t} \\ 0 & \epsilon^{-2t} \end{bmatrix} \mathbf{x}(0)$$

**6.10**    From the previous page:

$$\mathbf{X}_F(s) = \begin{bmatrix} X_{1_F}(s) \\ X_{2_F}(s) \end{bmatrix} = \begin{bmatrix} & \\ & \end{bmatrix}\begin{bmatrix} & \\ & \end{bmatrix}$$

$\uparrow$
(*note*)

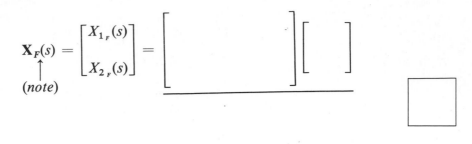

---

**6.11**    If $u_1(t) = 3\delta(t)$, where $\delta(t)$ is a unit impulse, and $u_2(t) = -4$, FIND $x_{1_F}(t)$ and $x_{2_F}(t)$:

---

### SUMMARY

**6.12**    We started this section with the state equation:

$$\dot{\mathbf{x}} = \mathbf{Ax} + \mathbf{Bu}$$

This was transformed to yield:

$$s\mathbf{X}(s) = \mathbf{x}(0) + \mathbf{AX}(s) + \mathbf{BU}(s)$$

Then, the S.F.G. followed at once, and using the Mason gain rule, we found:

$$\mathbf{X}(s) = \mathbf{\Phi}(s)\mathbf{x}(0) + \mathbf{H}(s)\mathbf{U}(s)$$

$$= \mathbf{X}_{\text{I.C.}}(s) + \mathbf{X}_F(s)$$

Finally, taking the inverse transform, we obtained the solution:

$\mathbf{x}(t) = \mathbf{x}_{\text{I.C.}}(t) + \mathbf{x}_F(t)$, where $\mathbf{x}_{\text{I.C.}}(t)$ is the initial condition part of the solution, and $\mathbf{x}_F(t)$ is the forced part of the solution.

---

Section 7 will take you 20 to 35 minutes to complete.

$$\mathbf{X}_F(s) = \begin{bmatrix} X_{1_F}(s) \\ \\ X_{2_F}(s) \end{bmatrix} = \begin{bmatrix} \dfrac{1}{(s+1)(s+2)} & \dfrac{1}{s+1} \\ \\ \dfrac{1}{s+2} & 0 \end{bmatrix} \begin{bmatrix} U_1(s) \\ \\ U_2(s) \end{bmatrix}$$

$$\mathscr{L}[u_1(t)] = \mathscr{L}[3\delta(t)] = 3$$

$$\mathscr{L}[u_2(t)] = \mathscr{L}[-4] = -\frac{4}{s}$$

$$X_{1_F}(s) = \frac{3}{(s+1)(s+2)} - \frac{4}{s(s+1)}$$

and $\quad \underline{x_{1_F}(t) = 3\epsilon^{-t} - 3\epsilon^{-2t} - 4 + 4\epsilon^{-t}} \qquad t \geqslant 0 \qquad \checkmark$

$$X_{2_F}(s) = \frac{3}{s+2}$$

and $\quad \underline{x_{2_F}(t) = 3\epsilon^{-2t}} \qquad t \geqslant 0$

In the last section you have learned to solve the state equation, $\dot{\mathbf{x}} = \mathbf{Ax} + \mathbf{Bu}$, using signal flow graphs and Mason's gain rule.

Here we will consider an alternative procedure—that of matrix algebra.

**7.1** Let's return to the example of frame **6.7**:

$$\begin{bmatrix} \dot{x}_1 \\ \dot{x}_2 \end{bmatrix} = \begin{bmatrix} -1 & 1 \\ 0 & -2 \end{bmatrix} \begin{bmatrix} x_1 \\ x_2 \end{bmatrix} + \begin{bmatrix} 0 & 1 \\ 1 & 0 \end{bmatrix} \begin{bmatrix} u_1(t) \\ u_2(t) \end{bmatrix}$$

As in the S.F.G. solution, the first step of the matrix solution is to transform the state equation, thereby obtaining:

$$\begin{bmatrix} sX_1(s) \\ sX_2(s) \end{bmatrix} = \begin{bmatrix} x_1(0) \\ x_2(0) \end{bmatrix} + \begin{bmatrix} -1 & 1 \\ 0 & -2 \end{bmatrix} \begin{bmatrix} X_1(s) \\ X_2(s) \end{bmatrix} + \begin{bmatrix} 0 & 1 \\ 1 & 0 \end{bmatrix} \begin{bmatrix} U_1(s) \\ U_2(s) \end{bmatrix}$$

If we were solving an algebraic equation, the next step would be to move all terms involving the unknown onto one side of the equation. Here the equivalent is to REARRANGE the matrix equation to get all terms in $\mathbf{X}(s)$ onto one side:

$$\begin{bmatrix} sX_1(s) \\ sX_2(s) \end{bmatrix} - \begin{bmatrix} \phantom{xxxx} \\ \phantom{xxxx} \end{bmatrix}\begin{bmatrix} \phantom{xxxx} \\ \phantom{xxxx} \end{bmatrix} = \begin{bmatrix} x_1(0) \\ x_2(0) \end{bmatrix} + \begin{bmatrix} 0 & 1 \\ 1 & 0 \end{bmatrix} \begin{bmatrix} U_1(s) \\ U_2(s) \end{bmatrix}$$

**7.2** In matrix form this equation reads:

$$s\mathbf{X}(s) - \mathbf{AX}(s) = \mathbf{x}(0) + \mathbf{BU}(s)$$

If we were to proceed algebraically we would factor out $(s - \mathbf{A})$ on the left. However, this is *not* an algebraic equation, and $(s - \mathbf{A})$ is meaningless. Why?

$$\begin{bmatrix} sX_1(s) \\ sX_2(s) \end{bmatrix} - \begin{bmatrix} -1 & 1 \\ 0 & -2 \end{bmatrix} \begin{bmatrix} X_1(s) \\ X_2(s) \end{bmatrix} = \begin{bmatrix} x_1(0) \\ x_2(0) \end{bmatrix} + \begin{bmatrix} 0 & 1 \\ 1 & 0 \end{bmatrix} \begin{bmatrix} U_1(s) \\ U_2(s) \end{bmatrix}$$

*In your own words:*                                                          or the $1 \times 1$ matrix
The $2 \times 2$ matrix, **A**, cannot be subtracted from the scalar, $s$.

**7.3**　On the previous page we noted that:

$$sX(s) - AX(s) \neq (s - A)X(s)$$

However, we *do* want to combine the two terms. First, to review the appropriate notation, recall that:

$$\begin{bmatrix} 1 & 0 \\ 0 & 1 \end{bmatrix}, \quad \begin{bmatrix} 1 & 0 & 0 \\ 0 & 1 & 0 \\ 0 & 0 & 1 \end{bmatrix}, \quad \begin{bmatrix} 1 & 0 & 0 & 0 \\ 0 & 1 & 0 & 0 \\ 0 & 0 & 1 & 0 \\ 0 & 0 & 0 & 1 \end{bmatrix}, \quad \text{etc.}$$

are called _____ matrices and are represented by the symbol _____.

---

**7.4**　Now PERFORM the matrix multiplication:

$$sIX(s) = s\underset{\uparrow I}{\begin{bmatrix} 1 & 0 \\ 0 & 1 \end{bmatrix}}\begin{bmatrix} X_1(s) \\ X_2(s) \end{bmatrix} = \begin{bmatrix} \quad \end{bmatrix}\begin{bmatrix} X_1(s) \\ X_2(s) \end{bmatrix} = \begin{bmatrix} \quad \end{bmatrix}$$

$$= \text{\_\_\_\_} X(s)$$

---

**7.5**　That is, $sX(s)$ may be replaced by _____ $X(s)$.

---

**7.6**　Now we can write:

$$sX(s) - AX(s) = \text{\_\_\_\_\_} X(s) - AX(s)$$

$$= (\text{_____})X(s)$$

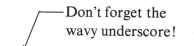

—Don't forget the
wavy underscore!

unit or identity matrices, symbolized by **I**.

*Comment:*

The identity matrix is a square matrix and is always chosen with the proper number of rows and columns.

---

$$s \begin{bmatrix} 1 & 0 \\ 0 & 1 \end{bmatrix} \begin{bmatrix} X_1(s) \\ X_2(s) \end{bmatrix} = \begin{bmatrix} s & 0 \\ 0 & s \end{bmatrix} \begin{bmatrix} X_1(s) \\ X_2(s) \end{bmatrix} = \begin{bmatrix} sX_1(s) \\ sX_2(s) \end{bmatrix}$$

$$= s\mathbf{X}(s)$$

---

$s\mathbf{X}(s)$ may be replaced by $s\mathbf{I}\mathbf{X}(s)$

---

$$s\mathbf{X}(s) - \mathbf{A}\mathbf{X}(s) = s\mathbf{I}\mathbf{X}(s) - \mathbf{A}\mathbf{X}(s)$$

$$= (s\mathbf{I} - \mathbf{A})\mathbf{X}(s)$$

└*this* subtraction is legitimate

---

**7.7**    To recapitulate, we started with the state equation:

$$\dot{x} = Ax + Bu$$

Then, TRANSFORMING,

$$sX(s) = \underline{\hspace{4cm}}$$

REARRANGING,

$$sX(s) - AX(s) = \underline{\hspace{4cm}}$$

$$\therefore \quad (\underline{\hspace{1cm}})X(s) = \underline{\hspace{4cm}}$$

---

**7.8**    Recalling that matrix division is not defined, that a matrix multiplied by its inverse yields the identity matrix, and that the *order* of a matrix product is important, it follows that the last equation can be "solved" for **X**(*s*), yielding:

$$X(s) = \underline{\hspace{5cm}}$$

---

**7.9**    In the problem posed in frame **7.1**, $\quad A = \begin{bmatrix} -1 & 1 \\ 0 & -2 \end{bmatrix}$

$$\therefore \quad (sI - A) = s\begin{bmatrix} & \\ & \end{bmatrix} - \begin{bmatrix} & \\ & \end{bmatrix}$$

$$= \begin{bmatrix} & \\ & \end{bmatrix} - \begin{bmatrix} & \\ & \end{bmatrix} = \begin{bmatrix} & \\ & \end{bmatrix}$$

---

**7.10**    Use scratch paper to FIND the inverse of $(sI - A)$:

$$(sI - A)^{-1} = \begin{bmatrix} & \\ & \end{bmatrix}$$

(see MASK for procedure)

$$sX(s) = \underline{x(0)} + AX(s) + BU(s)$$

$$sX(s) - AX(s) = \underline{x(0)} + BU(s)$$

$$\underline{(sI - A)X(s)} = \underline{x(0)} + BU(s) \qquad \text{since } sX(s) - AX(s) = sIX(s) - AX(s)$$

and since $(sI - A)$ is a legitimate operation

*Note:*

It is important that you differentiate between matrices and scalars. So don't leave out the wavy underscore.

---

Premultiplying the above equation by $(sI - A)^{-1}$:

$$(sI - A)^{-1}(sI - A)X(s) = (sI - A)^{-1}x(0) + (sI - A)^{-1}BU(s)$$

$$\therefore \qquad \boxed{\begin{aligned} X(s) &= (sI - A)^{-1}x(0) + (sI - A)^{-1}BU(s) \\ &= X_{\text{I.C.}}(s) + X_F(s) \end{aligned}}$$

these results are provided on the MASK for reference

---

$$(sI - A) = s\begin{bmatrix} 1 & 0 \\ 0 & 1 \end{bmatrix} - \begin{bmatrix} -1 & 1 \\ 0 & -2 \end{bmatrix}$$

$$= \begin{bmatrix} s & 0 \\ 0 & s \end{bmatrix} - \begin{bmatrix} -1 & 1 \\ 0 & -2 \end{bmatrix} = \begin{bmatrix} s+1 & -1 \\ 0 & s+2 \end{bmatrix}$$

---

$$(sI - A)^{-1} = \frac{C^T}{|sI - A|} \qquad \text{where the matrix of cofactors, } C = \begin{bmatrix} s+2 & 0 \\ 1 & s+1 \end{bmatrix}$$

$$\therefore \quad (sI - A)^{-1} = \frac{\begin{bmatrix} s+2 & 1 \\ 0 & s+1 \end{bmatrix}}{(s+1)(s+2) - 0} = \begin{bmatrix} \dfrac{1}{s+1} & \dfrac{1}{(s+1)(s+2)} \\ 0 & \dfrac{1}{s+2} \end{bmatrix}$$

**7.11**    We found the solution of the transformed state equation to be:

$$\mathbf{X}(s) = (s\mathbf{I} - \mathbf{A})^{-1}\mathbf{x}(0) + (s\mathbf{I} - \mathbf{A})^{-1}\mathbf{B}\mathbf{U}(s)$$

Given $(s\mathbf{I} - \mathbf{A})^{-1}$ as on the previous page,

$$\mathbf{X}_{\text{I.C.}}(s) = \begin{bmatrix} & \\ & \\ & \end{bmatrix} \mathbf{x}(0)$$

---

**7.12**    It follows that:

$$\mathbf{x}_{\text{I.C.}}(t) = \begin{bmatrix} & \\ & \end{bmatrix} \mathbf{x}(0)$$

(use scratch paper if necessary)

---

**7.13**    Given $\mathbf{B} = \begin{bmatrix} 0 & 1 \\ 1 & 0 \end{bmatrix}$ and the matrix equation at the top of the page you can obtain:

$$\mathbf{X}_F(s) = \begin{bmatrix} & \\ & \end{bmatrix}\begin{bmatrix} \\ \end{bmatrix} \mathbf{U}(s)$$

$$= \begin{bmatrix} & \\ & \end{bmatrix} \mathbf{U}(s)$$

Allow about one hour for the next Section.

$$\mathbf{X}_{\text{I.C.}}(s) = \begin{bmatrix} \dfrac{1}{s+1} & \dfrac{1}{(s+1)(s+2)} \\ 0 & \dfrac{1}{s+2} \end{bmatrix} \mathbf{x}(0)$$

From frame **7.8**,

$$\mathbf{X}_{\text{I.C.}}(s) = (s\mathbf{I} - \mathbf{A})^{-1}\mathbf{x}(0)$$

$$\mathbf{x}_{\text{I.C.}}(t) = \begin{bmatrix} \epsilon^{-t} & \epsilon^{-t} - \epsilon^{-2t} \\ 0 & \epsilon^{-2t} \end{bmatrix} \mathbf{x}(0)$$

this agrees with the S.F.G. solution in frame **6.9**.

From frame **7.8**,

$$\mathbf{X}_F(s) = (s\mathbf{I} - \mathbf{A})^{-1} \mathbf{B}\mathbf{U}(s)$$

$$= \begin{bmatrix} \dfrac{1}{s+1} & \dfrac{1}{(s+1)(s+2)} \\ 0 & \dfrac{1}{s+2} \end{bmatrix} \begin{bmatrix} 0 & 1 \\ 1 & 0 \end{bmatrix} \mathbf{U}(s)$$

$$= \begin{bmatrix} \dfrac{1}{(s+1)(s+2)} & \dfrac{1}{s+1} \\ \dfrac{1}{s+2} & 0 \end{bmatrix} \mathbf{U}(s)$$

*Comments:*

1. We obtained the above result using the S.F.G. in frame **6.10**.
2. For given inputs, $u_1(t)$ and $u_2(t)$, we could find $\mathbf{x}_F(t)$, as we did in frame **6.11**.

## A SECOND EXAMPLE OF MATRIX SOLUTION

**8.1**     Let us suppose that we want to solve the state equation:

$$\dot{\mathbf{x}} = \begin{bmatrix} 0 & 1 \\ 0 & 0 \end{bmatrix} \mathbf{x} + \begin{bmatrix} 0 \\ k \end{bmatrix} \mathbf{u}$$

We have shown that the transform of the solution is given by:

$$\mathbf{X}(s) = (s\mathbf{I} - \mathbf{A})^{-1} \mathbf{x}(0) + (s\mathbf{I} - \mathbf{A})^{-1} \mathbf{B}U(s)$$

The first step is therefore to COMPUTE $(s\mathbf{I} - \mathbf{A})^{-1}$:

☐

---

**8.2**     Now COMPLETE the solution for $\mathbf{X}(s)$:

*Answer:* $\mathbf{X}(s) = \begin{bmatrix} \\ \\ \end{bmatrix} \mathbf{x}(0) + \begin{bmatrix} \\ \\ \end{bmatrix} U(s)$

☐

$$\mathbf{A} = \begin{bmatrix} 0 & 1 \\ 0 & 0 \end{bmatrix}$$

$$\therefore \quad (s\mathbf{I} - \mathbf{A}) = \begin{bmatrix} s & 0 \\ 0 & s \end{bmatrix} - \begin{bmatrix} 0 & 1 \\ 0 & 0 \end{bmatrix} = \begin{bmatrix} s & -1 \\ 0 & s \end{bmatrix}$$

$$\therefore \quad \mathbf{C} = \begin{bmatrix} s & 0 \\ 1 & s \end{bmatrix} \quad \text{(matrix of cofactors)}$$

$$\text{and } (s\mathbf{I} - \mathbf{A})^{-1} = \frac{\begin{bmatrix} s & 1 \\ 0 & s \end{bmatrix}}{\begin{vmatrix} s & -1 \\ 0 & s \end{vmatrix}} = \frac{1}{s^2} \begin{bmatrix} s & 1 \\ 0 & s \end{bmatrix} = \begin{bmatrix} \dfrac{1}{s} & \dfrac{1}{s^2} \\ 0 & \dfrac{1}{s} \end{bmatrix}$$

$$(s\mathbf{I} - \mathbf{A})^{-1}\mathbf{B} = \begin{bmatrix} \dfrac{1}{s} & \dfrac{1}{s^2} \\ 0 & \dfrac{1}{s} \end{bmatrix} \begin{bmatrix} 0 \\ k \end{bmatrix} = \begin{bmatrix} \dfrac{k}{s^2} \\ \dfrac{k}{s} \end{bmatrix}$$

$$\therefore \quad \mathbf{X}(s) = \begin{bmatrix} \dfrac{1}{s} & \dfrac{1}{s^2} \\ 0 & \dfrac{1}{s} \end{bmatrix} \mathbf{x}(0) + \begin{bmatrix} \dfrac{k}{s^2} \\ \dfrac{k}{s} \end{bmatrix} \mathbf{U}(s)$$

*Comment:*

This is what you obtained in frame **6.5** from the S.F.G.

You could now proceed as in frame **6.6** to find $\mathbf{x}(t)$ for given $\mathbf{x}(0)$ and $\mathbf{U}(s)$.

## A REVIEW PROBLEM—MATRIX SOLUTION

**8.3**   Consider the differential equation:

$$\frac{d^3\theta}{dt^3} + 2\frac{d^2\theta}{dt^2} = 3r(t).$$

The corresponding state equation is:

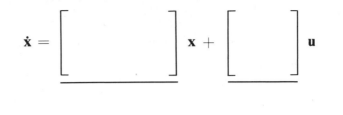

$$\dot{\mathbf{x}} = \begin{bmatrix} & \\ & \end{bmatrix} \mathbf{x} + \begin{bmatrix} \\ \end{bmatrix} \mathbf{u}$$

---

**8.4**   FIND $(s\mathbf{I}-\mathbf{A})^{-1}$:

(use scratch paper if necessary)

---

**8.5**   The equation $\mathbf{X}(s) = (s\mathbf{I} - \mathbf{A})^{-1}\mathbf{x}(0) + (s\mathbf{I} - \mathbf{A})^{-1}\mathbf{B}\mathbf{U}(s)$ can be written in the form:

$$\mathbf{X}(s) = \mathbf{\Phi}(s)\mathbf{x}(0) + \mathbf{H}(s)\mathbf{U}(s).$$

FIND $\mathbf{\Phi}(s)$ and $\mathbf{H}(s)$:

*Comment:*

Although $\dfrac{d\theta}{dt}$ and $\theta$ do not appear explicitly in the differential equation, the equation is still of *third* order, and there must be *three* states.

Representing $\theta$ by $x_1$, $\dot{\theta}$ by $x_2$, $\ddot{\theta}$ by $x_3$, and $r(t)$ by $u_1(t)$:

$$\dot{x}_1 = x_2$$
$$\dot{x}_2 = x_3 \qquad \text{and} \quad \dot{\mathbf{x}} = \begin{bmatrix} 0 & 1 & 0 \\ 0 & 0 & 1 \\ 0 & 0 & -2 \end{bmatrix} \mathbf{x} + \begin{bmatrix} 0 \\ 0 \\ 3 \end{bmatrix} \mathbf{u}$$
$$\dot{x}_3 = -2x_3 + 3u_1(t)$$

---

$$(s\mathbf{I} - \mathbf{A}) = \begin{bmatrix} s & -1 & 0 \\ 0 & s & -1 \\ 0 & 0 & s+2 \end{bmatrix} \quad \text{and} \quad \mathbf{C} = \begin{bmatrix} s(s+2) & 0 & 0 \\ s+2 & s(s+2) & 0 \\ 1 & s & s^2 \end{bmatrix}$$

$$(s\mathbf{I} - \mathbf{A})^{-1} = \frac{\begin{bmatrix} s(s+2) & s+2 & 1 \\ 0 & s(s+2) & s \\ 0 & 0 & s^2 \end{bmatrix}}{\begin{vmatrix} s & -1 & 0 \\ 0 & s & -1 \\ 0 & 0 & s+2 \end{vmatrix}} = \begin{bmatrix} \dfrac{1}{s} & \dfrac{1}{s^2} & \dfrac{1}{s^2(s+2)} \\[2mm] 0 & \dfrac{1}{s} & \dfrac{1}{s(s+2)} \\[2mm] 0 & 0 & \dfrac{1}{s+2} \end{bmatrix}$$

---

$$\boldsymbol{\Phi}(s) = (s\mathbf{I} - \mathbf{A})^{-1} \text{ (as above)}$$

$$\mathbf{H}(s) = (s\mathbf{I} - \mathbf{A})^{-1}\mathbf{B} = \begin{bmatrix} \dfrac{3}{s^2(s+2)} \\[3mm] \dfrac{3}{s(s+2)} \\[3mm] \dfrac{3}{s+2} \end{bmatrix}$$

**8.6**     Our state equation on the previous page was:

$$\dot{\mathbf{x}} = \begin{bmatrix} 0 & 1 & 0 \\ 0 & 0 & 1 \\ 0 & 0 & -2 \end{bmatrix} \mathbf{x} + \begin{bmatrix} 0 \\ 0 \\ 3 \end{bmatrix} \mathbf{u}$$

As an alternative to the matrix solution, let's now solve the same equation using the S.F.G. First, **TRANSFORM**, and then **DRAW** the graph:

**8.7**     Now apply the Mason gain rule to FIND $\mathbf{X}(s)$:

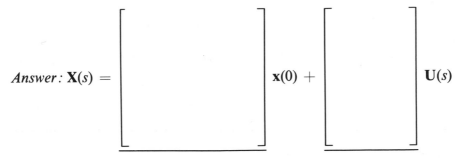

$$Answer: \mathbf{X}(s) = \begin{bmatrix} \phantom{xxxxxxxx} \\ \phantom{xxxxxxxx} \\ \phantom{xxxxxxxx} \end{bmatrix} \mathbf{x}(0) + \begin{bmatrix} \phantom{xxxxxxxx} \\ \phantom{xxxxxxxx} \\ \phantom{xxxxxxxx} \end{bmatrix} \mathbf{U}(s)$$

(use scratch paper if necessary)

$$sX(s) = \mathbf{x}(0) + \begin{bmatrix} 0 & 1 & 0 \\ 0 & 0 & 1 \\ 0 & 0 & -2 \end{bmatrix} X(s) + \begin{bmatrix} 0 \\ 0 \\ 3 \end{bmatrix} U(s)$$

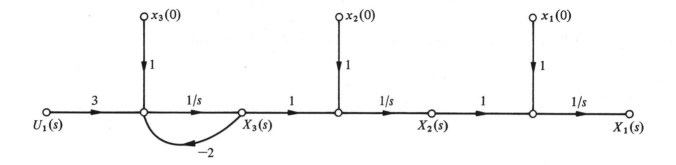

$$\Delta = 1 + \frac{2}{s} = \frac{s + 2}{s}$$

$$X(s) = \begin{bmatrix} \dfrac{1}{s} & \dfrac{1}{s^2} & \dfrac{1}{s^2(s+2)} \\[2ex] 0 & \dfrac{1}{s} & \dfrac{1}{s(s+2)} \\[2ex] 0 & 0 & \dfrac{1}{s+2} \end{bmatrix} \mathbf{x}(0) + \begin{bmatrix} \dfrac{3}{s^2(s+2)} \\[2ex] \dfrac{3}{s(s+2)} \\[2ex] \dfrac{3}{s+2} \end{bmatrix} U(s)$$

note that this is what we found in frame **8.5** by the matrix method

**8.8**　The transform of our system's response has been found both by S.F.G. and matrix methods to be:

$$\mathbf{X}(s) = \begin{bmatrix} \dfrac{1}{s} & \dfrac{1}{s^2} & \dfrac{1}{s^2(s+2)} \\[2ex] 0 & \dfrac{1}{s} & \dfrac{1}{s(s+2)} \\[2ex] 0 & 0 & \dfrac{1}{s+2} \end{bmatrix} \mathbf{x}(0) + \begin{bmatrix} \dfrac{3}{s^2(s+2)} \\[2ex] \dfrac{3}{s(s+2)} \\[2ex] \dfrac{3}{s+2} \end{bmatrix} U(s) = \mathbf{X}_{\text{I.C.}}(s) + \mathbf{X}_F(s)$$

FIND the initial condition response, $\mathbf{x}_{\text{I.C.}}(t)$, in terms of $\mathbf{x}(0)$:

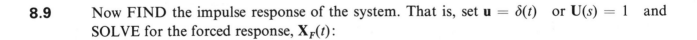

**8.9**　Now FIND the impulse response of the system. That is, set $\mathbf{u} = \delta(t)$　or $U(s) = 1$　and SOLVE for the forced response, $\mathbf{X}_F(t)$:

$$\mathbf{X}_{\text{I.C.}}(s) = \mathbf{\Phi}(s)\mathbf{x}(0)$$

$$\therefore \quad \mathbf{x}_{\text{I.C.}}(t) = \mathscr{L}^{-1}[\mathbf{\Phi}(s)\mathbf{x}(0)]$$

$$= \mathscr{L}^{-1}[\mathbf{\Phi}(s)]\mathbf{x}(0) \quad \textit{since } \mathbf{x}(0) \textit{ is a matrix of constants}$$

Taking the inverse transform of each element in the $\mathbf{\Phi}(s)$ matrix:

$$\mathbf{x}_{\text{I.C.}}(t) = \begin{bmatrix} 1 & t & \frac{1}{4}\epsilon^{-2t} + \frac{1}{2}t - \frac{1}{4} \\[2mm] 0 & 1 & \frac{1}{2} - \frac{1}{2}\epsilon^{-2t} \\[2mm] 0 & 0 & \epsilon^{-2t} \end{bmatrix} \mathbf{x}(0)$$

---

From frame **8.8**:

$$\mathbf{X}_F(s) = \begin{bmatrix} \dfrac{3}{s^2(s + 2)} \\[3mm] \dfrac{3}{s(s + 2)} \\[3mm] \dfrac{3}{s + 2} \end{bmatrix} \overset{\displaystyle\longleftarrow U(s) \text{ is a scalar}}{[1]}$$

$$\mathbf{x}_F(t) = \begin{bmatrix} \frac{3}{4}\epsilon^{-2t} + \frac{3}{2}t - \frac{3}{4} \\[2mm] \frac{3}{2} - \frac{3}{2}\epsilon^{-2t} \\[2mm] 3\epsilon^{-2t} \end{bmatrix}$$

## SUMMARY

**8.10**   The last problem (frames **8.3–8.9**) should serve as a useful review of all the topics developed up to this point. The normal procedure has been to

1. *Define* new (state) variables so that the given differential equation can be written in first order form:

$$\dot{\mathbf{x}} = \mathbf{A}\mathbf{x} + \mathbf{B}\mathbf{u}$$

2. *Transform* the state equation to obtain:

$$s\mathbf{X}(s) = \mathbf{x}(0) + \mathbf{A}\mathbf{X}(s) + \mathbf{B}\mathbf{U}(s)$$

3. *Draw* the S.F.G. and use the Mason gain rule to obtain $\mathbf{X}(s)$;
   or by matrix methods,

$$\textit{Compute, } \mathbf{X}(s) = (s\mathbf{I} - \mathbf{A})^{-1}\mathbf{x}(0) + (s\mathbf{I} - \mathbf{A})^{-1}\mathbf{B}\mathbf{U}(s)$$

4. In either case (S.F.G. or matrix solution) the transformed solution is of the form:

$$\mathbf{X}(s) = \mathbf{\Phi}(s)\mathbf{x}(0) + \mathbf{H}(s)\mathbf{U}(s)$$

$$= \mathbf{X}_{\text{I.C.}}(s) + \mathbf{X}_F(s)$$

5. Finally, *taking the inverse transform*, one obtains the solution:

$$\mathbf{x}(t) = \mathbf{x}_{\text{I.C.}}(t) + \mathbf{x}_F(t)$$

*NOTE:*

Steps 3, 4, and 5 above can become *very* tedious if the system is of high order. If the system is of order $n$, then $\mathbf{\Phi}(s)$ will be an $n \times n$ matrix, requiring in its evaluation $n^2$ applications of the Mason gain rule, or the computation of the inverse of an $n \times n$ matrix. The corresponding inverse transformation of $n^2$ terms in $\mathbf{\Phi}(s)$ will generally be equally frustrating!

However, once we become familiar with the nature of the state equations and their solution, we will be in a position to rely upon computers to relieve us of much of the effort.

You will take about 45 minutes to work through the next section—*which starts opposite.*

## PREVIEW OF THE TIME DOMAIN SOLUTION

We set out with two objectives (frame **2.11**):

1. To put a system's equations into state variable form, and

2. To solve the resulting state equation, $\dot{\mathbf{x}} = \mathbf{A}\mathbf{x} + \mathbf{B}\mathbf{u}$.

You have already had a considerable amount of practice in the first of these—most recently in frame **8.3**.

You have also seen how we may solve the *transformed* state equation, either by S.F.G. methods or by matrices—most recently in the review problem of frames **8.3–8.9**.

These transform methods become quite cumbersome if the system is of high order, and although they *can* be adapted to computer solution, we generally find it more convenient to work entirely in the "time domain" if we are going to use a computer. That is, we *do not transform* the state equation and instead work directly with $\dot{\mathbf{x}}(t) = \mathbf{A}\mathbf{x}(t) + \mathbf{B}\mathbf{u}(t)$, which we describe as working in the time domain.

The next three sections will prepare the ground for computer solution in the time domain, which should be regarded as a major objective of the program.

Have you READ the PREVIEW on the previous page?

**9.1** Before we attempt to solve the *matrix* equation $\dot{\mathbf{x}} = \mathbf{Ax} + \mathbf{Bu}$, let's refresh our memory concerning the solution of the *scalar* equation $\frac{dx(t)}{dt} = ax(t) + bu(t)$. First consider the I.C. (homogeneous) solution, which requires that we solve:

$$\frac{dx(t)}{dt} - ax(t) = 0$$

Multiplying by the integrating factor, $\epsilon^{-at}$, one obtains:

$$\frac{dx(t)}{dt}\epsilon^{-at} - ax(t)\epsilon^{-at} = 0$$

That is,

$$\frac{d}{dt}\{ \underline{\hspace{3cm}} \} = 0$$

**9.2** Now we can integrate:

$$\int_0^t \frac{d}{dt}\{ \hspace{2cm} \} \, dt = 0$$

or

$$\{ \hspace{2cm} \}\Big|_0^t = 0$$

or

$$\underline{\hspace{3cm}} = 0$$

**9.3** Therefore,

$$x(t) = \underline{\hspace{3cm}}$$

$$\frac{d}{dt}\{x(t)\epsilon^{-at}\} = 0$$

*Comment:*
We know that there are easier methods for solving a first order scalar equation!

---

$$\int_0^t \frac{d}{dt}\{x(t)\epsilon^{-at}\}\,dt = 0$$

or $\qquad \{x(t)\epsilon^{-at}\}\Big|_0^t = 0$

Substituting the limits,

$$x(t)\epsilon^{-at} - x(0)\epsilon^{-a0} = 0$$

or $\qquad x(t)\epsilon^{-at} - x(0) = 0$

---

Solving the above equation for $x(t)$:

$$x(t) = \epsilon^{at}x(0) \quad \text{or} \quad \frac{x(0)}{\epsilon^{-at}}$$

*Comment:*
This is the initial condition solution which we have written $x_{\text{I.C.}}(t)$.

---

**9.4**    We have seen, in the scalar case, that:

$$\frac{dx}{dt} = ax \implies x_{\text{I.C.}}(t) = \epsilon^{at}x(0)$$

We might therefore hope that in the matrix case:

$$\dot{\mathbf{x}} = \mathbf{A}\mathbf{x} \implies \mathbf{x}_{\text{I.C.}}(t) = \epsilon^{\mathbf{A}t}\mathbf{x}(0)$$

This is in fact the correct I.C. solution,[†] but you are not likely to be impressed until you know a little more about $\epsilon^{\mathbf{A}t}$.

First, if $\mathbf{A}$ is any square matrix, we can *define*:

$$\epsilon^{\mathbf{A}t} = \mathbf{I} + \mathbf{A}t + \mathbf{A}^2\frac{t^2}{2!} + \cdots + \mathbf{A}^n\frac{t^n}{n!} + \cdots$$

For example:

If $\mathbf{A} = \begin{bmatrix} -1 & 0 \\ 0 & -2 \end{bmatrix}$, then the first two terms of the series will be:

$$\mathbf{I} + \mathbf{A}t = \begin{bmatrix} & \\ & \end{bmatrix} + \begin{bmatrix} & \\ & \end{bmatrix}$$

---

**9.5**    The next term in the series will be:

$$\mathbf{A}^2\frac{t^2}{2!} = \begin{bmatrix} & \\ & \end{bmatrix}\begin{bmatrix} & \\ & \end{bmatrix}\frac{t^2}{2} = \begin{bmatrix} & \\ & \end{bmatrix}\frac{t^2}{2} = \begin{bmatrix} & \\ & \end{bmatrix}$$

---

† Richard Bellman, *Introduction to Matrix Analysis* (New York: McGraw-Hill Book Company, 1960), pp. 165–169.

$$\mathbf{I} + \mathbf{A}t = \begin{bmatrix} 1 & 0 \\ 0 & 1 \end{bmatrix} + \begin{bmatrix} -1 & 0 \\ 0 & -2 \end{bmatrix} t \quad \text{or} \quad \begin{bmatrix} 1 & 0 \\ 0 & 1 \end{bmatrix} + \begin{bmatrix} -t & 0 \\ 0 & -2t \end{bmatrix}$$

*Comment:*

The definition of $\epsilon^{\mathbf{A}t}$ parallels the scalar case:

$$\epsilon^{at} = 1 + at + a^2 \frac{t^2}{2!} + \cdots + a^n \frac{t^n}{n!} + \cdots$$

---

$$\mathbf{A}^2 \frac{t^2}{2} = \begin{bmatrix} -1 & 0 \\ 0 & -2 \end{bmatrix} \overset{\mathbf{A}^2}{\begin{bmatrix} -1 & 0 \\ 0 & -2 \end{bmatrix}} \frac{t^2}{2} = \begin{bmatrix} 1 & 0 \\ 0 & 4 \end{bmatrix} \frac{t^2}{2} = \begin{bmatrix} \dfrac{t^2}{2} & 0 \\ 0 & 2t^2 \end{bmatrix}$$

*Comment:*

We will find it convenient to include the scalar multiplier, here $t^2/2$, inside the final matrix.

---

**9.6**    We have found the first three terms in the series for $\epsilon^{At}$, given

$A = \begin{bmatrix} -1 & 0 \\ 0 & -2 \end{bmatrix}$. Find the fourth term (Look back to the previous page if you wish):

<br>

□

---

**9.7**    Thus, knowing that $\epsilon^{At} = I + At + A^2 \dfrac{t^2}{2!} + A^3 \dfrac{t^3}{3!} + \cdots$

you can COMBINE the results of the last three frames to obtain:

$$\epsilon^{-At} = \begin{bmatrix} 1 - t + \frac{1}{2}t^2 - \frac{1}{6}t^3 + \cdots & \underline{\phantom{xxxx}} \\ \underline{\phantom{xxxx}} & \underline{\phantom{xxxxxxxxxx}} \end{bmatrix}$$

□

---

**9.8**    We see that $\epsilon^{At}$ can be written as a matrix with the same number of rows and columns as **A**. Each element in the $\epsilon^{At}$ matrix will be an infinite series—which will always converge for any finite value of $t$.

EVALUATE the above $\epsilon^{At}$ matrix when $t = 0.1$. That is, sum the first three terms of each series:

$$\epsilon^{0.1A} \doteq \begin{bmatrix} \phantom{xxxxxxxx} \end{bmatrix} \doteq \begin{bmatrix} \phantom{xxxx} \end{bmatrix}$$

□

---

The fourth term is $\mathbf{A}^3 \dfrac{t^3}{3!} = \mathbf{A}^2 \mathbf{A} \dfrac{t^3}{3!}$ or $\mathbf{A}\mathbf{A}^2 \dfrac{t^3}{3!}$

$$= \begin{bmatrix} 1 & 0 \\ 0 & 4 \end{bmatrix} \begin{bmatrix} -1 & 0 \\ 0 & -2 \end{bmatrix} \frac{t^3}{3!}$$

$$= \begin{bmatrix} -1 & 0 \\ 0 & -8 \end{bmatrix} \frac{t^3}{3!} = \begin{bmatrix} -\dfrac{t^3}{6} & 0 \\ 0 & -\dfrac{8}{6}t^3 \end{bmatrix}$$

$$\epsilon^{\mathbf{A}t} = \begin{bmatrix} 1 - t + \frac{1}{2}t^2 - \frac{1}{6}t^3 + \cdots & \underline{0} \\ \underline{0} & \underline{1 - 2t + 2t^2 - \frac{8}{6}t^3 + \cdots} \end{bmatrix}$$

Substituting $t = 0.1$:

$$\therefore \epsilon^{0.1\mathbf{A}} = \begin{bmatrix} 1 - 0.1 + \frac{1}{2}(0.1)^2 - \cdots & 0 \\ 0 & 1 - 2(0.1) + 2(0.1)^2 - \cdots \end{bmatrix}$$

$$\doteq \begin{bmatrix} 0.905 & 0 \\ 0 & 0.82 \end{bmatrix}$$

*Comment:*
Usually one would use a digital computer to sum each series. As a result of summing more terms, one obtains:

$$\epsilon^{0.1\mathbf{A}} \doteq \begin{bmatrix} 0.9048 & 0 \\ 0 & 0.8187 \end{bmatrix}$$

**9.9**    Summarizing, we claim that $\dot{\mathbf{x}} = \mathbf{Ax}$ has an I.C. solution $\mathbf{x}_{\text{I.C.}}(t) = \epsilon^{\mathbf{A}t}\mathbf{x}(0)$.

When $\mathbf{A} = \begin{bmatrix} -1 & 0 \\ 0 & -2 \end{bmatrix}$ we found

$$\epsilon^{\mathbf{A}t} = \begin{bmatrix} 1 - t + \frac{1}{2}t^2 - \frac{1}{6}t^3 + \cdots & 0 \\ 0 & 1 - 2t + 2t^2 - \frac{8}{6}t^3 + \cdots \end{bmatrix}$$

$$\therefore \quad \mathbf{x}_{\text{I.C.}}(t) = \begin{bmatrix} \phantom{xxxxxxxxxxxxxxxxxx} \end{bmatrix}$$

$\square$

---

**9.10**    Putting $t = 0.1$ we found:

$$\epsilon^{0.1\mathbf{A}} \doteq \begin{bmatrix} 0.905 & 0 \\ 0 & 0.82 \end{bmatrix}$$

Given also the initial conditions $x_1(0) = 2$ and $x_2(0) = 1$, it follows that:

$$\mathbf{x}_{\text{I.C.}}(0.1) = \begin{bmatrix} \phantom{xxxx} \end{bmatrix}$$

$\square$

---

**9.11**    Given the $\epsilon^{\mathbf{A}t}$ matrix in frame **9.9**, FIND $\mathbf{x}_{\text{I.C.}}(0.5)$ if $\mathbf{x}(0)$ remains equal to $\begin{bmatrix} 2 \\ 1 \end{bmatrix}$:

$\square$

$$\mathbf{x}_{\text{I.C.}}(t) = \begin{bmatrix} 1 - t + \frac{1}{2}t^2 - \frac{1}{6}t^3 + \cdots & 0 \\[2mm] 0 & 1 - 2t + 2t^2 - \frac{8}{6}t^3 + \cdots \end{bmatrix} \mathbf{x}(0)$$

and $\mathbf{x}_{\text{I.C.}}(0.1) \doteq \begin{bmatrix} 0.905 & 0 \\[2mm] 0 & 0.82 \end{bmatrix} \begin{bmatrix} 2 \\[2mm] 1 \end{bmatrix} = \begin{bmatrix} 1.81 \\[2mm] 0.82 \end{bmatrix}$

For this (larger) value of $t$, one needs at least four terms. If you used three terms (as in frame **9.8**) your answer will be slightly different.

$$\epsilon^{0.5A} = \begin{bmatrix} 1 - 0.5 + \frac{1}{2}(0.5)^2 - \frac{1}{6}(0.5)^3 + \cdots & 0 \\[2mm] 0 & 1 - 2(0.5) + 2(0.5)^2 - \frac{8}{6}(0.5)^3 + \cdots \end{bmatrix}$$

$$\doteq \begin{bmatrix} 0.604 & 0 \\[2mm] 0 & 0.334 \end{bmatrix}$$

$$\therefore \quad \mathbf{x}_{\text{I.C.}}(0.5) = \begin{bmatrix} 0.604 & 0 \\[2mm] 0 & 0.334 \end{bmatrix} \begin{bmatrix} 2 \\[2mm] 1 \end{bmatrix} \quad \text{or} \quad \begin{bmatrix} 1.208 \\[2mm] 0.334 \end{bmatrix}$$

*Comment:*

As $t$ becomes larger, even a digital computer will be inadequate for this calculation. In Sections 13 and 14 we will discuss a more intelligent numerical procedure.

## A SECOND EXAMPLE OF I.C. SOLUTION IN THE TIME DOMAIN

**9.12**    Let's solve the state equation $\dot{\mathbf{x}} = \begin{bmatrix} 0 & 1 \\ 0 & 0 \end{bmatrix} \mathbf{x}$ for $\mathbf{x}_{I.C.}(t)$. The first step is to EVALUATE:

$$\epsilon^{\mathbf{A}t} = \mathbf{I} + \mathbf{A}t + \mathbf{A}^2 \frac{t^2}{2!} + \cdots$$

$$= \begin{bmatrix} \phantom{xx} \end{bmatrix}$$

---

**9.13**    Now FIND $\mathbf{x}_{I.C.}(t)$, given $x_1(0) = 2$ and $x_2(0) = -3$:
(look back at frame **9.9** if you need help)

---

**9.14**    EVALUATE $\mathbf{x}_{I.C.}\left(\frac{2}{3}\right)$, and COMPLETE the sketches:

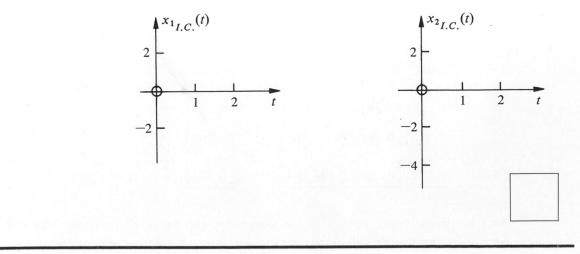

---

Time for Section 10—35 to 50 minutes.

$$\epsilon^{At} = \begin{bmatrix} 1 & 0 \\ 0 & 1 \end{bmatrix} + \begin{bmatrix} 0 & 1 \\ 0 & 0 \end{bmatrix} t + \overbrace{\begin{bmatrix} 0 & 1 \\ 0 & 0 \end{bmatrix}\begin{bmatrix} 0 & 1 \\ 0 & 0 \end{bmatrix}}^{A^2 = 0} \frac{t^2}{2!} + \cdots$$

$$= \begin{bmatrix} 1 & t \\ 0 & 1 \end{bmatrix}$$

*Comment:*

In this simple example the series terminates after two terms.
This won't happen often!

---

$$\mathbf{x}_{I.C.}(t) = \epsilon^{At}\mathbf{x}(0)$$

$$= \begin{bmatrix} 1 & t \\ 0 & 1 \end{bmatrix}\begin{bmatrix} 2 \\ -3 \end{bmatrix} \quad \text{or} \quad \begin{bmatrix} 2 - 3t \\ -3 \end{bmatrix}$$

---

$$\mathbf{x}_{I.C.}\left(\tfrac{2}{3}\right) = \begin{bmatrix} 0 \\ -3 \end{bmatrix}$$

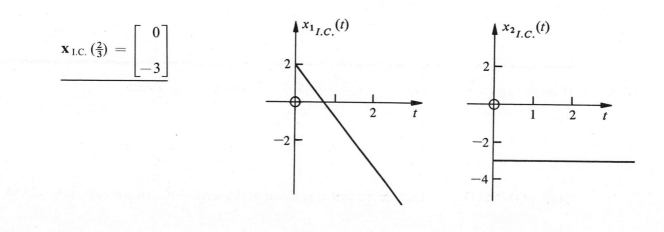

---

## A VACUUM TUBE CIRCUIT

**10.1**

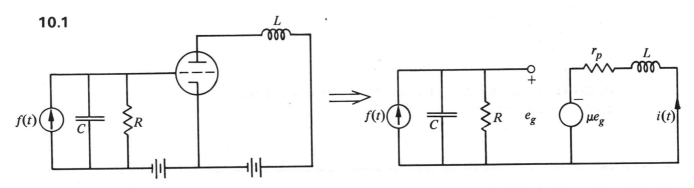

For small signals about the operating point the circuit on the left can be replaced by the small-signal equivalent on the right. Then:

$$L\frac{di}{dt} + r_p i - \mu e_g = 0$$

$$\text{and} \quad C\frac{de_g}{dt} + \frac{1}{R}e_g = f(t)$$

where $R$, $L$, $C$, $r_p$, and $\mu$ are circuit constants, and $f(t)$ is a current source.

Representing $i$ by $x_1$, $e_g$ by $x_2$, and $f(t)$ by $\mathbf{u}$,

$$\dot{\mathbf{x}} = \begin{bmatrix} \phantom{xxxx} \\ \phantom{xxxx} \end{bmatrix} \mathbf{x} + \begin{bmatrix} \phantom{x} \\ \phantom{x} \end{bmatrix} \mathbf{u}$$

---

**10.2**  If we are given $\mu = 10$, $L = 10$, $r_p = 10$, $R = 10$, and $C = \frac{1}{20}$, then:

$$\mathbf{A} = \begin{bmatrix} -1 & 1 \\ 0 & -2 \end{bmatrix}$$

Now COMPUTE $\epsilon^{At}$. Include the first four terms in the series—which is listed on the MASK.

$$\frac{di}{dt} = -\frac{r_p}{L}i + \frac{\mu}{L}e_g$$

$$\frac{de_g}{dt} = -\frac{1}{RC}e_g + \frac{1}{C}f(t)$$

$$\therefore \quad \dot{\mathbf{x}} = \begin{bmatrix} \dfrac{-r_p}{L} & \dfrac{\mu}{L} \\ \\ 0 & -\dfrac{1}{RC} \end{bmatrix} \mathbf{x} + \begin{bmatrix} 0 \\ \\ \dfrac{1}{C} \end{bmatrix} \mathbf{u}$$

$$\epsilon^{\mathbf{A}t} = \begin{bmatrix} 1 & 0 \\ 0 & 1 \end{bmatrix} + \begin{bmatrix} -1 & 1 \\ 0 & -2 \end{bmatrix}t + \begin{bmatrix} 1 & -3 \\ 0 & 4 \end{bmatrix}\frac{t^2}{2!} + \begin{bmatrix} -1 & 7 \\ 0 & -8 \end{bmatrix}\frac{t^3}{3!} + \cdots$$

$$= \begin{bmatrix} 1 - t + \dfrac{t^2}{2} - \dfrac{t^3}{6} + \cdots & t - \dfrac{3}{2}t^2 + \dfrac{7}{6}t^3 - \cdots \\ \\ 0 & 1 - 2t + 2t^2 - \dfrac{8}{6}t^3 + \cdots \end{bmatrix}$$

**10.3** We have found:

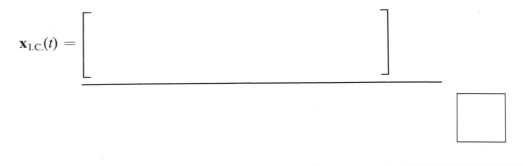

$$\epsilon^{At} = \begin{bmatrix} 1 - t + \dfrac{t^2}{2} - \dfrac{t^3}{6} + \cdots & t - \dfrac{3}{2}t^2 + \dfrac{7}{6}t^3 - \cdots \\ 0 & 1 - 2t + 2t^2 - \dfrac{8}{6}t^3 + \cdots \end{bmatrix}$$

Therefore the I.C. response of the circuit will be:

$$\mathbf{x}_{\text{I.C.}}(t) = \left[ \rule{0pt}{40pt} \hspace{300pt} \right]$$

☐

---

## SOME PROPERTIES OF $\epsilon^{At}$

**10.4** We have suggested that the matrix exponential, $\epsilon^{At}$, plays an important role in the solution of the matrix state equation. It behooves us, therefore, to investigate its properties.

We have defined $\quad \epsilon^{At} = \mathbf{I} + \mathbf{A}t + \mathbf{A}^2 \dfrac{t^2}{2!} + \cdots + \mathbf{A}^n \dfrac{t^n}{n!} + \cdots$

---

**10.5** First, $\qquad \epsilon^{-At} = $ _____

☐

---

**10.6** And $\qquad \epsilon^{-A\tau} = $ _____

☐

---

**10.7** Also, $\qquad \epsilon^{A0} = $ _____

☐

---

**10.8** And $\qquad \epsilon^{0t} = $ _____

☐

(**0** represents a null matrix)

---

92

$\mathbf{x}_{\text{I.C.}}(t) = \epsilon^{\mathbf{A}t}\mathbf{x}(0)$—SEE MASK

$$= \begin{bmatrix} 1 - t + \dfrac{t^2}{2} - \dfrac{t^3}{6} + \cdots & t - \dfrac{3}{2}t^2 + \dfrac{7}{6}t^3 - \cdots \\[4mm] 0 & 1 - 2t + 2t^2 - \dfrac{8}{6}t^3 + \cdots \end{bmatrix} \mathbf{x}(0)$$

*Comment:*

If you inspect the above series carefully, you will see that $\mathbf{x}_{\text{I.C.}}(t)$ may be written in the following closed form:

$$\mathbf{x}_{\text{I.C.}}(t) = \begin{bmatrix} \epsilon^{-t} & \epsilon^{-t} - \epsilon^{-2t} \\[3mm] 0 & \epsilon^{-2t} \end{bmatrix} \mathbf{x}(0)$$

This problem was also solved in frames **6.7–6.9** by S.F.G.—with the same result.

---

note the signs!

$$\epsilon^{-\mathbf{A}t} = \mathbf{I} - \mathbf{A}t + \mathbf{A}^2 \frac{t^2}{2!} - \mathbf{A}^3 \frac{t^3}{3!} + \cdots$$

(substitute $-t$ for $t$ in the series for $\epsilon^{\mathbf{A}t}$)

---

$$\epsilon^{-\mathbf{A}\tau} = \mathbf{I} - \mathbf{A}\tau + \mathbf{A}^2 \frac{\tau^2}{2!} - \mathbf{A}^3 \frac{\tau^3}{3!} + \cdots$$

---

$$\epsilon^{\mathbf{A}0} = \underline{\mathbf{I}}$$

---

$$\epsilon^{0t} = \underline{\mathbf{I}}$$

---

**10.9**  Using data from the previous page:

$$\epsilon^{At}\,\epsilon^{-At} = \Big(\phantom{xxxxxxxxxxxxxxxxxxxx}\Big)\Big(\phantom{xxxxxxxxxxxxxxxxxxxxxxxxxxxxx}\Big)$$

$$\boxed{\phantom{xx}}$$

---

**10.10**  Multiplying out the product, term by term:

$$\epsilon^{At}\,\epsilon^{-At} = \quad \mathbf{I}\Big(\mathbf{I} - \mathbf{A}t + \mathbf{A}^2\frac{t^2}{2!} - \mathbf{A}^3\frac{t^3}{3!} + \cdots\Big) = \qquad - \quad + \quad - \quad + \cdots$$

$$+ \quad \mathbf{A}t\Big(\mathbf{I} - \mathbf{A}t + \mathbf{A}^2\frac{t^2}{2!} - \cdots \phantom{xx}\Big) = \qquad\qquad - \quad + \quad - \cdots$$

$$+ \mathbf{A}^2\frac{t^2}{2!}\Big(\mathbf{I} - \mathbf{A}t + \cdots \phantom{xxx}\Big) = \qquad\qquad\qquad - \quad + \cdots$$

$$+ \mathbf{A}^3\frac{t^3}{3!}\Big(\mathbf{I} - \cdots \phantom{xxxxx}\Big) = \qquad\qquad\qquad\qquad - \cdots$$

And so on!        Summing, $\epsilon^{At}\,\epsilon^{-At} = $ _____

$$\boxed{\phantom{xx}}$$

---

**10.11**  Since $\epsilon^{At}\,\epsilon^{-At} = \mathbf{I}$, it follows that the inverse of the exponential matrix is:

$$\big[\epsilon^{At}\big]^{-1} = \underline{\phantom{xxx}}$$

$$\boxed{\phantom{xx}}$$

---

**10.12**  However, one would *not* calculate $\epsilon^{-At}$ by taking the inverse of the matrix $\epsilon^{At}$—it is too much work!

Given $\epsilon^{At} = \begin{bmatrix} 1 & t \\ 0 & 1 \end{bmatrix}$, FIND $\epsilon^{-At}$ *without* calculating an inverse.

(if you need help, look back at the note opposite frame **10.5**)

$$\epsilon^{-At} = \begin{bmatrix} \phantom{xxxx} \end{bmatrix}$$

$$\boxed{\phantom{xx}}$$

---

$$\epsilon^{At}\epsilon^{-At} = \left(\mathbf{I} + \mathbf{A}t + \mathbf{A}^2\frac{t^2}{2!} + \mathbf{A}^3\frac{t^3}{3!} + \cdots\right)\left(\mathbf{I} - \mathbf{A}t + \mathbf{A}^2\frac{t^2}{2!} - \mathbf{A}^3\frac{t^3}{3!} + \cdots\right)$$

$$\epsilon^{At}\epsilon^{-At} = \quad \mathbf{I}\left(\mathbf{I} - \mathbf{A}t + \mathbf{A}^2\frac{t^2}{2!} - \mathbf{A}^3\frac{t^3}{3!} + \cdots\right) \overset{\text{or } \mathbf{I}^2}{=} \mathbf{I} - \mathbf{A}t + \mathbf{A}^2\frac{t^2}{2!} - \mathbf{A}^3\frac{t^3}{3!} + \cdots$$

$$+ \quad \mathbf{A}t\left(\mathbf{I} - \mathbf{A}t + \mathbf{A}^2\frac{t^2}{2!} - \mathbf{A}^3\frac{t^3}{3!} + \cdots\right) = \quad \mathbf{A}t - \mathbf{A}^2 t^2 + \mathbf{A}^3\frac{t^3}{2!} - \cdots$$

$$+ \mathbf{A}^2\frac{t^2}{2!}\left(\mathbf{I} - \mathbf{A}t + \mathbf{A}^2\frac{t^2}{2!} - \mathbf{A}^3\frac{t^3}{3!} + \cdots\right) = \quad \mathbf{A}^2\frac{t^2}{2!} - \mathbf{A}^3\frac{t^3}{2!} + \cdots$$

$$+ \mathbf{A}^3\frac{t^3}{3!}\left(\mathbf{I} - \mathbf{A}t + \mathbf{A}^2\frac{t^2}{2!} - \mathbf{A}^3\frac{t^3}{3!} + \cdots\right) = \quad \mathbf{A}^3\frac{t^3}{3!} - \cdots$$

Summing: $\quad \epsilon^{At}\epsilon^{-At} = \mathbf{I}$

or $\mathbf{I}^2$

$$\left[\epsilon^{At}\right]^{-1} = \epsilon^{-At} \qquad \text{(a matrix multiplied by its inverse equals } \mathbf{I}\text{)}$$

*Comment:*
It follows, of course, that the order of the product can be interchanged; that is, $\epsilon^{At}\epsilon^{-At} = \epsilon^{-At}\epsilon^{At} = \mathbf{I}$.

Replacing $t$ with $-t$, we get:

$$\epsilon^{-At} = \begin{bmatrix} 1 & -t \\ 0 & 1 \end{bmatrix}$$

# DERIVATIVE OF THE MATRIX EXPONENTIAL

**10.13** It can be shown that it is legitimate to differentiate the exponential series term by term. Therefore, since

$$\epsilon^{At} = I + At + A^2 \frac{t^2}{2!} + \cdots + A^n \frac{t^n}{n!} + \cdots$$

$$\frac{d\,\epsilon^{At}}{dt} = \qquad + \qquad + \qquad + \cdots + \qquad + \cdots$$

$$= A(\underline{\qquad})$$

---

**10.14** If $A = \begin{bmatrix} 0 & 1 \\ 0 & 0 \end{bmatrix}$, $\epsilon^{At} = \begin{bmatrix} 1 & t \\ 0 & 1 \end{bmatrix}$ Therefore, *using the above result*, FIND the time derivative of $\epsilon^{At}$:

---

**10.15** Check the above result by differentiating the $\epsilon^{At}$ matrix directly:

---

$$\frac{d\,\epsilon^{\mathbf{A}t}}{dt} = \frac{d}{dt}(\mathbf{I}) + \frac{d}{dt}(\mathbf{A}t) + \frac{d}{dt}\left(\mathbf{A}^2\,\frac{t^2}{2!}\right) + \cdots + \frac{d}{dt}\left(\mathbf{A}^n\frac{t^n}{n!}\right) + \cdots$$

$$= \mathbf{0} \quad + \mathbf{A}\frac{d(t)}{dt} + \mathbf{A}^2\,\frac{d}{dt}\left(\frac{t^2}{2!}\right) + \cdots + \mathbf{A}^n\,\frac{d}{dt}\left(\frac{t^n}{n!}\right) + \cdots$$

$$= \mathbf{0} \quad + \mathbf{A} + \mathbf{A}^2 t + \cdots + \mathbf{A}^n\,\frac{t^{n-1}}{(n-1)!} + \cdots$$

$$= \mathbf{A}\left(\mathbf{I} + \mathbf{A}t + \cdots + \mathbf{A}^{n-1}\,\frac{t^{n-1}}{(n-1)!} + \cdots\right)$$

$$= \mathbf{A}(\epsilon^{\mathbf{A}t})$$

the next term will be $\mathbf{A}^n\,\dfrac{t^n}{n!}$

(A may also be factored out as a postmultiplier, thus $\mathbf{A}\epsilon^{\mathbf{A}t} = \epsilon^{\mathbf{A}t}\mathbf{A}$)

---

$$\frac{d\epsilon^{\mathbf{A}t}}{dt} = \mathbf{A}\;\epsilon^{\mathbf{A}t}$$

$$= \begin{bmatrix} 0 & 1 \\ 0 & 0 \end{bmatrix}\begin{bmatrix} 1 & t \\ 0 & 1 \end{bmatrix}$$

$$= \begin{bmatrix} 0 & 1 \\ 0 & 0 \end{bmatrix}$$

---

$$\epsilon^{\mathbf{A}t} = \begin{bmatrix} 1 & t \\ 0 & 1 \end{bmatrix}$$

$$\frac{d\,\epsilon^{\mathbf{A}t}}{dt} = \begin{bmatrix} 0 & 1 \\ 0 & 0 \end{bmatrix}$$ differentiating each element in the $\epsilon^{\mathbf{A}t}$ matrix

**10.16**    In frame **9.4** we asserted that $\mathbf{x}(t) = \epsilon^{\mathbf{A}t}\,\mathbf{x}(0)$ is the I.C. solution of the equation $\dot{\mathbf{x}}(t) = \mathbf{A}\mathbf{x}(t) + \mathbf{B}\mathbf{u}(t)$.

CONFIRM this by substituting the above I.C. solution into both sides of the (homogeneous) equation $\dot{\mathbf{x}}(t) = \mathbf{A}\mathbf{x}(t)$.

## SOME COMMENTS ON MATRIX CALCULUS

**10.17**    We have already been using matrix calculus without having made any special point of the fact. Thus in frame **10.15** we wrote:

$$\frac{d}{dt}\begin{bmatrix} 1 & t \\ 0 & 1 \end{bmatrix} = \begin{bmatrix} 0 & 1 \\ 0 & 0 \end{bmatrix}$$

Thus, in general, if a matrix $\alpha(t)$ is a function of time $t$, then one computes $d\alpha(t)/dt$ or $\int\alpha(t)dt$ by differentiating or integrating each term in the original matrix, $\alpha(t)$.

First, differentiate the asserted I.C. solution, $\mathbf{x}(t) = \epsilon^{\mathbf{A}t}\mathbf{x}(0)$. This yields:

$$\dot{\mathbf{x}}(t) = \mathbf{A}\,\epsilon^{\mathbf{A}t}\mathbf{x}(0)$$

a matrix of constants

Then substitute for $\dot{\mathbf{x}}$ and $\mathbf{x}$ in the (homogeneous) equation $\dot{\mathbf{x}}(t) = \mathbf{A}\mathbf{x}(t)$. That is:

$$\dot{\mathbf{x}}(t) = \mathbf{A}\mathbf{x}(t)$$

$$\mathbf{A}\,\epsilon^{\mathbf{A}t}\mathbf{x}(0) = \mathbf{A}(\epsilon^{\mathbf{A}t}\mathbf{x}(0))$$

Since this is clearly an identity, we have confirmed that $\mathbf{x} = \epsilon^{\mathbf{A}t}\mathbf{x}(0)$ is indeed the I.C. (homogeneous) solution of the state equation $\dot{\mathbf{x}} = \mathbf{A}\mathbf{x} + \mathbf{B}\mathbf{u}$

**10.18** Let's now consider the derivative of a matrix product. Suppose $\mathbf{Q}(t) = [q_1(t) \quad q_2(t) \quad \cdots]$ and that $\mathbf{R}(t) = \begin{bmatrix} r_1(t) \\ r_2(t) \\ \vdots \end{bmatrix}$

Here $\mathbf{Q}(t)\mathbf{R}(t) = \underline{\hspace{2cm}} + \underline{\hspace{2cm}} + \cdots$

□

---

**10.19** Then $\dfrac{d}{dt}\{\mathbf{Q}(t)\mathbf{R}(t)\} = \dfrac{d}{dt}\{\underline{\hspace{2cm}} + \underline{\hspace{2cm}} + \cdots\}$

$= \underline{\hspace{3cm}} + \underline{\hspace{2cm}}$

$\underline{\hspace{2cm}} + \underline{\hspace{2cm}} + \cdots$

□

---

**10.20** If you group alternate terms, you should see that the derivative of the product can be written:

$$\frac{d}{dt}\{\mathbf{Q}(t)\mathbf{R}(t)\} = \underline{\hspace{0.5cm}\frac{d}{dt}\hspace{0.5cm} + \hspace{0.5cm}\frac{d}{dt}\hspace{0.5cm}}$$

□

---

## DERIVATIVE OF A MATRIX PRODUCT

**10.21** If one extends the above demonstration to the product of general matrices $\mathbf{Q}(t)$ and $\mathbf{R}(t)$, one can show that in general:

$$\frac{d}{dt}\{\mathbf{Q}(t)\mathbf{R}(t)\} = \mathbf{Q}(t)\frac{d\mathbf{R}(t)}{dt} + \frac{d\mathbf{Q}(t)}{dt}\mathbf{R}(t),$$

but note that the *order* of each product must be preserved, and that the product $\mathbf{Q}(t)\mathbf{R}(t)$ must be conformable.

---

You should anticipate spending 40–60 minutes on the next section, where we will apply these matrix methods to the time domain solution of $\dot{\mathbf{x}} = \mathbf{A}\mathbf{x} + \mathbf{B}\mathbf{u}$.

$$\mathbf{Q}(t)\mathbf{R}(t) = \underline{q_1(t)r_1(t) + q_2(t)r_2(t) + \cdots}$$

*Comments:*
1. This product is a scalar.
2. Both the $\mathbf{Q}(t)$ and $\mathbf{R}(t)$ matrices must have the same number of elements.

---

$$\frac{d}{dt}\{\mathbf{Q}(t)\mathbf{R}(t)\} = \frac{d}{dt}\{q_1(t)r_1(t) + q_2(t)r_2(t) + \cdots\}$$

$$= \underline{q_1(t)\frac{dr_1(t)}{dt} + \frac{dq_1(t)}{dt}r_1(t)}$$

$$\underline{+ q_2(t)\frac{dr_2(t)}{dt} + \frac{dq_2(t)}{dt}r_2(t) + \cdots}$$

---

$$\frac{d}{dt}\{\mathbf{Q}(t)\mathbf{R}(t)\} = \underline{\mathbf{Q}(t)\frac{d\mathbf{R}(t)}{dt} + \frac{d\mathbf{Q}(t)}{dt}\mathbf{R}(t)}$$

---

**11.1**   We have learned how to solve the equation $\dot{x} = Ax$ in the time domain. In other words, we have found the *I.C. solution* of the state equation $\dot{x} = Ax + Bu$. We must now obtain the total solution. First, we *pre*multiply the state equation by the matrix integrating factor $\epsilon^{-At}$, and move all terms containing $x$ and $\dot{x}$ to the left of the equation. Thus:

$$\underline{\hspace{5cm}} = \epsilon^{-At} Bu$$

□

---

**11.2**   Then  $\dfrac{d}{dt} \left\{ \underline{\hspace{3cm}} \right\} = \epsilon^{-At} Bu$

*Hint:* What product has $\epsilon^{-At}\dfrac{dx}{dt} - A\,\epsilon^{-At}x$ for its time derivative?

(if you need more help, look back at frame **9.1**)

□

---

**11.3**   Next, integrating both sides from zero to $t$:

$$\left\{ \underline{\hspace{2cm}} \right\}\Big|_0^t = \int_0^t \underline{\hspace{3cm}}\, dt$$

□

---

**11.4**   SUBSTITUTING the limits, on the left,

$$\underline{\hspace{3cm}} - \underline{\hspace{1cm}} = \int_0^t \epsilon^{-At} Bu\, dt$$

□

---

**11.5**   It is convenient to change the variable of the integration (which is a "dummy") from $t$ to $\tau$. That is,

$$\int_0^t \epsilon^{-At} Bu\, dt = \int_0^t \underline{\hspace{3cm}}\, d\tau$$

□

---

$$\epsilon^{-At}\dot{\mathbf{x}} = \epsilon^{-At}\mathbf{Ax} + \epsilon^{-At}\mathbf{Bu}$$

$$\epsilon^{-At}\dot{\mathbf{x}} - \epsilon^{-At}\mathbf{Ax} = \epsilon^{-At}\mathbf{Bu}$$

*NOTE:*

As we saw in frame **10.13**, $\epsilon^{-At}\mathbf{A} = \mathbf{A}\epsilon^{-At}$. This fact is used in the hint to the next frame.

---

$$\frac{d}{dt}\{\epsilon^{-At}\mathbf{x}\} = \epsilon^{-At}\mathbf{Bu}$$

($\mathbf{x}\epsilon^{-At}$ is *not* correct—the product does not even exist)

---

$$\{\epsilon^{-At}\mathbf{x}\}\Big|_0^t = \int_0^t \epsilon^{-At}\mathbf{Bu}\,dt$$

---

since $\epsilon^{A0} = \mathbf{I}$

$$\epsilon^{-At}\mathbf{x}(t) - \mathbf{I}\mathbf{x}(0) \quad \text{or} \quad \epsilon^{-At}\mathbf{x}(t) - \mathbf{x}(0) = \int_0^t \epsilon^{-At}\mathbf{Bu}\,dt$$

or simply $\mathbf{x}$

---

strictly $\mathbf{u}(\tau)$

$$= \int_0^t \epsilon^{-At}\mathbf{Bu}\,d\tau$$

**11.6**    On the previous page we obtained:

$$\epsilon^{-At}\mathbf{x} - \mathbf{x}(0) = \int_0^t \epsilon^{-A\tau}\,\mathbf{Bu}(\tau)d\tau$$

Now PREMULTIPLY throughout by $\epsilon^{At}$, and then SOLVE for $\mathbf{x}$:

$$\mathbf{x} = \underline{\hspace{6cm}}$$

---

**11.7**    We see that, as before, $\mathbf{x}_{I.C.} = \underline{\hspace{3cm}}$

and now we know that $\mathbf{x}_F = \underline{\hspace{3cm}}$

---

**11.8**    Now let's *apply* the above result to a simple problem. If you LOOK at the solution above, you will see that $\epsilon^{At}$ appears in both $\mathbf{x}_{I.C.}$ and $\mathbf{x}_F$. Therefore, the first step will still entail the evaluation of this matrix. In an earlier example we considered the state equation:

$$\dot{\mathbf{x}} = \begin{bmatrix} 0 & 1 \\ 0 & 0 \end{bmatrix}\mathbf{x} + \begin{bmatrix} 0 \\ k \end{bmatrix}\mathbf{u}$$

We have already calculated $\epsilon^{At}$ for this system, namely:

$$\epsilon^{At} = \begin{bmatrix} 1 & t \\ 0 & 1 \end{bmatrix} \text{ (see frame 9.12.)}$$

In order to compute $\mathbf{x}_F(t)$ we need the matrix $\epsilon^{-A\tau}$. WRITE this down:

$$\epsilon^{-A\tau} = \begin{bmatrix} \phantom{xx} & \phantom{xx} \\ \phantom{xx} & \phantom{xx} \end{bmatrix}$$

---

**11.9**    Therefore:

$$\mathbf{x}_F(t) = \begin{bmatrix} \phantom{xx} \\ \phantom{xx} \end{bmatrix} \int_0^t \begin{bmatrix} \phantom{xx} \end{bmatrix}\begin{bmatrix} \phantom{xx} \end{bmatrix}\mathbf{u}(\tau)d\tau$$

Premultiplying by $\epsilon^{At}$,

$$\mathbf{x} - \epsilon^{At}\mathbf{x}(0) = \epsilon^{At}\int_0^t \epsilon^{-A\tau}\mathbf{B}\mathbf{u}(\tau)d\tau$$

Rearranging,

$$\boxed{\mathbf{x} = \epsilon^{At}\mathbf{x}(0) + \epsilon^{At}\int_0^t \epsilon^{-A\tau}\mathbf{B}\mathbf{u}(\tau)d\tau}$$

(this result is
listed on
the MASK)

$$\mathbf{x}_{I.C.} = \underline{\epsilon^{At}\mathbf{x}(0)}$$

$$\mathbf{x}_F = \underline{\epsilon^{At}\int_0^t \epsilon^{-A\tau}\mathbf{B}\mathbf{u}(\tau)d\tau}$$

Replacing $t$ with $-\tau$:

$$\epsilon^{-A\tau} = \begin{bmatrix} 1 & -\tau \\ 0 & 1 \end{bmatrix}$$

$$\mathbf{x}_F(t) = \underline{\begin{bmatrix} 1 & t \\ 0 & 1 \end{bmatrix}\int_0^t \begin{bmatrix} 1 & -\tau \\ 0 & 1 \end{bmatrix}\begin{bmatrix} 0 \\ k \end{bmatrix}\mathbf{u}(\tau)d\tau}$$

**11.10** In the previous frame we had:

$$\mathbf{x}_F(t) = \begin{bmatrix} 1 & t \\ 0 & 1 \end{bmatrix} \int_0^t \begin{bmatrix} 1 & -\tau \\ 0 & 1 \end{bmatrix} \begin{bmatrix} 0 \\ k \end{bmatrix} \mathbf{u}(\tau)d\tau$$

If we are given as data that $k = 1$ and $\mathbf{u}(t) = \mathbf{u}(\tau) = 10$,

$$\mathbf{x}_F(t) = \begin{bmatrix} 1 & t \\ 0 & 1 \end{bmatrix} \int_0^t \begin{bmatrix} \phantom{xx} \\ \phantom{xx} \end{bmatrix} d\tau$$

□

---

**11.11** Next,

$$\mathbf{x}_F(t) = \begin{bmatrix} \phantom{xx} \end{bmatrix} \left\{ \begin{bmatrix} \phantom{xx} \end{bmatrix} \Big|_0^t \right\} = \begin{bmatrix} \phantom{xx} \end{bmatrix} \begin{bmatrix} \phantom{xx} \end{bmatrix}$$

□

---

**11.12** Finally,

$$\mathbf{x}_F(t) = \begin{bmatrix} \phantom{xx} \end{bmatrix}$$

□

---

**11.13** Referring to the time domain solution on the MASK, and given $x_1(0) = 2$ and $x_2(0) = -3$,

$$\mathbf{x}_{\text{I.C.}}(t) = \begin{bmatrix} \phantom{xx} \end{bmatrix} \begin{bmatrix} \phantom{xx} \end{bmatrix} = \begin{bmatrix} \phantom{xx} \end{bmatrix}$$

□

---

**11.14** Therefore the total solution is:

$$x_1(t) = \underline{\hphantom{xxxxxxxxxx}}$$

and $x_2(t) = \underline{\hphantom{xxxxxxxxxx}}$ or $\mathbf{x}(t) = \begin{bmatrix} \phantom{xx} \end{bmatrix}$

□

---

$$\mathbf{x}_F(t) = \begin{bmatrix} 1 & t \\ 0 & 1 \end{bmatrix} \int_0^t \begin{bmatrix} -10\tau \\ 10 \end{bmatrix} d\tau$$

---

$$\mathbf{x}_F(t) = \begin{bmatrix} 1 & t \\ 0 & 1 \end{bmatrix} \left\{ \begin{bmatrix} -5\tau^2 \\ 10\tau \end{bmatrix} \Big|_0^t \right\} = \begin{bmatrix} 1 & t \\ 0 & 1 \end{bmatrix} \begin{bmatrix} -5t^2 \\ 10t \end{bmatrix}$$

---

$$\mathbf{x}_F(t) = \begin{bmatrix} 5t^2 \\ 10t \end{bmatrix}$$

---

$$\mathbf{x}_{I.C.}(t) = \begin{bmatrix} 1 & t \\ 0 & 1 \end{bmatrix} \begin{bmatrix} 2 \\ -3 \end{bmatrix} = \begin{bmatrix} 2 - 3t \\ -3 \end{bmatrix}$$

---

Summing the results of the last two frames:

$$\mathbf{x}(t) = \begin{bmatrix} 2 - 3t + 5t^2 \\ -3 + 10t \end{bmatrix}$$

GO BACK and REVIEW the derivation of frames **11.1–11.6**. Note especially that we are now able to find the *total* solution, $\mathbf{x}(t) = \mathbf{x}_{I.C.}(t) + \mathbf{x}_F(t)$, entirely in the time domain.

## ANOTHER TIME DOMAIN PROBLEM

**11.15** Suppose we wish to solve:

$$\dot{\mathbf{x}} = \begin{bmatrix} 1 & 0 \\ 0 & -2 \end{bmatrix} \mathbf{x} + \begin{bmatrix} 3 & 0 \\ 0 & -4 \end{bmatrix} \mathbf{u}$$

As usual the first step is to DETERMINE $\epsilon^{At}$. Keep only the first three terms in the series—see the MASK.

Answer: $\epsilon^{At} =$ 

---

**11.16** Therefore,

$$\epsilon^{-A\tau} =$$

---

**11.17** To find the *forced* solution, we first write:

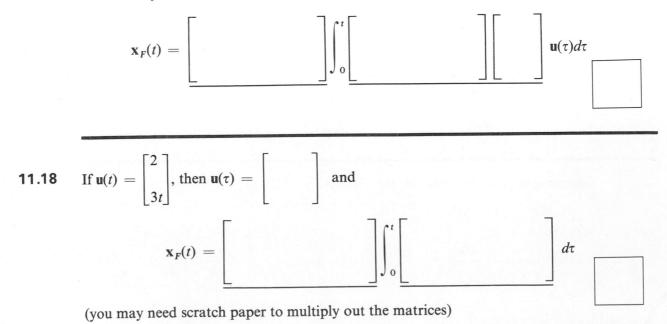

$$\mathbf{x}_F(t) = \begin{bmatrix} \quad \end{bmatrix} \int_0^t \begin{bmatrix} \quad \end{bmatrix} \begin{bmatrix} \quad \end{bmatrix} \mathbf{u}(\tau)d\tau$$

---

**11.18** If $\mathbf{u}(t) = \begin{bmatrix} 2 \\ 3t \end{bmatrix}$, then $\mathbf{u}(\tau) = \begin{bmatrix} \quad \end{bmatrix}$ and

$$\mathbf{x}_F(t) = \begin{bmatrix} \quad \end{bmatrix} \int_0^t \begin{bmatrix} \quad \end{bmatrix} d\tau$$

(you may need scratch paper to multiply out the matrices)

with $\quad \mathbf{A} = \begin{bmatrix} 1 & 0 \\ 0 & -2 \end{bmatrix}$

$$\epsilon^{\mathbf{A}t} = \begin{bmatrix} 1 & 0 \\ 0 & 1 \end{bmatrix} + \begin{bmatrix} 1 & 0 \\ 0 & -2 \end{bmatrix} t + \begin{bmatrix} 1 & 0 \\ 0 & 4 \end{bmatrix} \frac{t^2}{2!} + \cdots$$

$$= \begin{bmatrix} 1 + t + \dfrac{t^2}{2} + \cdots & 0 \\ 0 & 1 - 2t + 2t^2 - \cdots \end{bmatrix}$$

$$\epsilon^{-\mathbf{A}\tau} = \begin{bmatrix} 1 - \tau + \dfrac{\tau^2}{2} - \cdots & 0 \\ 0 & 1 + 2\tau + 2\tau^2 + \cdots \end{bmatrix} \qquad \text{(substituting } -\tau \text{ for } t \text{ in } \epsilon^{\mathbf{A}t})$$

$$\mathbf{x}_F(t) = \begin{bmatrix} 1 + t + \dfrac{t^2}{2} + \cdots & 0 \\ 0 & 1 - 2t + 2t^2 - \cdots \end{bmatrix} \int_0^t \begin{bmatrix} 1 - \tau + \dfrac{\tau^2}{2} - \cdots & 0 \\ 0 & 1 + 2\tau + 2\tau^2 + \cdots \end{bmatrix} \begin{bmatrix} 3 & 0 \\ 0 & -4 \end{bmatrix} \mathbf{u}(\tau)d\tau$$

If $\mathbf{u}(t) = \begin{bmatrix} 2 \\ 3t \end{bmatrix}$ then $\mathbf{u}(\tau) = \begin{bmatrix} 2 \\ 3\tau \end{bmatrix}$ and

$$\mathbf{x}_F(t) = \begin{bmatrix} 1 + t + \dfrac{t^2}{2} + \cdots & 0 \\ 0 & 1 - 2t + 2t^2 - \cdots \end{bmatrix} \int_0^t \begin{bmatrix} 6 - 6\tau + 3\tau^2 - \cdots \\ -12\tau - 24\tau^2 - 24\tau^3 - \cdots \end{bmatrix} d\tau$$

**11.19**   EVALUATE:

$$\mathbf{x}_F(t) = \begin{bmatrix} 1 + t + \dfrac{t^2}{2} + \cdots & 0 \\ \\ 0 & 1 - 2t + 2t^2 - \cdots \end{bmatrix} \int_0^t \begin{bmatrix} 6 - 6\tau + 3\tau^2 - \cdots \\ \\ -12\tau - 24\tau^2 - 24\tau^3 - \cdots \end{bmatrix} d\tau$$

Answer: $\mathbf{x}_F(t) = \begin{bmatrix} \phantom{xxxxxxxxxxxx} \\ \\ \end{bmatrix}$ $\begin{bmatrix} \phantom{xx} \end{bmatrix}$

---

## SUMMARY

Given $\mathbf{A}$, $\mathbf{B}$, $\mathbf{x}(0)$ and $\mathbf{u}(t)$, one can solve the state equation $\dot{\mathbf{x}} = \mathbf{Ax} + \mathbf{Bu}$ entirely in the time domain.

The evaluation of $\mathbf{x}_{I.C.}(t) = \epsilon^{\mathbf{A}t}\,\mathbf{x}(0)$ is accomplished by expanding $\epsilon^{\mathbf{A}t}$ as a series. The same is true of $\mathbf{x}_F(t) = \epsilon^{\mathbf{A}t}\int_0^t \epsilon^{-\mathbf{A}\tau}\mathbf{Bu}(\tau)d\tau$.

*However,* the amount of work can be considerable, particularly if one wants to find $\mathbf{x}(t)$ for several or many values of $t$—by summing the various series for each value of $t$. Later we will show that this time domain approach is well suited to numerical (computer) techniques.

---

Take a break before you start the next Section, which is a 60–90 minute REVIEW of all the techniques you have learned so far.

Integrating:

$$\mathbf{x}_F(t) = \left\{ \begin{bmatrix} 1 + t + \dfrac{t^2}{2} + \cdots & 0 \\ 0 & 1 - 2t + 2t^2 - \cdots \end{bmatrix} \begin{bmatrix} 6\tau - 3\tau^2 + \tau^3 - \cdots \\ -6\tau^2 - 8\tau^3 - 6\tau^4 - \cdots \end{bmatrix} \Bigg|_0^t \right\}$$

Substituting the limits:

$$\mathbf{x}_F(t) = \begin{bmatrix} 1 + t + \dfrac{t^2}{2} + \cdots & 0 \\ 0 & 1 - 2t + 2t^2 - \cdots \end{bmatrix} \begin{bmatrix} 6t - 3t^2 + t^3 - \cdots \\ -6t^2 - 8t^3 - 6t^4 - \cdots \end{bmatrix}$$

$$= \begin{bmatrix} (1 + t + \dfrac{t^2}{2} + \cdots)(6t - 3t^2 + t^3 + \cdots) \\ (1 - 2t + 2t^2 - \cdots)(-6t^2 - 8t^3 - 6t^4 - \cdots) \end{bmatrix}$$

$$= \begin{bmatrix} 6t + 3t^2 + t^3 + \cdots \\ -6t^2 + 4t^3 - 2t^4 + \cdots \end{bmatrix}$$

*Comment:*

Here we have only found the *forced* solution—due to $\mathbf{u}(t)$. We could, if we wished, also find the *I.C.* solution—due to $\mathbf{x}(0)$, and hence the *total* solution $\mathbf{x}(t) = \mathbf{x}_{I.C.}(t) + \mathbf{x}_F(t)$.

In this section you will solve a problem by the three state variable methods that you have at your disposal. Use the MASK as much as is necessary, and don't be too discouraged if you find some of the calculations to be tedious—they often are!

## REVIEW OF TIME DOMAIN SOLUTION

**12.1**

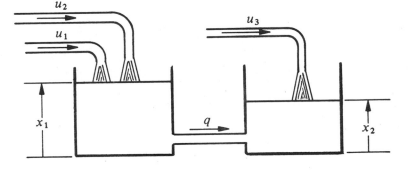

Two tanks, both of cross-sectional area $\alpha$, are connected by a narrow pipe as shown. Fluid is introduced to the system in the form of three inputs—also shown.

The applicable linearized equations are:

$$\alpha\dot{x}_1 = u_1 + u_2 - q; \quad \alpha\dot{x}_2 = u_3 + q; \quad \text{and } q = k(x_1 - x_2).$$

Put these equations into state matrix form:
(use scratch paper if necessary)

---

**12.2**    Given $\dfrac{k}{\alpha} = 1$, $x_1(0) = 2$, and $x_2(0) = 3$, SOLVE for $\mathbf{x}_{\text{I.C.}}(t)$ in the time domain:

These equations are first order in $x_1$, first order in $x_2$, and zero order in $q$. Therefore the total system order is two, and we need two state equations—$q$ is *not* a state.

Substituting for $q$ in the first two equations:

$$\alpha \dot{x}_1 = u_1 + u_2 - k(x_1 - x_2)$$

$$\alpha \dot{x}_2 = u_3 + k(x_1 - x_2)$$

In matrix form:

$$\begin{bmatrix} \dot{x}_1 \\ \\ \dot{x}_2 \end{bmatrix} = \begin{bmatrix} -\dfrac{k}{\alpha} & \dfrac{k}{\alpha} \\ \\ \dfrac{k}{\alpha} & -\dfrac{k}{\alpha} \end{bmatrix} \begin{bmatrix} x_1 \\ \\ x_2 \end{bmatrix} + \begin{bmatrix} \dfrac{1}{\alpha} & \dfrac{1}{\alpha} & 0 \\ \\ 0 & 0 & \dfrac{1}{\alpha} \end{bmatrix} \begin{bmatrix} u_1(t) \\ u_2(t) \\ u_3(t) \end{bmatrix}$$

---

$$\epsilon^{At} = I + At + A^2 \frac{t^2}{2!} + \cdots + A^n \frac{t^n}{n!} + \cdots$$

$$= \begin{bmatrix} 1 & 0 \\ 0 & 1 \end{bmatrix} + \begin{bmatrix} -1 & 1 \\ 1 & -1 \end{bmatrix} t + \begin{bmatrix} 2 & -2 \\ -2 & 2 \end{bmatrix} \frac{t^2}{2!} + \cdots$$

$$\therefore \quad \mathbf{x}_{\text{I.C.}}(t) = \begin{bmatrix} 1 - t + t^2 - \cdots & t - t^2 + \cdots \\ \\ t - t^2 + \cdots & 1 - t + t^2 - \cdots \end{bmatrix} \begin{bmatrix} 2 \\ 3 \end{bmatrix}$$

$$= \begin{bmatrix} 2 - 2t + 2t^2 - \cdots + 3t - 3t^2 + \cdots \\ \\ 2t - 2t^2 + \cdots + 3 - 3t + 3t^2 - \cdots \end{bmatrix} = \begin{bmatrix} 2 + t - t^2 - \cdots \\ \\ 3 - t + t^2 - \cdots \end{bmatrix}$$

---

**12.3**    Given the data on the previous page and on the MASK, and given that $\alpha = 0.5$, $u_1(t) = 0$, $u_2(t) = 5t$, and $u_3(t) = 0$, FIND $\mathbf{x}_F(t)$. There is some hard labor involved. Terminate each of the initial series at the squared terms, and include only the terms to $t^4$ in the final matrix product which leads to the answer.

$$\mathbf{x}_F(t) = \epsilon^{\mathbf{A}t} \int_0^t \epsilon^{-\mathbf{A}\tau} \mathbf{B}u(\tau)d\tau$$

$$= \begin{bmatrix} 1 - t + t^2 - \cdots & t - t^2 + \cdots \\ t - t^2 + \cdots & 1 - t + t^2 - \cdots \end{bmatrix} \int_0^t \begin{bmatrix} 1 + \tau + \tau^2 + \cdots & -\tau - \tau^2 - \cdots \\ -\tau - \tau^2 - \cdots & 1 + \tau + \tau^2 + \cdots \end{bmatrix}$$
$$\begin{bmatrix} 2 & 2 & 0 \\ 0 & 0 & 2 \end{bmatrix} \begin{bmatrix} 0 \\ 5\tau \\ 0 \end{bmatrix} d\tau$$

$$= \begin{bmatrix} & \\ & \end{bmatrix} \int_0^t \begin{bmatrix} 2 + 2\tau + 2\tau^2 + \cdots + 2 + 2\tau + 2\tau^2 + \cdots - 2\tau - 2\tau^2 - \cdots \\ -2\tau - 2\tau^2 - \cdots - 2\tau - 2\tau^2 - \cdots + 2 + 2\tau + 2\tau^2 + \cdots \end{bmatrix} \begin{bmatrix} 0 \\ 5\tau \\ 0 \end{bmatrix} d\tau$$

$$= \begin{bmatrix} & \\ & \end{bmatrix} \int_0^t \begin{bmatrix} 10\tau + 10\tau^2 + 10\tau^3 + \cdots \\ -10\tau^2 - 10\tau^3 - \cdots \end{bmatrix} d\tau$$

$$= \begin{bmatrix} & \\ & \end{bmatrix} \begin{bmatrix} 5\tau^2 + \dfrac{10}{3}\tau^3 + \dfrac{10}{4}\tau^4 + \cdots \\ -\dfrac{10}{3}\tau^3 - \dfrac{10}{4}\tau^4 - \cdots \end{bmatrix} \Bigg|_0^t$$

$$= \begin{bmatrix} 1 - t + t^2 - \cdots & t - t^2 + \cdots \\ t - t^2 + \cdots & 1 - t + t^2 - \cdots \end{bmatrix} \begin{bmatrix} 5t^2 + \dfrac{10}{3}t^3 + \dfrac{10}{4}t^4 + \cdots \\ -\dfrac{10}{3}t^3 - \dfrac{10}{4}t^4 - \cdots \end{bmatrix}$$

$$= \begin{bmatrix} 5t^2 + \dfrac{10}{3}t^3 + \dfrac{10}{4}t^4 - 5t^3 - \dfrac{10}{3}t^4 + 5t^4 + \cdots - \dfrac{10}{3}t^4 + \cdots \\ 5t^3 + \dfrac{10}{3}t^4 - 5t^4 + \cdots - \dfrac{10}{3}t^3 - \dfrac{10}{4}t^4 + \dfrac{10}{3}t^4 + \cdots \end{bmatrix}$$

$$\therefore \quad \mathbf{x}_F(t) = \begin{bmatrix} 5t^2 - \dfrac{5}{3}t^3 + \dfrac{10}{12}t^4 + \cdots \\ \dfrac{5}{3}t^3 - \dfrac{10}{12}t^4 + \cdots \end{bmatrix}$$

*Comment:*
The *total* solution $\mathbf{x}(t)$ is the sum of $\mathbf{x}_{\text{I.C.}}(t)$ and $\mathbf{x}_F(t)$ from this and the previous frame.

## REVIEW OF THE MATRIX SOLUTION

**12.4**     Let's now solve the same problem by the matrix method.  The system state equation is:

$$\dot{\mathbf{x}} = \begin{bmatrix} -1 & 1 \\ 1 & -1 \end{bmatrix} \begin{bmatrix} x_1 \\ x_2 \end{bmatrix} + \begin{bmatrix} 2 & 2 & 0 \\ 0 & 0 & 2 \end{bmatrix} \begin{bmatrix} 0 \\ 5t \\ 0 \end{bmatrix} \text{ with } \mathbf{x}(0) = \begin{bmatrix} 2 \\ 3 \end{bmatrix}$$

Use the method of matrix solution (see MASK) to FIND $\mathbf{X}_{I.C.}(s)$ *and* $\mathbf{X}_F(s)$:

The first step is to find $(s\mathbf{I} - \mathbf{A})^{-1}$—SEE MASK

$$(s\mathbf{I} - \mathbf{A}) = \begin{bmatrix} s+1 & -1 \\ -1 & s+1 \end{bmatrix}$$

$$\mathbf{C} = \begin{bmatrix} s+1 & 1 \\ 1 & s+1 \end{bmatrix} \qquad \text{(matrix of cofactors)}$$

and $(s\mathbf{I} - \mathbf{A})^{-1} = \dfrac{\mathbf{C}^T}{|s\mathbf{I} - \mathbf{A}|} = \dfrac{\begin{bmatrix} s+1 & 1 \\ 1 & s+1 \end{bmatrix}}{(s+1)(s+1)-1} = \begin{bmatrix} \dfrac{s+1}{s(s+2)} & \dfrac{1}{s(s+2)} \\[2mm] \dfrac{1}{s(s+2)} & \dfrac{s+1}{s(s+2)} \end{bmatrix}$

Now $\mathbf{X}_{\text{I.C.}}(s) = (s\mathbf{I} - \mathbf{A})^{-1}\mathbf{x}(0)$   (see MASK)

$$\therefore\ \mathbf{X}_{\text{I.C.}}(s) = \begin{bmatrix} \dfrac{s+1}{s(s+2)} & \dfrac{1}{s(s+2)} \\[2mm] \dfrac{1}{s(s+2)} & \dfrac{s+1}{s(s+2)} \end{bmatrix} \begin{bmatrix} 2 \\ 3 \end{bmatrix} = \begin{bmatrix} \dfrac{2s+5}{s(s+2)} \\[2mm] \dfrac{3s+5}{s(s+2)} \end{bmatrix}$$

If you were to take the inverse transform, you would find:

$$\mathbf{x}_{\text{I.C.}}(t) = \begin{bmatrix} \dfrac{5}{2} - \dfrac{1}{2}\epsilon^{-2t} \\[2mm] \dfrac{5}{2} + \dfrac{1}{2}\epsilon^{-2t} \end{bmatrix}$$

Also, $\mathbf{X}_F(s) = (s\mathbf{I} - \mathbf{A})^{-1}\mathbf{B}\mathbf{U}(s)$   (see MASK)

$$= \begin{bmatrix} \dfrac{s+1}{s(s+2)} & \dfrac{1}{s(s+2)} \\[2mm] \dfrac{1}{s(s+2)} & \dfrac{s+1}{s(s+2)} \end{bmatrix} \begin{bmatrix} 2 & 2 & 0 \\ 0 & 0 & 2 \end{bmatrix} \begin{bmatrix} 0 \\ 5/s^2 \\ 0 \end{bmatrix}$$

or $\mathbf{X}_F(s) = \begin{bmatrix} \dfrac{s+1}{s(s+2)} & \dfrac{1}{s(s+2)} \\[2mm] \dfrac{1}{s(s+2)} & \dfrac{s+1}{s+2} \end{bmatrix} \begin{bmatrix} \dfrac{10}{s^2} \\[2mm] 0 \end{bmatrix} = \begin{bmatrix} \dfrac{10(s+1)}{s^3(s+2)} \\[2mm] \dfrac{10}{s^3(s+2)} \end{bmatrix}$

Again, if you were to take the inverse transform, you would find:

$$\mathbf{X}_F(t) = \begin{bmatrix} -\dfrac{5}{4} + \dfrac{5}{2}t + \dfrac{5}{2}t^2 + \dfrac{5}{4}\epsilon^{-2t} \\[3mm] \dfrac{5}{4} - \dfrac{5}{2}t + \dfrac{5}{2}t^2 - \dfrac{5}{4}\epsilon^{-2t} \end{bmatrix}$$

**12.5**   Given the same state equation:

$$\dot{\mathbf{x}} = \begin{bmatrix} -1 & 1 \\ 1 & -1 \end{bmatrix} \mathbf{x} + \begin{bmatrix} 2 & 2 & 0 \\ 0 & 0 & 2 \end{bmatrix} \mathbf{u}$$

use the S.F.G. method to FIND $\mathbf{X}_{\text{I.C.}}(s)$ and $\mathbf{X}_F(s)$:
[*Don't* substitute any data for $\mathbf{x}(0)$ and $\mathbf{u}(t)$]

Transforming and rearranging we obtain:

$$\begin{bmatrix} sX_1(s) \\ sX_2(s) \end{bmatrix} = \begin{bmatrix} x_1(0) \\ x_2(0) \end{bmatrix} + \begin{bmatrix} -1 & 1 \\ 1 & -1 \end{bmatrix} \begin{bmatrix} X_1(s) \\ X_2(s) \end{bmatrix} + \begin{bmatrix} 2 & 2 & 0 \\ 0 & 0 & 2 \end{bmatrix} \begin{bmatrix} U_1(s) \\ U_2(s) \\ U_3(s) \end{bmatrix}$$

Drawing the S.F.G.:

$$\Delta = 1 - \left( -\frac{1}{s} - \frac{1}{s} + \frac{1}{s^2} \right) + \frac{1}{s^2} = \frac{s^2 + 2s}{s^2} = \frac{s + 2}{s}$$

$$X_1(s) = \frac{(1/s)(1 + 1/s)}{\Delta} x_1(0) + \frac{(1/s^2)(1)}{\Delta} x_2(0) + \frac{(2/s)(1 + 1/s)}{\Delta} U_1(s)$$

$$+ \frac{(2/s)(1 + 1/s) \cdot}{\Delta} U_2(s) + \frac{(2/s^2)(1)}{\Delta} U_3(s)$$

Similarly for $X_2(s)$. In matrix form,

$$\mathbf{X}(s) = \underbrace{\begin{bmatrix} \dfrac{s + 1}{s(s + 2)} & \dfrac{1}{s(s + 2)} \\[4mm] \dfrac{1}{s(s + 2)} & \dfrac{s + 1}{s(s + 2)} \end{bmatrix}}_{\mathbf{X}_{I.C.}(s)} \mathbf{x}(0) + \underbrace{\begin{bmatrix} \dfrac{2(s + 1)}{s(s + 2)} & \dfrac{2(s + 1)}{s(s + 2)} & \dfrac{2}{s(s + 2)} \\[4mm] \dfrac{2}{s(s + 2)} & \dfrac{2}{s(s + 2)} & \dfrac{2(s + 1)}{s(s + 2)} \end{bmatrix}}_{\mathbf{X}_F(s)} \mathbf{U}(s)$$

*Comment:*
Given $\mathbf{x}(0)$ and $\mathbf{u}(t)$ one could calculate $\mathbf{x}_{I.C.}(t)$ and $\mathbf{x}_F(t)$ as in the previous frame.

## SOME COMMENTS

You have now seen how one may take a system's differential equations and put them into the state variable form:

$$\dot{x} = Ax + Bu$$

As you may have realized, it is possible to write a system's equations in state form from the outset—that is, directly from the laws governing the behavior of the physical system. However, as there are many possible approaches to this topic, it has been left to your instructor to make the appropriate selection. If you want to study the topic on your own, Appendix 3, together with References 7 and 8 is a good place to start.

\* \* \*

Three methods for *solving* the state equation have been introduced:

1. The S.F.G. method,
2. The matrix method, and
3. The time domain method.

We would agree that each of these requires an excessive amount of computation, but a familiarity with all three is almost essential to your understanding of state variable methods. In section 15—AN OVERVIEW—these concepts will again be reviewed and interrelated.

\* \* \*

The basic advantage of the state variable approach—which we now propose to exploit—is that the state equation is a standard form: a set of simultaneous first order equations. This suggests that a digital computer should be able to relieve us of much of the computational effort.

Although the computer may be used to mechanize each of the three basic methods of solution, we will develop only the most directly useful—the time domain approach. This is taken up in the next Section, which will require 40–70 minutes of your time.

Before you start this section, you may wish to GO BACK and REVIEW the mathematical basis of the time domain solution, in frames **11.1–11.6**. You should certainly REREAD the comments on the previous page. Our present objective is to mechanize the time domain solution.

**13.1**  Given $\dot{\mathbf{x}} = \mathbf{A}\mathbf{x} + \mathbf{B}\mathbf{u}$, we know that the time domain solution is:

$$\mathbf{x}(t) = \epsilon^{\mathbf{A}t}\mathbf{x}(0) + \epsilon^{\mathbf{A}t}\int_0^t \epsilon^{-\mathbf{A}\tau}\mathbf{B}\mathbf{u}(\tau)\,d\tau$$

Now, suppose we want to compute $\mathbf{x}(t)$ at the particular time $t = T$. Then:

$$\mathbf{x}(T) = \underline{\hspace{5cm}}$$

☐

---

**13.2**  Further, suppose that $u_1(t) = u_1(0)$ during the period $0 \leqslant t < T$, as shown; that $u_2(t) = u_2(0)$, and so on. Then

$$\mathbf{u}(t) = \underline{\hspace{3cm}} \quad \text{for } 0 \leqslant t < T$$

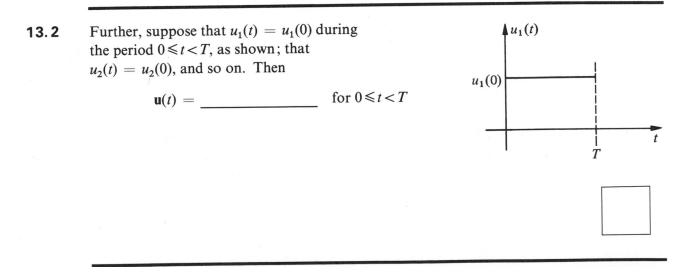

☐

---

**13.3**  Now **B** is also a matrix of constants, so that $\mathbf{B}\mathbf{u}(0)$ can be taken out of the integral. Thus the state vector at $t = T$ can be written:

$$\underline{\hspace{4cm}} = \underline{\hspace{4cm}}$$

(remember that the *order* of a matrix product must be preserved)

☐

*matrix* of initial conditions (given)

*matrix* of inputs (given)

$$\mathbf{x}(T) = \epsilon^{AT}\mathbf{x}(0) + \epsilon^{AT}\int_0^T \epsilon^{-A\tau}\mathbf{Bu}(\tau)d\tau$$

a matrix of *constants*

$$\mathbf{u}(t) = \underline{\mathbf{u}(0)} \quad \text{for} \quad 0 \leqslant t < T$$

*Comment:*

If the given inputs are *not* constant in the interval, then we must *approximate* them by constants.

$$\mathbf{x}(T) = \epsilon^{AT}\mathbf{x}(0) + \epsilon^{AT}\left[\int_0^T \epsilon^{-A\tau}d\tau\right]\mathbf{Bu}(0)$$

*NOTE:*

The order of the matrix product is preserved—$\mathbf{Bu}(0)$ must *follow* the integral.

**13.4**  On the previous page we solved the equation $\dot{\mathbf{x}} = \mathbf{A}\mathbf{x} + \mathbf{B}\mathbf{u}$ at $t = T$, on the assumption that $\mathbf{u}(t) = \mathbf{u}(0)$, a matrix of constants, for $0 \leqslant t < T$.  We found the solution to be:

$$\mathbf{x}(T) = \epsilon^{\mathbf{A}T}\mathbf{x}(0) + \epsilon^{\mathbf{A}T}\int_0^T \epsilon^{-\mathbf{A}\tau}d\tau\,\mathbf{B}\mathbf{u}(0)$$

or   $\mathbf{x}(T) = \boldsymbol{\varphi}(T)\mathbf{x}(0) + \boldsymbol{\Delta}(T)\mathbf{u}(0)$

where we have now introduced the notation:

$\boldsymbol{\varphi}(T) = $ _____   and   $\boldsymbol{\Delta}(T) = $ _____

(shortly we will see how $\boldsymbol{\varphi}(T)$ and $\boldsymbol{\Delta}(T)$ can be calculated using a digital computer)

**13.5**  Now, suppose we were to call the initial time $t_0$ rather than 0.  This is no more than a change of notation, and

$\mathbf{x}(0)$ will become _____ , while

$\mathbf{u}(0)$ becomes _____ .

**13.6**  In the same way, the solution after $T$ seconds becomes:

$$\mathbf{x}(\underline{\quad} + \underline{\quad})$$

**13.7**  Merely changing the notation cannot, of course, change the solution, so the multipliers $\boldsymbol{\varphi}(T)$ and $\boldsymbol{\Delta}(T)$ are unchanged.  Therefore:

$$\mathbf{x}(\underline{\qquad}) = \underline{\qquad}\mathbf{x}(t_0) + \underline{\qquad}\mathbf{u}(t_0)$$

called the "phi-matrix"

called the "del-matrix"

$$\boldsymbol{\varphi}(T) = \underline{\epsilon^{\mathbf{A}T}} \quad \text{and} \quad \boldsymbol{\Delta}(T) = \underline{\epsilon^{\mathbf{A}T} \int_0^T \epsilon^{-\mathbf{A}\tau} d\tau \mathbf{B}}$$

$\underline{\mathbf{x}(t_0)}$

$\underline{\mathbf{u}(t_0)}$

$\underline{\mathbf{x}(t_0 + T)}$

$\underline{\mathbf{x}(t_0 + T)} = \underline{\boldsymbol{\varphi}(T)}\mathbf{x}(t_0) + \underline{\boldsymbol{\Delta}(T)}\mathbf{u}(t_0)$

**13.8** Given the equation $\dot{\mathbf{x}} = \mathbf{Ax} + \mathbf{Bu}$ with initial conditions $\mathbf{x}(t_0)$ and an input matrix equal to $\mathbf{u}(t_0)$ for $t_0 \leqslant t < t_0 + T$, then we have shown that:

$$\mathbf{x}(t_0 + T) = \boldsymbol{\varphi}(T)\mathbf{x}(t_0) + \boldsymbol{\Delta}(T)\mathbf{u}(t_0).$$

Let's look at some special values of $t_0$:

1. $t_0 = 0$

$\mathbf{x}(\underline{\phantom{xxxxxx}}) = \underline{\phantom{xxxxxxxxxxxxxxxxxxxxxxxxx}}$

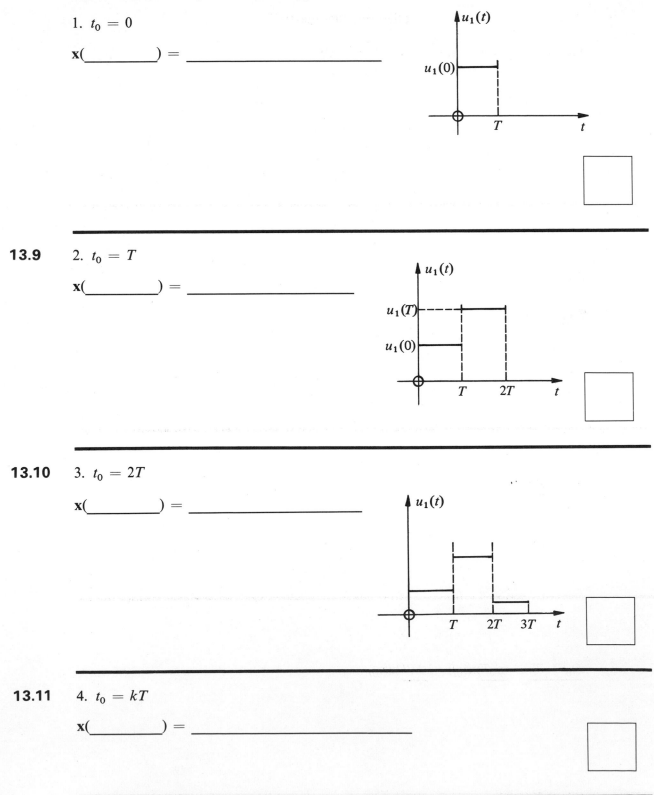

**13.9**    2. $t_0 = T$

$\mathbf{x}(\underline{\phantom{xxxxxx}}) = \underline{\phantom{xxxxxxxxxxxxxxxxxxx}}$

**13.10**    3. $t_0 = 2T$

$\mathbf{x}(\underline{\phantom{xxxxxx}}) = \underline{\phantom{xxxxxxxxxxxxxxxxxxx}}$

**13.11**    4. $t_0 = kT$

$\mathbf{x}(\underline{\phantom{xxxxxx}}) = \underline{\phantom{xxxxxxxxxxxxxxxxxxxxxxxxx}}$

$$\mathbf{x}(\underline{T}) = \varphi(T)\mathbf{x}(0) + \Delta(T)\mathbf{u}(0)$$

*Comments:*
1. *All* of the inputs are constant over the interval $0 \leqslant t < T$.
2. This is the same result as was obtained in Frame **13.4**.

---

$$\mathbf{x}(\underline{2T}) = \varphi(T)\mathbf{x}(T) + \Delta(T)\mathbf{u}(T) \qquad \text{(setting } t_0 = T \text{ in the basic solution)}$$

*Comments:*
1. We have simply started a new solution at $t = T$. $\mathbf{x}(2T)$ is then dependent on $\mathbf{x}(T)$ and $\mathbf{u}(T)$ in the same way that $\mathbf{x}(T)$ was dependent on $\mathbf{x}(0)$ and $\mathbf{u}(0)$ in the previous frame.

2. $\mathbf{u}(T)$ is a matrix of constants over the interval $T \leqslant t < 2T$.

---

$$\mathbf{x}(\underline{3T}) = \varphi(T)\mathbf{x}(2T) + \Delta(T)\mathbf{u}(2T)$$

*Comment:*
This is a new solution, starting at $t = 2T$.

---

$$\mathbf{x}(\underline{kT + T}) = \varphi(T)\mathbf{x}(kT) + \Delta(T)\mathbf{u}(kT) \qquad \text{this is called a ``difference equation''}$$

---

## A SIMPLE PROBLEM

**13.12** To make sure that you have the idea, let's do a little hand calculation before turning to the digital computer. We will suppose that we have already computed:

$$\varphi(T) = \begin{bmatrix} 1 & T \\ 0 & 1 \end{bmatrix} \quad \text{and} \quad \Delta(T) = \begin{bmatrix} 50T^2 & T \\ 100T & 0 \end{bmatrix}$$

and that we are given:

$$\mathbf{x}(0) = \begin{bmatrix} 2 \\ -1 \end{bmatrix} \quad \text{and}$$

We know that $\mathbf{x}(t_0 + T) = \varphi(T)\mathbf{x}(t_0) + \Delta(T)\mathbf{u}(t_0)$, and, starting our computation at $t_0 = 0$, it follows that:

$$\mathbf{u}(t_0) = \mathbf{u}(\underline{\quad}) = \begin{bmatrix} \\ \end{bmatrix}$$

---

**13.13** Given $T = 0.1$,

$$\varphi(0.1) = \begin{bmatrix} \\ \end{bmatrix} \quad \text{and} \quad \Delta(0.1) = \begin{bmatrix} \\ \end{bmatrix}$$

---

**13.14** Combining the above data:

$$\mathbf{x}(0.1) = \begin{bmatrix} \\ \end{bmatrix}\begin{bmatrix} \\ \end{bmatrix} + \begin{bmatrix} \\ \end{bmatrix}\begin{bmatrix} \\ \end{bmatrix}$$

---

**13.15** And $\mathbf{x}(0.1) = \begin{bmatrix} \\ \end{bmatrix} + \begin{bmatrix} \\ \end{bmatrix} = \begin{bmatrix} \\ \end{bmatrix}$

---

$$\mathbf{u}(t_0) = \mathbf{u}(0) = \overbrace{\begin{bmatrix} 1 \\ 3 \end{bmatrix}}^{\text{from the graphs of } u_1(t) \text{ and } u_2(t)}$$

$$\boldsymbol{\varphi}(0.1) = \begin{bmatrix} 1 & 0.1 \\ 0 & 1 \end{bmatrix} \quad \text{and} \quad \boldsymbol{\Delta}(0.1) = \begin{bmatrix} 0.5 & 0.1 \\ 10 & 0 \end{bmatrix}$$

$$\mathbf{x}(0.1) = \overset{\boldsymbol{\varphi}(0.1)}{\begin{bmatrix} 1 & 0.1 \\ 0 & 1 \end{bmatrix}} \overset{\mathbf{x}(0)}{\begin{bmatrix} 2 \\ -1 \end{bmatrix}} + \overset{\boldsymbol{\Delta}(0.1)}{\begin{bmatrix} 0.5 & 0.1 \\ 10 & 0 \end{bmatrix}} \overset{\mathbf{u}(0)}{\begin{bmatrix} 1 \\ 3 \end{bmatrix}}$$

$$\mathbf{x}(0.1) = \begin{bmatrix} 1.9 \\ -1 \end{bmatrix} + \begin{bmatrix} 0.8 \\ 10 \end{bmatrix} = \begin{bmatrix} 2.7 \\ 9 \end{bmatrix}$$

**13.16** Now let's see how to use the same facts to find $\mathbf{x}(0.2)$.
We have:

$$\mathbf{x}(t_0 + T) = \boldsymbol{\varphi}(T)\mathbf{x}(t_0) + \Delta(T)\mathbf{u}(t_0),$$

$$\boldsymbol{\varphi}(0.1) = \begin{bmatrix} 1 & 0.1 \\ 0 & 1 \end{bmatrix}, \quad \Delta(0.1) = \begin{bmatrix} 0.5 & 0.1 \\ 10 & 0 \end{bmatrix}, \quad \mathbf{x}(0.1) = \begin{bmatrix} 2.7 \\ 9 \end{bmatrix},$$

and the graphs of $\mathbf{u}(t)$ on the previous page.

To calculate $\mathbf{x}(0.2)$ we would *now* set $t_0 = $ _____ and $T = $ _____ .

$$\boxed{\phantom{xx}}$$

---

**13.17** From the available data, then:

$$\mathbf{x}(t_0) = \mathbf{x}(\underline{\phantom{xx}}) = \begin{bmatrix} \phantom{xxx} \\ \phantom{xxx} \end{bmatrix} \quad \text{and} \quad \mathbf{u}(t_0) = \mathbf{u}(\underline{\phantom{xx}}) = \begin{bmatrix} \phantom{xxx} \\ \phantom{xxx} \end{bmatrix}$$

$$\boxed{\phantom{xx}}$$

---

**13.18** It follows that:

$$\mathbf{x}(0.2) = \begin{bmatrix} \phantom{xx} \end{bmatrix}\begin{bmatrix} \phantom{x} \end{bmatrix} + \begin{bmatrix} \phantom{xx} \end{bmatrix}\begin{bmatrix} \phantom{x} \end{bmatrix} = \begin{bmatrix} \phantom{x} \end{bmatrix} + \begin{bmatrix} \phantom{x} \end{bmatrix} = \begin{bmatrix} \phantom{x} \end{bmatrix}$$

$$\boxed{\phantom{xx}}$$

---

$$t_0 = \underline{0.1} \quad \text{and} \quad T = \underline{0.1}$$

*Note:*
Using this method one *cannot* calculate directly from $t = 0$ to $t = 0.2$. The inputs are *not* constant during this time interval. (That is: $t_0 = 0$ and $T = 0.2$ is wrong! We must calculate from $t = 0.1$ forward to $t = 0.2$.)

from the graphs in
frame **13.12**

$$\mathbf{x}(t_0) = \mathbf{x}(\underline{0.1}) = \begin{bmatrix} 2.7 \\ 9 \end{bmatrix} \quad \text{and} \quad \mathbf{u}(t_0) = \mathbf{u}(\underline{0.1}) = \begin{bmatrix} 2 \\ 3 \end{bmatrix}$$

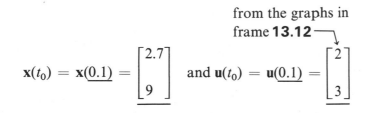

**13.19**   How about calculating $x(0.3)$? You have all the data, and you can, if necessary, refer to the method on the previous page.

**13.20**   Finally, FIND $x(0.4)$:

Here we set $t_0 = 0.2$; from the graphs, $\mathbf{u}(0.2) = \begin{bmatrix} 3 \\ 3 \end{bmatrix}$; and from the previous page,

$$\mathbf{x}(0.2) = \begin{bmatrix} 4.9 \\ 29 \end{bmatrix}.$$

$$\therefore \quad \mathbf{x}(0.3) = \begin{bmatrix} 1 & 0.1 \\ 0 & 1 \end{bmatrix} \begin{bmatrix} 4.9 \\ 29 \end{bmatrix} + \begin{bmatrix} 0.5 & 0.1 \\ 10 & 0 \end{bmatrix} \begin{bmatrix} 3 \\ 3 \end{bmatrix}$$

$$= \begin{bmatrix} 7.8 \\ 29 \end{bmatrix} + \begin{bmatrix} 1.8 \\ 30 \end{bmatrix} = \begin{bmatrix} 9.6 \\ 59 \end{bmatrix}$$

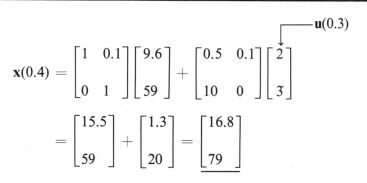

$$\mathbf{x}(0.4) = \begin{bmatrix} 1 & 0.1 \\ 0 & 1 \end{bmatrix} \begin{bmatrix} 9.6 \\ 59 \end{bmatrix} + \begin{bmatrix} 0.5 & 0.1 \\ 10 & 0 \end{bmatrix} \begin{bmatrix} 2 \\ 3 \end{bmatrix} \xleftarrow{\mathbf{u}(0.3)}$$

$$= \begin{bmatrix} 15.5 \\ 59 \end{bmatrix} + \begin{bmatrix} 1.3 \\ 20 \end{bmatrix} = \begin{bmatrix} 16.8 \\ 79 \end{bmatrix}$$

*Comment:*

We started at $t = 0$ and calculated forward to $t = 0.4$ using steps of $T = 0.1$. The results are summarized below:

| $t$ | $x_1(t)$ | $x_2(t)$ |
|-----|----------|----------|
| 0   | 2        | 1        |
| 0.1 | 2.7      | 9        |
| 0.2 | 4.9      | 29       |
| 0.3 | 9.6      | 59       |
| 0.4 | 16.8     | 79       |

## THE DIGITAL COMPUTER PROGRAM

Here we will see how the foregoing procedure may be implemented as a computer program.

**13.21**    We have seen that the solution of $\dot{\mathbf{x}} = \mathbf{Ax} + \mathbf{Bu}$ may be written:

$$\mathbf{x}(t_0 + T) = \underline{\hspace{2cm}} \mathbf{x}(t_0) + \mathbf{\Delta}(T) \underline{\hspace{2cm}}$$

*provided that* $\mathbf{u}(t) = \mathbf{u}(t_0)$, a matrix of $\underline{\hspace{2cm}}$, for $t_0 \leqslant t < t_0 + T$.

---

**13.22**    As a special case, if we put $t_0 = kT$,

$$\mathbf{x}(kT + T) = \mathbf{x}(\overline{k + 1}T) = \underline{\hspace{3cm}} + \underline{\hspace{2cm}}$$

the bar above $k + 1$ serves
as a bracket

---

**13.23**    Now if we start with $k = 0$, we can calculate $\mathbf{x}(T)$, given $\mathbf{x}(0)$ and $\mathbf{u}(0)$. Then, by putting $k = 1$, we can calculate $\mathbf{x}(\underline{\hspace{1cm}})$, knowing $\mathbf{x}(T)$ from the previous calculation, and given $\mathbf{u}(\underline{\hspace{1cm}})$.

That is, incrementing $k$ through the sequence $k = 0, 1, 2 \ldots$ will allow us to compute $\mathbf{x}(\underline{\hspace{1cm}}), \mathbf{x}(\underline{\hspace{1cm}}), \mathbf{x}(\underline{\hspace{1cm}}), \ldots$, provided that we are given $\mathbf{x}(0), \mathbf{u}(\underline{\hspace{1cm}}), \mathbf{u}(\underline{\hspace{1cm}}), \mathbf{u}(\underline{\hspace{1cm}})$, $\ldots$, as data.

$$\mathbf{x}(t_0 + T) = \underline{\boldsymbol{\varphi}(T)}\mathbf{x}(t_0) + \boldsymbol{\Delta}(T)\underline{\mathbf{u}(t_0)}$$

<u>constants</u>

---

$$\boxed{\mathbf{x}(kT + T) = \mathbf{x}(\overline{k + 1}T) = \boldsymbol{\varphi}(T)\mathbf{x}(kT) + \boldsymbol{\Delta}(T)\mathbf{u}(kT)}$$

(this result is provided on the MASK for reference)

---

For $k = 1$ we get $\mathbf{x}(\underline{2T})$ using $\mathbf{x}(T)$ and $\mathbf{u}(T)$.

We compute $\mathbf{x}(\underline{T})$, $\mathbf{x}(\underline{2T})$, $\mathbf{x}(\underline{3T})$, . . . knowing the values of $\mathbf{x}(0)$ and $\mathbf{u}(\underline{0})$, $\mathbf{u}(\underline{T})$, $\mathbf{u}(\underline{2T})$, . . .

**13.24** Even if you have not had experience with digital computer programming, you should have no difficulty following the flow chart for the process described on the previous page:

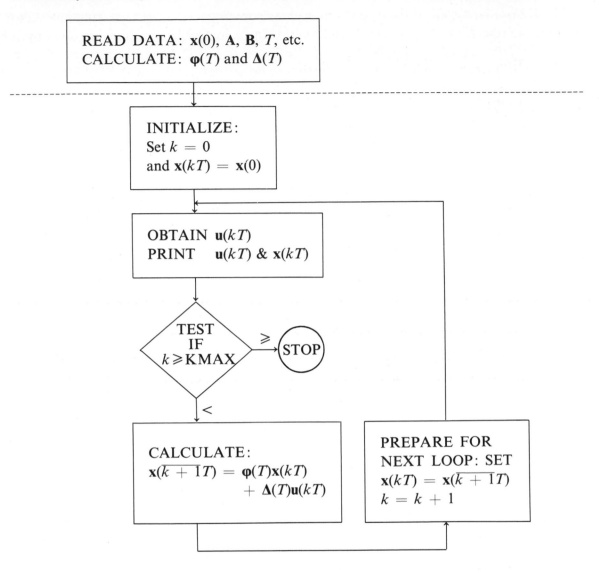

We have yet to discuss the calculation of $\varphi(T)$ and $\Delta(T)$ as indicated in the top box, but the remainder of the chart simply describes the process summarized on the previous page. The corresponding FORTRAN program (for all but the top box of the flow chart) is shown opposite.

Allow one hour for Section 14.

## FORTRAN PROGRAM

For clarity, all of the operations such as copying a vector (i.e. making one vector equal to another), printing a vector, and multiplying a matrix by a vector, are done by subroutines (CPYVEC, PRINTV, MVMULT, etc.†). With this in mind, the program can be related to the flow chart quite easily, even by those who are not familiar with FORTRAN. $N$ represents the system order, and $M$ the number of inputs.

```
C          INITIALIZE LOOP
C
      K=0
      CALL CPYVEC(X0,XK,N)
      WRITE(6,118)
  118 FORMAT('1SYSTEM INPUT AND RESPONSE --')
C
C          START THE LOOP TO PRINT THE X(KT) AND U(KT) MATRICES, AND TO
C                   CALCULATE   X(KT + T) = PHI * X(KT) + DEL * U(KT).
   20 FK=K
      TIME=FK*T
C
C        CALL SUBROUTINE INPUT TO GET THE UK'S
C
      CALL INPUT(M,T,K,TIME,XK,UK)
      WRITE(6,119) K,TIME
  119 FORMAT(//,' K =',I3, '   TIME =', F10.5,//,' INPUT MATRIX, U(K) --
     1 ')
      CALL PRINTV (UK,M)
      WRITE(6,120)
  120 FORMAT(/, ' RESPONSE MATRIX, X(K) --')
      CALL PRINTV (XK,N)
      IF(K-KMAX)300,301,301
C
C          CALCULATE X(KT+T) = PHI * X(KT) + DEL * U(KT)
C
  300 CALL MVMULT(PHI,XK,P,N,N)
      CALL MVMULT(DEL,UK,Q,N,M)
      CALL ADDVEC(P,Q,XKPLS1,N)
      CALL CPYVEC(XKPLS1,XK,N)
      K=K+1
      GO TO 20
  301 STOP
```

The user must write his own SUBROUTINE INPUT to generate the input matrix specified for each problem. This subroutine is standard except for the "UK statement(s)" of which there must be one for each of the $M$ inputs. A simple example, where $M = 1$ and $\mathbf{u} = u_1 = 0.5$, now follows:

```
      SUBROUTINE INPUT(M,T,K,TIME,XK,UK)
      DIMENSION UK(8), XK(8)
C
C          SUBROUTINE INPUT MUST BE REWRITTEN FOR EACH NEW
C              PROBLEM.  WHEN CALLED BY FIDEL, IT MUST
C              CALCULATE THE INPUT MATRIX, UK.
C      FIDEL PROVIDES THE VALUES OF
C              M, THE NUMBER OF INPUTS
C              T, THE TIME INCREMENT
C              K, THE TIME INDEX
C              TIME, WHOSE CURRENT VALUE IS K * T, AND
C              XK, THE (CURRENT) RESPONSE MATRIX.
C      THESE MAY BE USED AS NECESSARY TO CALCULATE
C              THE UK'S, BUT THEY MUST NOT BE CHANGED IN
C              THIS SUBROUTINE.
C
      UK(1) = 0.5
      RETURN
      END
```

† The subroutines are listed in Appendix 1.

**14.1**  Let's review the previous section, and then see how one may calculate the quantities $\varphi(T)$ and $\Delta(T)$ on a computer. We know that the solution of the equation:

$$\dot{\mathbf{x}}(t) = \mathbf{A}\mathbf{x}(t) + \mathbf{B}\mathbf{u}(t)$$

is:

$$\mathbf{x}(t) = \epsilon^{\mathbf{A}t}\,\mathbf{x}(0) + \epsilon^{\mathbf{A}t}\int_0^t \epsilon^{-\mathbf{A}\tau}\mathbf{B}\mathbf{u}(\tau)d\tau$$

In particular, substituting $t = T$ in the above solution:

$$\mathbf{x}(T) = \underline{\hspace{5cm}}$$

---

**14.2**  If the input matrix $\mathbf{u}(t) = \mathbf{u}(0)$, a matrix of constants, for $0 \leqslant t < T$ then $\mathbf{u}(\tau)$ as well as **B** may be taken out of the integral:

$$\mathbf{x}(T) = \epsilon^{\mathbf{A}T}\mathbf{x}(0) + \underline{\hspace{5cm}}$$

$$= \varphi(T)\mathbf{x}(0) + \Delta(T)\mathbf{u}(0)$$

$$\therefore \quad \varphi(T) = \underline{\hspace{3cm}}$$

and:

$$\Delta(T) = \underline{\hspace{4cm}}$$

$$\overset{\text{this is } \mathbf{x}(t) \text{ at time } T}{\mathbf{x}(T)} = \epsilon^{\mathbf{A}T}\mathbf{x}(0) + \epsilon^{\mathbf{A}T}\int_0^T \epsilon^{-\mathbf{A}\tau}\mathbf{B}\mathbf{u}(\tau)\,d\tau$$

$$\mathbf{x}(T) = \epsilon^{\mathbf{A}T}\mathbf{x}(0) + \epsilon^{\mathbf{A}T}\int_0^T \epsilon^{-\mathbf{A}\tau}\,d\tau\,\mathbf{B}\mathbf{u}(0)$$

$$\boldsymbol{\varphi}(T) = \epsilon^{\mathbf{A}T}$$

and

$$\boldsymbol{\Delta}(T) = \epsilon^{\mathbf{A}T}\int_0^T \epsilon^{-\mathbf{A}\tau}\,d\tau\,\mathbf{B}$$

**14.3** If we now regard $t_0$ rather than 0 as the initial time, the solution after the same $T$ seconds as before must be:

$$\mathbf{x}(\underline{\quad}+\underline{\quad}) = \boldsymbol{\varphi}(T) \underline{\quad\quad} + \underline{\quad\quad}\mathbf{u}(t_0)$$

[ ]

**14.4** Finally, if $t_0 = kT$:

$$\mathbf{x}(\underline{\quad\quad}) = \underline{\quad\quad} + \underline{\quad\quad}$$

[ ]

**14.5** The above is known as a difference equation, and its solution clearly depends upon knowing $\boldsymbol{\varphi}(T)$ and $\boldsymbol{\Delta}(T)$. First, we can find $\boldsymbol{\varphi}(T)$ by summing the series:

$$\boldsymbol{\varphi}(T) = \epsilon^{AT} = (\underline{\quad}+\underline{\quad}+\underline{\quad}+\underline{\quad}+\cdots)$$

[ ]

**14.6** Looking at the above series you can see:

that one multiplies the 1st term by _____ to obtain the 2nd,

the 2nd term by _____ to obtain the 3rd,

the 3rd term by _____ to obtain the 4th,

and the $L$th term by _____ to obtain the $L + 1$st.

[ ]

$$\mathbf{x}(t_0 + T) = \boldsymbol{\varphi}(T)\mathbf{x}(t_0) + \boldsymbol{\Delta}(T)\mathbf{u}(t_0)$$

---

or, $\mathbf{x}(\overline{k + 1}T)$

$$\mathbf{x}(kT + T) = \boldsymbol{\varphi}(T)\mathbf{x}(kT) + \boldsymbol{\Delta}(T)\mathbf{u}(kT)$$

---

As on the MASK:

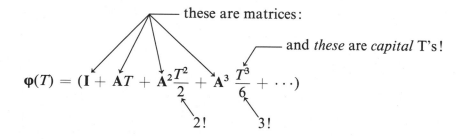

— these are matrices:

— and *these* are *capital* T's!

$$\boldsymbol{\varphi}(T) = (\mathbf{I} + \mathbf{A}T + \mathbf{A}^2\frac{T^2}{2} + \mathbf{A}^3\frac{T^3}{6} + \cdots)$$

2!  3!

---

1st  term by $\underline{\mathbf{A}T}$

2nd term by $\mathbf{A}\dfrac{T}{2}$

3rd  term by $\mathbf{A}\dfrac{T}{3}$

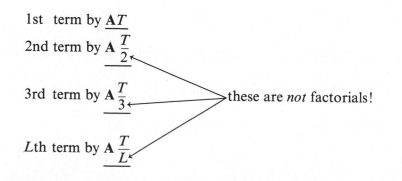

these are *not* factorials!

$L$th term by $\mathbf{A}\dfrac{T}{L}$

**14.7** A flow chart describing the process for computing $\varphi(T)$ follows. The corresponding computer program will be found in frame **14.12**.

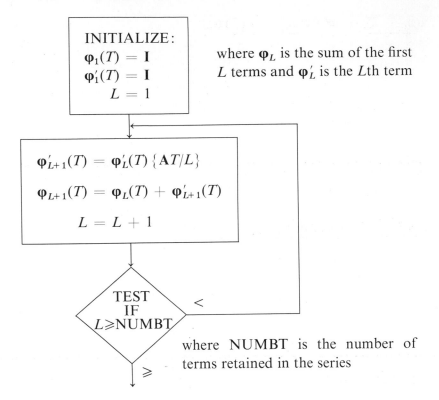

where $\varphi_L$ is the sum of the first $L$ terms and $\varphi'_L$ is the $L$th term

where **NUMBT** is the number of terms retained in the series

Using the above flow chart and some scratch paper, EVALUATE $\varphi(T)$ to *three* terms—that is, $\varphi_3(T)$.

Given:  $\mathbf{A} = \begin{bmatrix} -1 & 0 \\ 0 & -2 \end{bmatrix}$ and $T = 0.1$

*Answer:* $\varphi(0.1) \doteq \begin{bmatrix} & \\ & \end{bmatrix}$

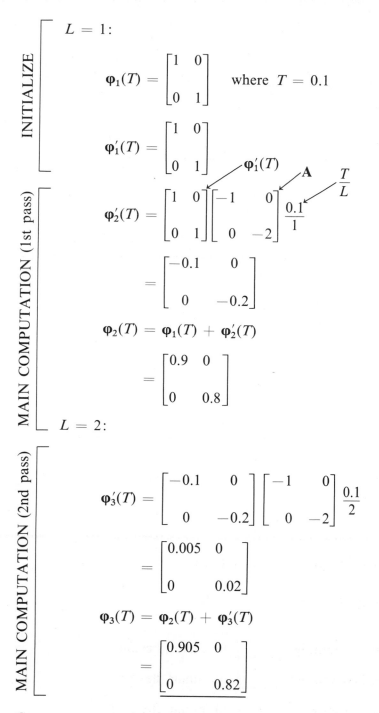

**INITIALIZE**

$L = 1$:

$$\varphi_1(T) = \begin{bmatrix} 1 & 0 \\ 0 & 1 \end{bmatrix} \quad \text{where } T = 0.1$$

**MAIN COMPUTATION (1st pass)**

$$\varphi_1'(T) = \begin{bmatrix} 1 & 0 \\ 0 & 1 \end{bmatrix}$$

$$\varphi_2'(T) = \overset{\varphi_1'(T)}{\begin{bmatrix} 1 & 0 \\ 0 & 1 \end{bmatrix}} \overset{\mathbf{A}}{\begin{bmatrix} -1 & 0 \\ 0 & -2 \end{bmatrix}} \overset{\frac{T}{L}}{\frac{0.1}{1}}$$

$$= \begin{bmatrix} -0.1 & 0 \\ 0 & -0.2 \end{bmatrix}$$

$$\varphi_2(T) = \varphi_1(T) + \varphi_2'(T)$$

$$= \begin{bmatrix} 0.9 & 0 \\ 0 & 0.8 \end{bmatrix}$$

$L = 2$:

**MAIN COMPUTATION (2nd pass)**

$$\varphi_3'(T) = \begin{bmatrix} -0.1 & 0 \\ 0 & -0.2 \end{bmatrix} \begin{bmatrix} -1 & 0 \\ 0 & -2 \end{bmatrix} \frac{0.1}{2}$$

$$= \begin{bmatrix} 0.005 & 0 \\ 0 & 0.02 \end{bmatrix}$$

$$\varphi_3(T) = \varphi_2(T) + \varphi_3'(T)$$

$$= \begin{bmatrix} 0.905 & 0 \\ 0 & 0.82 \end{bmatrix}$$

*Comment:*

We obtained this result earlier in frame **9.8**.

**14.8** Recalling that we wish to compute $\mathbf{x}(\overline{k + 1}T) = \varphi(T)\mathbf{x}(kT) + \Delta(T)\mathbf{u}(kT)$ and that we have just seen how to compute $\varphi(T)$ using a computer, it follows that we must now consider the evaluation of $\Delta(T)$.

From the MASK:

$$\Delta(T) = \epsilon^{\mathbf{A}T}\int_0^T \epsilon^{-\mathbf{A}\tau}d\tau\mathbf{B}$$

$$= \epsilon^{\mathbf{A}T}\int_0^T\left[\quad - \quad + \quad - \cdots\right]d\tau\mathbf{B}$$

<br>

□

---

**14.9** Integrating:

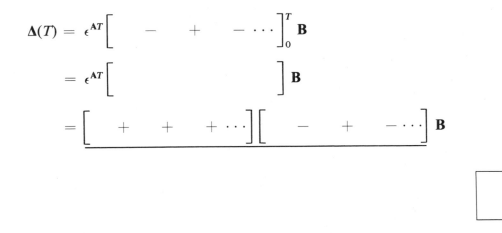

$$\Delta(T) = \epsilon^{\mathbf{A}T}\left[\quad - \quad + \quad - \cdots\right]_0^T \mathbf{B}$$

$$= \epsilon^{\mathbf{A}T}\left[\qquad\qquad\right]\mathbf{B}$$

$$= \left[\quad + \quad + \quad + \cdots\right]\left[\quad - \quad + \quad - \cdots\right]\mathbf{B}$$

□

---

**14.10** If one multiplies out the above product, one obtains:

$$\Delta(T) = \left[\mathbf{I}T + \mathbf{A}\frac{T^2}{2} + \mathbf{A}^2\frac{T^3}{6} + \mathbf{A}^3\frac{T^4}{24} + \cdots\right]\mathbf{B}$$

Thus, one multiplies the 1st term by _____ to obtain the 2nd,

the 2nd term by _____ to obtain the 3rd,

the 3rd term by _____ to obtain the 4th,

and the $L$th term by _____ to obtain the $L + 1$st.

□

$$\Delta(T) = \epsilon^{AT} \int_0^T \left[ \mathbf{I} - \mathbf{A}\tau + \mathbf{A}^2 \frac{\tau^2}{2} - \cdots \right] d\tau \mathbf{B}$$

---

$$\Delta(T) = \epsilon^{AT} \left[ \mathbf{I}\tau - \mathbf{A}\frac{\tau^2}{2} + \mathbf{A}^2 \frac{\tau^3}{6} - \cdots \right]_0^T \mathbf{B}$$

$$= \epsilon^{AT} \left[ \mathbf{I}T - \mathbf{A}\frac{T^2}{2} + \mathbf{A}^2 \frac{T^3}{6} - \cdots \right] \mathbf{B}$$

$$= \left[ \mathbf{I} + \mathbf{A}T + \mathbf{A}^2 \frac{T^2}{2} + \cdots \right] \left[ \mathbf{I}T - \mathbf{A}\frac{T^2}{2} + \mathbf{A}^2 \frac{T^3}{6} - \cdots \right] \mathbf{B}$$

---

1st  term by $\mathbf{A}\dfrac{T}{2}$

2nd term by $\mathbf{A}\dfrac{T}{3}$

3rd  term by $\mathbf{A}\dfrac{T}{4}$

$L$th term by $\mathbf{A}\dfrac{T}{L+1}$

**14.11**    A flow chart for the process of summing the series for $\Delta(T)$ now follows.  The corresponding FORTRAN program is listed in frame **14.12**.

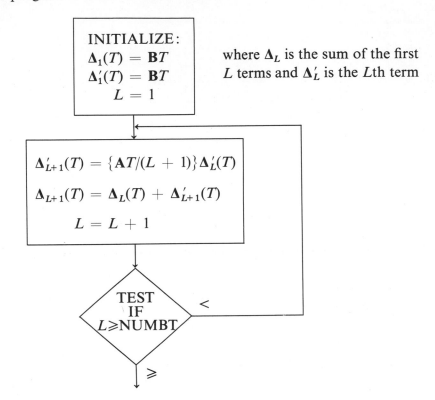

INITIALIZE:
$\Delta_1(T) = \mathbf{B}T$
$\Delta_1'(T) = \mathbf{B}T$
$L = 1$

where $\Delta_L$ is the sum of the first $L$ terms and $\Delta_L'$ is the $L$th term

$\Delta_{L+1}'(T) = \{\mathbf{A}T/(L + 1)\}\Delta_L'(T)$

$\Delta_{L+1}(T) = \Delta_L(T) + \Delta_{L+1}'(T)$

$L = L + 1$

TEST IF $L \geqslant$ NUMBT

$<$

$\geqslant$

Using the above flow chart and some scratch paper, EVALUATE $\Delta(T)$ to *two* terms, given:

$$\mathbf{A} = \begin{bmatrix} -1 & 0 \\ 0 & -2 \end{bmatrix}, \quad \mathbf{B} = \begin{bmatrix} 0 \\ 1 \end{bmatrix} \quad \text{and} \quad T = 0.1$$

*Answer:*   $\Delta(0.1) \doteq \begin{bmatrix} \phantom{xxx} \\ \phantom{xxx} \end{bmatrix}$

$L = 1$:

$$\Delta_1(T) = \begin{bmatrix} 0 \\ 0.1 \end{bmatrix} \qquad \text{where } T = 0.1$$

$$\Delta_1'(T) = \begin{bmatrix} 0 \\ 0.1 \end{bmatrix}$$

$$\Delta_2'(T) = \left\{ \begin{bmatrix} -1 & 0 \\ 0 & -2 \end{bmatrix} \frac{0.1}{2} \begin{bmatrix} 0 \\ 0.1 \end{bmatrix} \right\}$$

where the arrows point to $\mathbf{A}$, $\dfrac{T}{L+1}$, and $\Delta_1'(T)$

$$= \begin{bmatrix} 0 \\ -0.01 \end{bmatrix}$$

$$\Delta_2(T) = \Delta_1(T) + \Delta_2'(T)$$

$$= \begin{bmatrix} 0 \\ 0.09 \end{bmatrix}$$

*Comment:*

If you go one stage further you will find:

$$\Delta_3(T) = \begin{bmatrix} 0 \\ 0.0907 \end{bmatrix}$$

**14.12** In the following FORTRAN program, which implements the procedures of frames **14.7** and **14.11**,

PHI corresponds to $\varphi_L(T)$ in the flow chart,

PHITRM corresponds to $\varphi_L'(T)$,

DEL corresponds to $\Delta_L(T)$, and

DELTRM corresponds to $\Delta_L'(T)$.

$N$ represents the system order, while

$M$ represents the number of inputs.

```
C           INITIALIZE
C
      CALL SETUNI(PHI,N)
      CALL SETUNI(PHITRM,N)
      CALL SMULT(T,B,DEL,N,M)
      CALL COPYM(DEL,DELTRM,N,M)
      CALL SMULT(T,A,AT,N,N)
      L = 1
C
C         SUM THE SERIES FOR PHI AND DEL TO NUMBT TERMS
C
   10 XL=L
      RPL=1./XL
      RPLP1=1./(XL+1.)
      CALL MMULT(PHITRM,AT,PHITRM,N,N,N)
      CALL SMULT(RPL,PHITRM,PHITRM,N,N)
      CALL MADD(PHI,PHITRM,PHI,N,N)
      CALL MMULT(AT,DELTRM,DELTRM,N,N,M)
      CALL SMULT(RPLP1,DELTRM,DELTRM,N,M)
      CALL MADD(DEL,DELTRM,DEL,N,M)
      L = L + 1
      IF(L-NUMBT)10,11,11
   11 CONTINUE
```

**PROCEDURAL NOTE:**

If you do *not* have access to a digital computer with FORTRAN IV capability, you should use a slide rule and the flow charts in frames **14.7**, **14.11**, and **13.24** (in that order) to complete at least the first few steps of the calculation corresponding to the problem in frame **14.13**. You should then proceed to frame **14.17**. Otherwise, CONTINUE OPPOSITE.

## THE COMPUTER PROGRAM

The main calculation (described opposite and in frame **13.24**) is performed by SUB-
ROUTINE FIDEL, which, together with its supporting subroutines, is listed in Appendix 1.
Assuming, for the moment, that these subroutines have been placed on your computer
system's FORTRAN library file, you will be required to prepare on cards and in the following
order:

1. The main program, which calls FIDEL—

```
CALL FIDEL
STOP
END
```

2. SUBROUTINE INPUT, which defines the inputs in the problem you are to solve. For
example, if $\mathbf{u} = u_1 = 0.5$—

```
      SUBROUTINE INPUT(M,T,K,TIME,XK,UK)
      DIMENSION UK(8), XK(8)
C
C        SUBROUTINE INPUT MUST BE REWRITTEN FOR EACH NEW
C            PROBLEM.  WHEN CALLED BY FIDEL, IT MUST
C            CALCULATE THE INPUT MATRIX, UK.
C        FIDEL PROVIDES THE VALUES OF
C            M, THE NUMBER OF INPUTS
C            T, THE TIME INCREMENT
C            K, THE TIME INDEX
C            TIME, WHOSE CURRENT VALUE IS K * T, AND
C            XK, THE (CURRENT) RESPONSE MATRIX.
C        THESE MAY BE USED AS NECESSARY TO CALCULATE
C            THE UK'S, BUT THEY MUST NOT BE CHANGED IN
C            THIS SUBROUTINE.
C
      UK(1) = 0.5
      RETURN
      END
```

(obviously it is not necessary to include the comment cards in your deck)

3. The data:

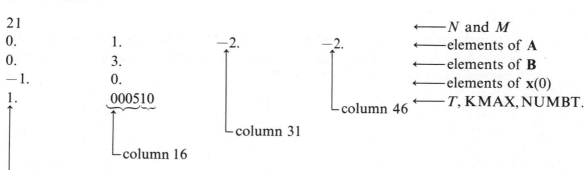

The data *must* be arranged as shown. The elements of each matrix are entered sequentially
by rows—for example, $a_{11}, a_{12}, a_{21}, a_{22}$—with up to *five* elements per card (the fifth element
would start in column 61). If there are more than five elements in a matrix, additional cards
must be added as appropriate.

**14.13**    The FORTRAN program on the previous page relates to the following problem:

*Given:*

$$\mathbf{A} = \begin{bmatrix} 0 & 1 \\ -2 & -2 \end{bmatrix}, \quad \mathbf{B} = \begin{bmatrix} 0 \\ 3 \end{bmatrix}, \quad \mathbf{x}(0) = \begin{bmatrix} -1 \\ 0 \end{bmatrix},$$

$N$ = System order = 2
$M$ = Number of inputs = 1
$T = 1.0$   KMAX = 5
        NUMBT = 10
$\mathbf{u} = u_1 = 0.5$

When your cards have been punched,† have the program run on your computer and enter the results below. *But*, see the NOTE at the bottom of the page.

$$\boldsymbol{\varphi}(T) = \boldsymbol{\varphi}(1.0) = \begin{bmatrix} & \\ & \end{bmatrix}$$

$$\boldsymbol{\Delta}(T) = \boldsymbol{\Delta}(1.0) = \begin{bmatrix} \\ \end{bmatrix}$$

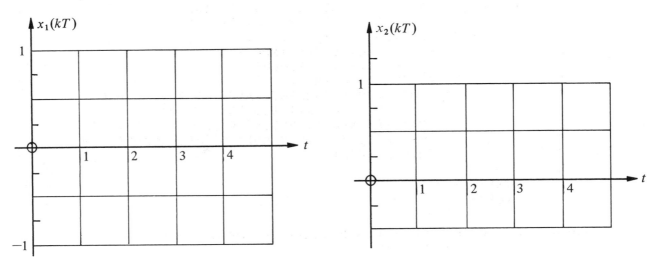

**NOTE:**
Getting cards punched and programs to run can be a time-consuming process!  To save time, you should continue this program at frame **14.17** without waiting for the computer results corresponding to frames **14.13–14.16**.

---

† If the subroutines of Appendix 1 have *not* been placed on your computer system's FORTRAN library file, you will have to get them punched on cards.  They should follow the main program in the card deck.

The computer program prints out the input data. CHECK this carefully to ensure that the computer is solving the correct problem.

$$\varphi(1.0) = \begin{bmatrix} 0.508 & 0.310 \\ -0.619 & -0.111 \end{bmatrix}$$

the last terms in the series for $\varphi$ and $\Delta$ are also printed; unless these terms are small, $\varphi(T)$ and $\Delta(T)$ are likely to be inaccurate

$$\Delta(1.0) = \begin{bmatrix} 0.738 \\ 0.929 \end{bmatrix}$$

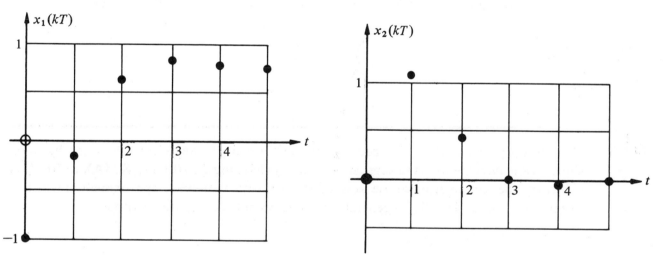

**14.14**   Next, let's solve the problem discussed in Section 12. There:

$$A = \begin{bmatrix} -1 & 1 \\ 1 & -1 \end{bmatrix}, \quad B = \begin{bmatrix} 2 & 2 & 0 \\ 0 & 0 & 2 \end{bmatrix}, \quad x(0) = \begin{bmatrix} 2 \\ 3 \end{bmatrix},$$

$u_1 = 0$, $u_2$ is as shown, and $u_3 = 0$.

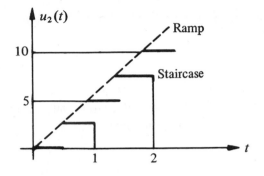

**NOTE:**
Since "time" is represented by TIME in the computer program, the "ramp" function $u_2(t) = 5t$ should be written:

UK(2) = 5. ∗ TIME

in SUBROUTINE INPUT. Further, the program assumes *piecewise constant* inputs over each time increment, $T$. Therefore the program will *approximate* the "ramp" by the "staircase" as shown.

OBTAIN your computer solution with $T = 0.5$, NUMBT = 10, and KMAX = 10.
(you will have to prepare SUBROUTINE INPUT and the data cards appropriately)

---

**14.15**   Now investigate the effect of improving the staircase approximation to the ramp by using shorter time increments. As a suggestion, start by changing $T$ to 0.1 and KMAX to 50. This will carry the computation to the same final time, with a staircase approximation which is five times as "fine." It will also generate five times as much computer printout!

$$\varphi(0.5) = \begin{bmatrix} 0.684 & 0.316 \\ 0.316 & 0.684 \end{bmatrix} \quad \Delta(0.5) = \begin{bmatrix} 0.816 & 0.816 & 0.184 \\ 0.184 & 0.184 & 0.816 \end{bmatrix}$$

$$\mathbf{x}(1) = \begin{bmatrix} 4.5 \\ 3.0 \end{bmatrix}, \quad \mathbf{x}(2) = \begin{bmatrix} 13.0 \\ 7.0 \end{bmatrix}, \quad \mathbf{x}(3) = \begin{bmatrix} 26.8 \\ 15.7 \end{bmatrix}$$

$$\mathbf{x}(4) = \begin{bmatrix} 45.5 \\ 29.5 \end{bmatrix} \quad \text{and} \quad \mathbf{x}(5) = \begin{bmatrix} 69.3 \\ 48.2 \end{bmatrix}$$

---

$$\varphi(0.1) = \begin{bmatrix} 0.909 & 0.091 \\ 0.091 & 0.909 \end{bmatrix} \quad \Delta(0.1) = \begin{bmatrix} 0.191 & 0.191 & 0.009 \\ 0.009 & 0.009 & 0.191 \end{bmatrix}$$

$$\mathbf{x}(1) = \begin{bmatrix} 6.0 \\ 3.5 \end{bmatrix} \quad \mathbf{x}(2) = \begin{bmatrix} 15.6 \\ 8.4 \end{bmatrix} \quad \mathbf{x}(3) = \begin{bmatrix} 30.4 \\ 18.1 \end{bmatrix}$$

$$\mathbf{x}(4) = \begin{bmatrix} 50.1 \\ 32.9 \end{bmatrix} \quad \mathbf{x}(5) = \begin{bmatrix} 74.9 \\ 52.6 \end{bmatrix}$$

*Comment:*

As $T$ is made smaller, the "staircase" becomes a better approximation of the ramp. The exact solution ($T \rightarrow 0$) is

$$\mathbf{x}(5) = \begin{bmatrix} 76.25 \\ 53.75 \end{bmatrix}$$

**14.16**  As a final computer problem we will consider the classical sampled-data feedback servo-mechanism shown:

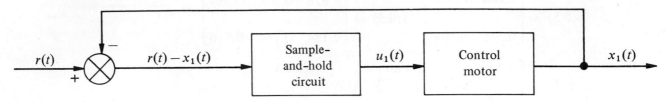

We will suppose that the control motor is described by the equation:

$$\frac{d^2x_1}{dt^2} + \frac{dx_1}{dt} = u_1(t) \quad \text{or} \quad \dot{\mathbf{x}} = \begin{bmatrix} 0 & 1 \\ 0 & -1 \end{bmatrix} \mathbf{x} + \begin{bmatrix} 0 \\ 1 \end{bmatrix} u_1$$

In this feedback system, $u_1(t)$ is given by:†

$$u_1(kT) = r(kT) - x_1(kT) \qquad kT \leqslant t < \overline{k+1}T$$

You will have to write the FORTRAN statement for UK(1), recalling that $x_1(kT)$ is represented by XK(1) in the program. Go ahead and solve the problem, given that the sample-and-hold circuit operates every $T = 1$ second. You are also given that $r(t) = 1$, and that $\mathbf{x}(0) = \mathbf{0}$. You could try NUMBT = 10 and KMAX = 20.

---

† The "sample-and-hold" circuit operates every $T$ seconds in such a way that its output is piecewise constant as indicated.

The "input" statement in your main program should read:

UK(1) = 1.0 − XK(1)

For the control motor:

$$\varphi(1) = \begin{bmatrix} 1.0 & 0.632 \\ 0. & 0.368 \end{bmatrix} \quad \text{and} \quad \Delta(1) = \begin{bmatrix} 0.368 \\ 0.632 \end{bmatrix}$$

The computed system output is:

$$\mathbf{x}(0) = \begin{bmatrix} 0.0 \\ 0.0 \end{bmatrix}, \quad \mathbf{x}(1) = \begin{bmatrix} 0.368 \\ 0.632 \end{bmatrix}, \quad \mathbf{x}(2) = \begin{bmatrix} 1.0 \\ 0.632 \end{bmatrix}$$

$$\mathbf{x}(3) = \begin{bmatrix} 1.400 \\ 0.233 \end{bmatrix}, \quad \mathbf{x}(4) = \begin{bmatrix} 1.400 \\ -0.167 \end{bmatrix}, \quad \mathbf{x}(5) = \begin{bmatrix} 1.147 \\ -0.314 \end{bmatrix}$$

$$\mathbf{x}(10) = \begin{bmatrix} 1.077 \\ 0.051 \end{bmatrix}, \quad \mathbf{x}(15) = \begin{bmatrix} 0.973 \\ 0.023 \end{bmatrix}, \quad \text{and} \quad \mathbf{x}(20) = \begin{bmatrix} 0.997 \\ -0.009 \end{bmatrix}$$

Note that $x_1(t)$ is the motor shaft position which approaches the reference input as $t \rightarrow \infty$, while $x_2(t)$ is the motor shaft velocity.

## SUMMARY OF THE COMPUTATIONAL TECHNIQUE

**14.17**  The equation $\dot{\mathbf{x}}(t) = \mathbf{A}\mathbf{x}(t) + \mathbf{B}\mathbf{u}(t)$ has for its time domain solution:

$\mathbf{x}(t) = $ _____ (see MASK)

and, at $t = T$,

$\mathbf{x}(T) = $ _____

Now **B** is a matrix of constants and *if* $\mathbf{u}(t) = \mathbf{u}(0)$, a matrix of _____ in the interval _____ $\leqslant t < $ _____ , then $\mathbf{B}\mathbf{u}(0)$ may be taken out of the integral. That is,

$\mathbf{x}(T) = $ _____

$= $ _____ $\mathbf{x}(0) + $ _____ $\mathbf{u}(0)$

where $\varphi(T) = $ _____ and $\Delta(T) = $ _____ .

Next, if we let the initial time be $t_0$ rather than zero:

$\mathbf{x}($_____$) = \varphi(T)$ _____ $+$ _____

and finally, if we let $t_0 = kT$:

$\mathbf{x}($_____$) = $ _____ $\quad kT \leqslant t < \overline{k+1}T$

$$\mathbf{x}(t) = \epsilon^{\mathbf{A}t}\mathbf{x}(0) + \epsilon^{\mathbf{A}t}\int_0^t \epsilon^{-\mathbf{A}\tau}\mathbf{B}u\,d\tau$$

$$\mathbf{x}(T) = \epsilon^{\mathbf{A}T}\mathbf{x}(0) + \epsilon^{\mathbf{A}T}\int_0^T \epsilon^{-\mathbf{A}\tau}\mathbf{B}u\,d\tau$$

$\mathbf{u}(t) = \mathbf{u}(0)$, a matrix of constants in the interval $0 \leqslant t < T$

$$\mathbf{x}(T) = \epsilon^{\mathbf{A}T}\mathbf{x}(0) + \left[\epsilon^{\mathbf{A}T}\int_0^T \epsilon^{-\mathbf{A}\tau}d\tau\mathbf{B}\right]\mathbf{u}(0)$$

$$= \boldsymbol{\varphi}(T)\mathbf{x}(0) + \boldsymbol{\Delta}(T)\mathbf{u}(0)$$

where $\boldsymbol{\varphi}(T) = \epsilon^{\mathbf{A}T}$ and $\boldsymbol{\Delta}(T) = \epsilon^{\mathbf{A}T}\int_0^T \epsilon^{-\mathbf{A}\tau}d\tau\mathbf{B}$

$$\mathbf{x}(t_0 + T) = \boldsymbol{\varphi}(T)\mathbf{x}(t_0) + \boldsymbol{\Delta}(T)\mathbf{u}(t_0)$$

$$\mathbf{x}(\overline{k + 1}T) = \boldsymbol{\varphi}(T)\mathbf{x}(kT) + \boldsymbol{\Delta}(T)\mathbf{u}(kT) \quad kT \leqslant t < \overline{k + 1}T$$

where, notice, $\mathbf{u}(t) = \mathbf{u}(kT)$ for $kT \leqslant t < \overline{k + 1}T$

**14.18**   The computer program implementing the process on the previous page first evaluates $\varphi(T)$ and $\Delta(T)$ from the appropriate series:

$$\varphi(T) = \epsilon^{AT} = I + AT + A^2 \frac{T^2}{2!} + \cdots$$

$$\Delta(T) = \epsilon^{AT} \int_0^T \epsilon^{-A\tau} d\tau \, B = \left[ IT + A \frac{T^2}{2!} + A^2 \frac{T^3}{3!} + \cdots \right] B$$

(see frames **14.8–14.10**)

Then, given $x(0)$ and $u(0)$, the program calculates:

$$\underline{\mathbf{x}(\quad) = \qquad\qquad + \qquad\qquad}$$

Next, given $u(T)$, and having just calculated $x(T)$, the program goes on to calculate:

$$\underline{\mathbf{x}(\quad) = \qquad\qquad + \qquad\qquad}$$

and so on . . .

---

The work you have done in this section, which is based on the summary of the last two frames, is the crux of this program.  You have seen and taken advantage of the fact that the solution of a state equation is easy—if you have a digital computer at hand. Further, you now appreciate that our computer solution is performed in the time domain.

This concept is central to the modern use of state variable techniques, although the transform methods of matrix algebra and the S.F.G. do find some application.

In the next section, of 35–50 minutes duration, we will review and interrelate all of the ideas we have developed so far.

$$\underline{\mathbf{x}(T) = \boldsymbol{\varphi}(T)\mathbf{x}(0) + \Delta(T)\mathbf{u}(0)}$$

$$\underline{\mathbf{x}(2T) = \boldsymbol{\varphi}(T)\mathbf{x}(T) + \Delta(T)\mathbf{u}(T)}$$

and so on to:

$$\mathbf{x}(\overline{k + 1}T) = \boldsymbol{\varphi}(T)\mathbf{x}(kT) + \Delta(T)\mathbf{u}(kT)$$

---

**NOTE:**

The computer program—and the theory—regard all inputs as *constant* during each interval, $kT \leqslant t < \overline{k + 1}T$, of the computation. Thus the program will replace each continuous function, such as $f(t)$ shown, by a piecewise constant approximation. The error introduced by this approximation may of course be minimized by reducing the interval size $T$.

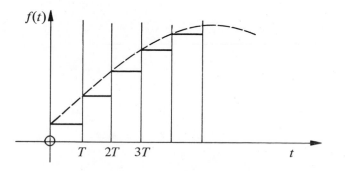

Let's review and summarize our progress.

S.F.G. SOLUTION

**15.1**   In the first three sections we saw how to write a set of differential equations in the form $\dot{\mathbf{x}}(t) = \mathbf{A}\mathbf{x}(t) + \mathbf{B}\mathbf{u}(t)$. (For REVIEW, see frames **3.17–3.20** and **5.11–5.13**.)

In general, if $n$ is the order of the system and $m$ is the number of inputs, then $\mathbf{A}$ and $\mathbf{B}$ will be of the form:

$$\mathbf{A} = \begin{bmatrix} a_{11} & a_{12} & \cdots & \underline{\phantom{x}} \\ a_{21} & a_{22} & \cdots & \underline{\phantom{x}} \\ & \cdot & \cdot & \cdot & \cdot \\ \underline{\phantom{x}} & \underline{\phantom{x}} & \cdots & \underline{\phantom{x}} \end{bmatrix} \quad \text{and} \quad \mathbf{B} = \begin{bmatrix} b_{11} & b_{12} & \cdots & \underline{\phantom{x}} \\ b_{21} & b_{22} & \cdots & \underline{\phantom{x}} \\ & \cdot & \cdot & \cdot & \cdot \\ \underline{\phantom{x}} & \underline{\phantom{x}} & \cdots & \underline{\phantom{x}} \end{bmatrix}$$

---

**15.2**   Next we noted that the Laplace transform of the state equation $\dot{\mathbf{x}} = \mathbf{A}\mathbf{x} + \mathbf{B}\mathbf{u}$ could be written:

$$s\mathbf{X}(s) = \underline{\hspace{5cm}}$$

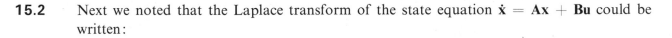

---

$$n \times n \text{ matrix}$$

$$\downarrow$$

$$\mathbf{A} = \begin{bmatrix} a_{11} & a_{12} & \cdots & a_{1n} \\ a_{21} & a_{22} & \cdots & a_{2n} \\ \cdot & \cdot & \cdot & \cdot \\ a_{n1} & a_{n2} & \cdots & a_{nn} \end{bmatrix} \quad \text{and} \quad \mathbf{B} = \begin{bmatrix} b_{11} & b_{12} & \cdots & b_{1m} \\ b_{21} & b_{22} & \cdots & b_{2m} \\ \cdot & \cdot & \cdot & \cdot \\ b_{n1} & b_{n2} & \cdots & b_{nm} \end{bmatrix}$$

$$n \times m \text{ matrix} \quad \downarrow$$

*Comment:*

Recall that we have assumed throughout that **A** and **B** are matrices of *constants*.

---

I.C. matrix

$$s\mathbf{X}(s) = \mathbf{x}(0) + \mathbf{A}\mathbf{X}(s) + \mathbf{B}\mathbf{U}(s)$$

*Comment:*

These three terms may be in any order, since the order of matrix addition is unimportant.

---

**15.3**    Combining the last two frames:

$$\begin{bmatrix} sX_1(s) \\ \cdot \\ \cdot \\ \hline \end{bmatrix} = \begin{bmatrix} x_1(0) \\ \cdot \\ \cdot \\ \hline \end{bmatrix} + \begin{bmatrix} - & - & \cdots & - \\ \cdot & \cdot & \cdots & \cdot \\ \cdot & \cdot & \cdots & \cdot \\ \hline - & - & \cdots & - \end{bmatrix} \begin{bmatrix} X_1(s) \\ \cdot \\ \cdot \\ \hline \end{bmatrix} + \begin{bmatrix} - & - & \cdots & - \\ \cdot & \cdot & \cdots & \cdot \\ \cdot & \cdot & \cdots & \cdot \\ \hline - & - & \cdots & - \end{bmatrix} \begin{bmatrix} - \\ \cdot \\ \cdot \\ \hline \end{bmatrix}$$

---

**15.4**    Now COMPLETE the labeling of the nodes and gains in the corresponding S.F.G.:

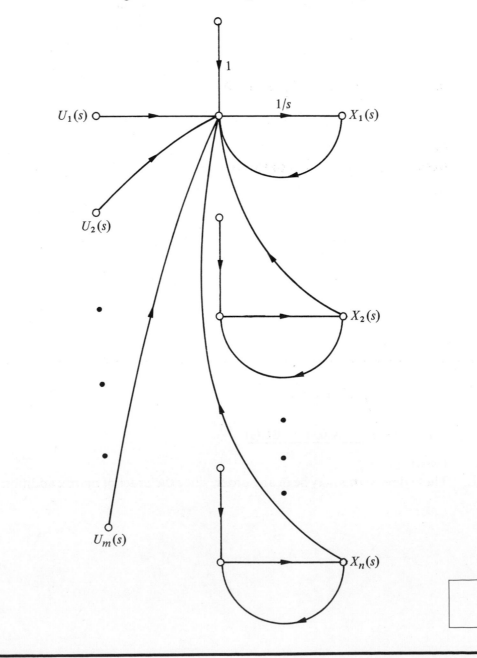

$$\begin{bmatrix} sX_1(s) \\ . \\ . \\ sX_n(s) \end{bmatrix} = \begin{bmatrix} x_1(0) \\ . \\ . \\ x_n(0) \end{bmatrix} + \begin{bmatrix} a_{11} & a_{12} & \cdots & a_{1n} \\ . & . & . & . \\ . & . & . & . \\ a_{n1} & a_{n2} & \cdots & a_{nn} \end{bmatrix} \begin{bmatrix} X_1(s) \\ . \\ . \\ X_n(s) \end{bmatrix} + \begin{bmatrix} b_{11} & b_{12} & \cdots & b_{1m} \\ . & . & . & . \\ . & . & . & . \\ b_{n1} & b_{n2} & \cdots & b_{nm} \end{bmatrix} \begin{bmatrix} U_1(s) \\ . \\ . \\ U_m(s) \end{bmatrix}$$

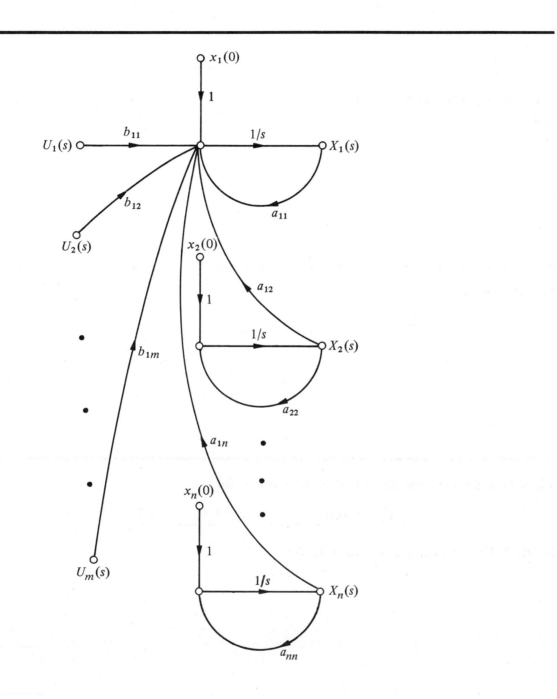

**15.5**  We know that the Mason gain formula may be used to calculate the transmission gain from any input or I.C. to any output. Thus we may write:

$$\begin{bmatrix} X_1(s) \\ X_2(s) \\ \cdot \\ X_n(s) \end{bmatrix} = \begin{bmatrix} \Phi_{11}(s) & \Phi_{12}(s) & \cdots & \underline{\quad} \\ \Phi_{21}(s) & \Phi_{22}(s) & \cdots & \underline{\quad} \\ \cdot & \cdot & \cdot & \cdot \\ \underline{\quad} & \underline{\quad} & \cdots & \underline{\quad} \end{bmatrix} \begin{bmatrix} x_1(0) \\ \underline{\quad} \\ \cdot \\ \underline{\quad} \end{bmatrix}$$

$$+ \begin{bmatrix} H_{11}(s) & H_{12}(s) & \cdots & \underline{\quad} \\ H_{21}(s) & H_{22}(s) & \cdots & \underline{\quad} \\ \cdot & \cdot & \cdot & \cdot \\ \underline{\quad} & \underline{\quad} & \cdots & \underline{\quad} \end{bmatrix} \begin{bmatrix} U_1(s) \\ \underline{\quad} \\ \cdot \\ \underline{\quad} \end{bmatrix}$$

where $\Phi_{11}(s)$ is the transmission gain from _____ to _____, and $H_{23}(s)$ is the transmission gain from _____ to _____.

$$\square$$

---

**15.6**  In matrix form:

$$\mathbf{X}(s) = \mathbf{\Phi}(s)\underline{\qquad} + \underline{\qquad\qquad}$$

$$\square$$

---

**15.7**  Thus the *solution* of the state equation $\dot{\mathbf{x}} = \mathbf{Ax} + \mathbf{Bu}$ is:

$$\mathbf{x}(t) = \boldsymbol{\varphi}(t)\underline{\qquad} + \mathscr{L}^{-1}\,[\underline{\qquad\qquad}]$$

(to REVIEW an example, see frame **12.5**)

$$\square$$

$$\begin{bmatrix} X_1(s) \\ X_2(s) \\ \cdot \\ X_n(s) \end{bmatrix} = \begin{bmatrix} \Phi_{11}(s) & \Phi_{12}(s) & \cdots & \Phi_{1n}(s) \\ \Phi_{21}(s) & \Phi_{22}(s) & \cdots & \Phi_{2n}(s) \\ \cdot & \cdot & \cdot & \cdot \\ \Phi_{n1}(s) & \Phi_{n2}(s) & \cdots & \Phi_{nn}(s) \end{bmatrix} \begin{bmatrix} x_1(0) \\ x_2(0) \\ \cdot \\ x_n(0) \end{bmatrix}$$

$$+ \begin{bmatrix} H_{11}(s) & H_{12}(s) & \cdots & H_{1m}(s) \\ H_{21}(s) & H_{22}(s) & \cdots & H_{2m}(s) \\ \cdot & \cdot & \cdot & \cdot \\ H_{n1}(s) & H_{n2}(s) & \cdots & H_{nm}(s) \end{bmatrix} \begin{bmatrix} U_1(s) \\ U_2(s) \\ \cdot \\ U_m(s) \end{bmatrix}$$

$\Phi_{11}(s)$ is the transmission gain from $\underline{x_1(0)}$ to $\underline{X_1(s)}$, and $H_{23}(s)$ is the transmission gain from $\underline{U_3(s)}$ to $\underline{X_2(s)}$.

$$\mathbf{X}(s) = \mathbf{\Phi}(s)\underline{\mathbf{x}(0)} + \underline{\mathbf{H}(s)\mathbf{U}(s)}$$

$$\mathbf{x}(t) = \mathbf{\phi}(t)\underline{\mathbf{x}(0)} + \mathscr{L}^{-1}[\underline{\mathbf{H}(s)\mathbf{U}(s)}]$$

*Comments:*
1. $\mathscr{L}^{-1}[\mathbf{\Phi}(s)\mathbf{x}(0)] = \mathbf{\phi}(t)\mathbf{x}(0)$ because $\mathbf{x}(0)$ is a matrix of constants. *But*, remember that $\mathscr{L}^{-1}[\mathbf{H}(s)\mathbf{U}(s)] \neq \mathbf{h}(t)\mathbf{u}(t)$!

2. If you are familiar with convolution, you will realize that:

$$\mathscr{L}^{-1}[\mathbf{H}(s)\mathbf{U}(s)] = \mathbf{h}(t) * \mathbf{u}(t) = \int_0^t \epsilon^{\mathbf{A}(t-\tau)}\mathbf{B}\mathbf{u}(\tau)d\tau = \epsilon^{\mathbf{A}t}\int_0^t \epsilon^{-\mathbf{A}\tau}\mathbf{B}\mathbf{u}(\tau)d\tau.$$

**MATRIX SOLUTION**

**15.8**    As an alternative to the S.F.G. solution, we next approached the problem from the point of view of matrices. Thus, to solve $\dot{\mathbf{x}} = \mathbf{A}\mathbf{x} + \mathbf{B}\mathbf{u}$, we first wrote:

$$s\mathbf{X}(s) = \underline{\hspace{4in}}$$

or, rearranging,

$$s\mathbf{X}(s) - \mathbf{A}\mathbf{X}(s) = \underline{\hspace{3in}}$$

**15.9**    Now $s\mathbf{X}(s) - \mathbf{A}\mathbf{X}(s) \neq (s - \mathbf{A})\mathbf{X}(s)$, since $\underline{\hspace{3.5in}}$.

However, we showed that:

$$s\mathbf{X}(s) - \mathbf{A}\mathbf{X}(s) = (\underline{\hspace{0.6in}})\mathbf{X}(s)$$

**15.10**    Combining the results of the last two frames:

$$(\underline{\hspace{0.6in}})\mathbf{X}(s) = \underline{\hspace{0.8in}} + \underline{\hspace{0.6in}}$$

**15.11**    Therefore;

$$\mathbf{X}(s) = \underline{\hspace{1in}} + \underline{\hspace{1.2in}}$$

(to REVIEW an example, see frame **12.4**)

$$sX(s) = \underline{x(0) + AX(s) + BU(s)}$$

$$sX(s) - AX(s) = \underline{x(0) + BU(s)}$$

---

since *s* is a scalar and **A** is a matrix  or equivalent

$$sX(s) - AX(s) = \underline{(sI - A)X(s)} \qquad \text{(see frames 7.3–7.6)}$$

---

$$\underline{(sI - A)X(s)} = \underline{x(0) + BU(s)}$$

---

Premultiplying by $(sI - A)^{-1}$;

$$\underline{X(s) = (sI - A)^{-1}x(0) + (sI - A)^{-1}BU(s)}$$

## THE TIME DOMAIN SOLUTION

**15.12**  Our third method of solution did not depend on Laplace transformation of the state equation. To solve $\dot{\mathbf{x}} = \mathbf{A}\mathbf{x} + \mathbf{B}\mathbf{u}$ we first *pre*multiplied through by the integrating factor $\epsilon^{-\mathbf{A}t}$:

$$\epsilon^{-\mathbf{A}t}\,\dot{\mathbf{x}} = \underline{\hspace{3in}}$$

or, rearranging,

$$\underline{\hspace{2.5in}} = \epsilon^{-\mathbf{A}t}\mathbf{B}\mathbf{u},$$

that is, $\dfrac{d}{dt}\{\underline{\hspace{0.6in}}\} = \epsilon^{-\mathbf{A}t}\mathbf{B}\mathbf{u}$

---

**15.13**  Integrating this equation between the limits 0 and $t$:

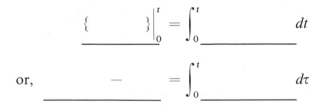

$$\{\underline{\hspace{0.8in}}\}\Big|_0^t = \int_0^t \underline{\hspace{0.8in}} \, dt$$

or, $\underline{\hspace{1in}} - \underline{\hspace{0.4in}} = \int_0^t \underline{\hspace{0.8in}} \, d\tau$

($\tau$ is a "dummy" variable of integration)

---

**15.14**  Finally, you can solve the last equation for $\mathbf{x}$:

$$\mathbf{x} = \underline{\hspace{3in}}$$

(to REVIEW an example, see frames **12.2, 12.3**)

$$\epsilon^{-At}\dot{\mathbf{x}} = \underline{\epsilon^{-At}\mathbf{A}\mathbf{x} + \epsilon^{-At}\mathbf{B}\mathbf{u}}$$

$$\underline{\epsilon^{-At}\dot{\mathbf{x}} - \epsilon^{-At}\mathbf{A}\mathbf{x}} = \epsilon^{-At}\mathbf{B}\mathbf{u}$$

— or $\mathbf{A}\,\epsilon^{-At}\,\mathbf{x}$

since $\epsilon^{-At}\mathbf{A} = \mathbf{A}\,\epsilon^{-At}$

(see frame **10.13**)

$$\frac{d}{dt}\{\epsilon^{-At}\mathbf{x}\} = \epsilon^{-At}\mathbf{B}\mathbf{u}$$

— *not* equal to $\mathbf{x}\,\epsilon^{-At}$

---

$$\underline{\{\epsilon^{-At}\mathbf{x}\}\Big|_0^t} = \underline{\int_0^t \epsilon^{-At}\mathbf{B}\mathbf{u}\,dt}$$

or

$$\underline{\epsilon^{-At}\mathbf{x} - \mathbf{x}(0)} = \underline{\int_0^t \epsilon^{-A\tau}\mathbf{B}\mathbf{u}\,d\tau}$$

$\tau$ \quad $\mathbf{u}(\tau)$

---

$$\mathbf{x} = \underline{\epsilon^{At}\mathbf{x}(0) + \epsilon^{At}\int_0^t \epsilon^{-A\tau}\mathbf{B}\mathbf{u}\,d\tau}$$

**15.15**   As we have seen, if $\dot{\mathbf{x}} = \mathbf{Ax} + \mathbf{Bu}$, then:

$$\mathbf{X}(s) = \mathbf{\Phi}(s)\mathbf{x}(0) + \mathbf{H}(s)\mathbf{U}(s) \qquad \text{(S.F.G. method)}$$

$$\text{or} \quad \mathbf{X}(s) = (s\mathbf{I} - \mathbf{A})^{-1}\mathbf{x}(0) + (s\mathbf{I} - \mathbf{A})^{-1}\mathbf{BU}(s) \qquad \text{(matrix method)}$$

$$\text{or} \quad \mathbf{x}(t) = \epsilon^{\mathbf{A}t}\mathbf{x}(0) + \epsilon^{\mathbf{A}t} \int_0^t \epsilon^{-\mathbf{A}\tau}\mathbf{Bu}d\tau \qquad \text{(time domain)}$$

These must of course be equivalent. So, comparing the three:

$$\epsilon^{\mathbf{A}t} = \mathscr{L}^{-1} [\underline{\qquad\qquad}] = \mathscr{L}^{-1} [\underline{\qquad\qquad}]$$

$$\text{(matrix method)} \qquad\qquad \text{(S.F.G. method)}$$

---

**15.16**   Also:

$$\mathbf{H}(s) = \frac{\phantom{\qquad\qquad}}{\text{(matrix method)}}$$

and:

$$\mathbf{H}(s)\mathbf{U}(s) = \mathscr{L}[\underline{\qquad\qquad\qquad}]$$

$$\text{(time domain method)}$$

or $\boldsymbol{\varphi}(t)$

$$\epsilon^{\mathbf{A}t} = \mathscr{L}^{-1}[(s\mathbf{I} - \mathbf{A})^{-1}] = \mathscr{L}^{-1}[\boldsymbol{\Phi}(s)]$$

*Comments:*

1. This is true only because $\mathbf{x}(0)$ is a matrix of constants.

That is, $\quad \mathscr{L}^{-1}[\boldsymbol{\Phi}(s)\mathbf{x}(0)] = \mathscr{L}^{-1}[\boldsymbol{\Phi}(s)]\mathbf{x}(0),$

and $\quad \mathscr{L}^{-1}[(s\mathbf{I} - \mathbf{A})^{-1}\mathbf{x}(0)] = \mathscr{L}^{-1}[(s\mathbf{I} - \mathbf{A})^{-1}]\mathbf{x}(0)$

2. $\boldsymbol{\varphi}(t)$ is often called the system's "transition matrix."

$$\mathbf{H}(s) = (s\mathbf{I} - \mathbf{A})^{-1}\mathbf{B}$$

$$\mathbf{H}(s)\mathbf{U}(s) = \mathscr{L}\left[\epsilon^{\mathbf{A}t}\int_0^t \epsilon^{-\mathbf{A}\tau}\mathbf{B}u\,d\tau\right]$$

*Comment:*

$\mathbf{H}(s)$ is often called the system's "transfer function matrix."

**15.17**    The three methods are summarized below:

   1. The S.F.G. is always useful in that it lets us "see" the system. The calculation of $\mathbf{x}(t)$ is lengthy because of the Mason gain rule calculations and the inverse Laplace transformation of $\mathbf{X}(s)$. For low order systems, this is not a problem.

   2. The matrix calculations are also lengthy because of the matrix inversion and the inverse transformation of $\mathbf{X}(s)$. Once again this is not serious for low order systems.

   3. The time domain solution is the most generally useful, since the equation can readily be modified into a form suitable for digital computation.†

---

**15.18**    Now what about the time domain solution? The calculation of $\mathbf{x}(t) = \epsilon^{\mathbf{A}t}\mathbf{x}(0) + \epsilon^{\mathbf{A}t}\int_0^t \epsilon^{-\mathbf{A}\tau}\mathbf{B}\mathbf{u}d\tau$, by hand, is also miserable. *But*, if we can *approximate* the inputs by piecewise constant functions,

$$\mathbf{u}(t) = \mathbf{u}(kT) \qquad kT \leqslant t < \overline{k+1}T$$

*then*, we showed that:

$$\mathbf{x}(\overline{k+1}T) = \underline{\hspace{4cm}}$$

---

**15.19**    This is very easy to calculate by iteration on a digital computer, as is the summation of the series for $\boldsymbol{\varphi}(T)$ and $\boldsymbol{\Delta}(T)$.

---

You will profit from looking back over this section *carefully*, including the frames referenced therein.

The time for the next section is about 45 minutes.

---

† A digital computer can also be used to solve the matrix equations: C. F. Chen and R. R. Parker, "Generalization of Heaviside's Expansion Technique to Transition Matrix Evaluation," *IEEE Trans. on Education*, December, 1966.

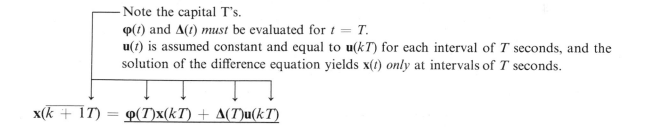

Note the capital T's.

$\varphi(t)$ and $\Delta(t)$ *must* be evaluated for $t = T$.

$\mathbf{u}(t)$ is assumed constant and equal to $\mathbf{u}(kT)$ for each interval of $T$ seconds, and the solution of the difference equation yields $\mathbf{x}(t)$ *only* at intervals of $T$ seconds.

$$\mathbf{x}(\overline{k + 1}T) = \underline{\varphi(T)\mathbf{x}(kT) + \Delta(T)\mathbf{u}(kT)}$$

We now know how to solve the state equation for the states, $\mathbf{x}(t)$. However, we will often want to solve for quantities which are different from those that have been chosen as states. Here we will see how to treat this situation.

**16.1** In the example below, $i_L$ and $v_C$ have been chosen as states, while $i_L$, $i_C$, and $v_R$ will be regarded as the required "outputs"—only one of which is a state. Of course, $v_1$ and $v_2$ are the inputs.

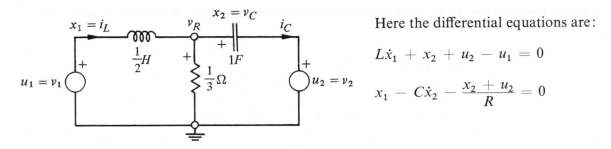

Here the differential equations are:

$$L\dot{x}_1 + x_2 + u_2 - u_1 = 0$$

$$x_1 - C\dot{x}_2 - \frac{x_2 + u_2}{R} = 0$$

Put these equations into state form and hence FIND **A** and **B**:

**16.2** SUBSTITUTE the values of $L$, $R$, and $C$ above to FIND the numerical values of the elements of **A** and **B**:

$$\dot{x}_1 = -\frac{1}{L} x_2 + \frac{1}{L} u_1 - \frac{1}{L} u_2$$

$$\dot{x}_2 = \frac{1}{C} x_1 - \frac{1}{RC} x_2 - \frac{1}{RC} u_2$$

Thus:

$$\mathbf{A} = \begin{bmatrix} 0 & -\dfrac{1}{L} \\[2mm] \dfrac{1}{C} & -\dfrac{1}{RC} \end{bmatrix} \quad \text{and} \quad \mathbf{B} = \begin{bmatrix} \dfrac{1}{L} & -\dfrac{1}{L} \\[2mm] 0 & -\dfrac{1}{RC} \end{bmatrix}$$

$$\mathbf{A} = \begin{bmatrix} 0 & -2 \\ 1 & -3 \end{bmatrix} \quad \text{and} \quad \mathbf{B} = \begin{bmatrix} 2 & -2 \\ 0 & -3 \end{bmatrix}$$

**16.3**    Let's suppose that we have calculated $\mathbf{x}(t)$, using one of the methods summarized in the last section. It remains to compute the outputs from $\mathbf{x}(t)$. By inspection of the circuit:

$$i_C = x_1 - \frac{x_2 + u_2}{R}$$

and
$$v_R = x_2 + u_2$$

Thus if we call the "output matrix"

$$\mathbf{y} = \begin{bmatrix} y_1 \\ y_2 \\ y_3 \end{bmatrix} = \begin{bmatrix} i_L \\ i_C \\ v_R \end{bmatrix}$$

Then:

$$\mathbf{y} = \begin{bmatrix} \phantom{xxxxxxxx} \\ \phantom{xx} \\ \underline{\phantom{xxxxxxxx}} \end{bmatrix} \mathbf{x} + \begin{bmatrix} \phantom{xxxxxxxx} \\ \phantom{xx} \\ \underline{\phantom{xxxxxxxx}} \end{bmatrix} \mathbf{u}$$

---

**16.4**    In general a system will be described by its state equation:

$$\dot{\mathbf{x}} = \mathbf{Ax} + \mathbf{Bu}$$

which we can solve for $\mathbf{x}(t)$. The desired outputs are not necessarily states but can be easily found from an output equation, which as you have just seen can be written in the form:

$$\mathbf{y} = \mathbf{Cx} + \mathbf{Du}$$

Note that calculating $\mathbf{x}$ is the most laborious part of the solution. It is easy to find $\mathbf{y}$ once $\mathbf{x}$ is known, since the outputs are simple linear combinations of the states and the inputs.
In the example of the previous frame:

$$\mathbf{C} = \begin{bmatrix} \phantom{xxxxxxxx} \\ \phantom{xx} \\ \underline{\phantom{xxxxxxxx}} \end{bmatrix} \quad \text{and} \quad \mathbf{D} = \begin{bmatrix} \phantom{xxxxxxxx} \\ \phantom{xx} \\ \underline{\phantom{xxxxxxxx}} \end{bmatrix}$$

$$y_1 = i_L = x_1$$

$$y_2 = i_C = x_1 - \frac{x_2}{R} - \frac{u_2}{R}$$

$$y_3 = v_R = x_2 + u_2$$

$$\therefore \; \mathbf{y} = \begin{bmatrix} 1 & 0 \\ 1 & -\dfrac{1}{R} \\ 0 & 1 \end{bmatrix} \mathbf{x} + \begin{bmatrix} 0 & 0 \\ 0 & -\dfrac{1}{R} \\ 0 & 1 \end{bmatrix} \mathbf{u}$$

$$\text{or } \mathbf{y} = \begin{bmatrix} 1 & 0 \\ 1 & -3 \\ 0 & 1 \end{bmatrix} \mathbf{x} + \begin{bmatrix} 0 & 0 \\ 0 & -3 \\ 0 & 1 \end{bmatrix} \mathbf{u}$$

$$\mathbf{C} = \begin{bmatrix} 1 & 0 \\ 1 & -3 \\ 0 & 1 \end{bmatrix} \quad \text{and} \quad \mathbf{D} = \begin{bmatrix} 0 & 0 \\ 0 & -3 \\ 0 & 1 \end{bmatrix}$$

**16.5**    Let's consider another example:

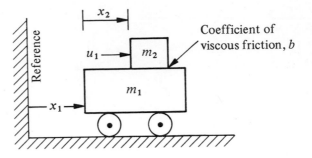

Here we will choose the states $x_1$, $x_2$, $x_3 = \dot{x}_1$, and $x_4 = \dot{x}_2$. We will suppose that we wish to find the outputs $y_1 = x_1$ and $y_2 = x_1 + x_2$, where $y_2$ is the position of the upper mass relative to the reference.

The relevant equations are:

$$m_1 \ddot{x}_1 = b\dot{x}_2$$

$$m_2(\ddot{x}_1 + \ddot{x}_2) = u_1 - b\dot{x}_2$$

FIND the **A**, **B**, **C**, and **D** matrices:

*Hint:* Eliminate $\ddot{x}_1$ from the second equation by substituting $\ddot{x}_1 = \dfrac{b}{m_1}\,\dot{x}_2$.

First, we set up the (four) state equations:

$$\dot{x}_1 = x_3 \tag{1}$$

$$\dot{x}_2 = x_4 \tag{2}$$

$$m_1\dot{x}_3 = bx_4 \quad \therefore \quad \dot{x}_3 = \frac{b}{m_1}x_4 \tag{3}$$

$$m_2\dot{x}_3 + m_2\dot{x}_4 = u_1 - bx_4$$

$$\therefore \quad m_2\left(\frac{b}{m_1}x_4\right) + m_2\dot{x}_4 = u_1 - bx_4$$

$$\text{and} \quad \dot{x}_4 = \left(-\frac{b}{m_2} - \frac{b}{m_1}\right)x_4 + \frac{1}{m_2}u_1 \tag{4}$$

Thus the state equation is:

$$\dot{x} = \begin{bmatrix} 0 & 0 & 1 & 0 \\ 0 & 0 & 0 & 1 \\ 0 & 0 & 0 & \dfrac{b}{m_1} \\ 0 & 0 & 0 & -\dfrac{b(m_1 + m_2)}{m_1 m_2} \end{bmatrix} \mathbf{x} + \begin{bmatrix} 0 \\ 0 \\ 0 \\ \dfrac{1}{m_2} \end{bmatrix} u_1 \qquad \text{or } \mathbf{u}$$

The output equation is:

$$\mathbf{y} = \begin{bmatrix} y_1 \\ y_2 \end{bmatrix} = \overset{\textstyle\mathbf{C}}{\begin{bmatrix} 1 & 0 & 0 & 0 \\ 1 & 1 & 0 & 0 \end{bmatrix}} \mathbf{x} + \overset{\textstyle\mathbf{D}}{\begin{bmatrix} 0 \\ 0 \end{bmatrix}} u_1$$

(since you were given that $y_1 = x_1$ and $y_2 = x_1 + x_2$)

**16.6**  A third example:

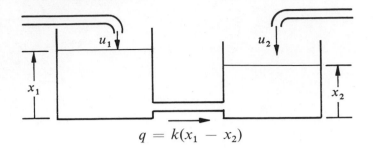

the two tanks have equal cross-sectional area, $\alpha$

$$q = k(x_1 - x_2)$$

Here  $\alpha \dot{x}_1 = -k(x_1 - x_2) + u_1 = Q_{net}$

$\alpha \dot{x}_2 = k(x_1 - x_2) + u_2$

We will suppose that we want to find the net flow rate, $Q_{net}$, into the left tank, and the flow rate, $q$, through the pipe.  That is,

$$\mathbf{y} = \begin{bmatrix} y_1 \\ y_2 \end{bmatrix} = \begin{bmatrix} Q_{net} \\ q \end{bmatrix}$$

FIND the appropriate **A**, **B**, **C**, and **D**:

$$\dot{x}_1 = -\frac{k}{\alpha}x_1 + \frac{k}{\alpha}x_2 + \frac{1}{\alpha}u_1$$

$$\dot{x}_2 = \frac{k}{\alpha}x_1 - \frac{k}{\alpha}x_2 + \frac{1}{\alpha}u_2$$

$\left.\right\}$ the state equations

$$\therefore \quad \mathbf{A} = \begin{bmatrix} -\dfrac{k}{\alpha} & \dfrac{k}{\alpha} \\[2ex] \dfrac{k}{\alpha} & -\dfrac{k}{\alpha} \end{bmatrix} \quad \text{and} \quad \mathbf{B} = \begin{bmatrix} \dfrac{1}{\alpha} & 0 \\[2ex] 0 & \dfrac{1}{\alpha} \end{bmatrix}$$

$$y_1 = -kx_1 + kx_2 + u_1$$

$$y_2 = kx_1 - kx_2$$

$\left.\right\}$ the output equations

Thus:

$$\mathbf{C} = \begin{bmatrix} -k & k \\ k & -k \end{bmatrix} \quad \text{and} \quad \mathbf{D} = \begin{bmatrix} 1 & 0 \\ 0 & 0 \end{bmatrix}$$

**16.7** If, in the previous problem, we put $k = 10$, $\alpha = 10$, $\mathbf{x}(0) = \mathbf{0}$, $u_1 = 5t$, and $u_2 = 0$, we can solve for $\mathbf{x}$. You did this in Section 12, where you found that:

$$\mathbf{x}(t) = \begin{bmatrix} -\dfrac{5}{4} + \dfrac{5}{2}t + \dfrac{5}{2}t^2 + \dfrac{5}{4}\epsilon^{-2t} \\[4mm] \dfrac{5}{4} - \dfrac{5}{2}t + \dfrac{5}{2}t^2 - \dfrac{5}{4}\epsilon^{-2t} \end{bmatrix}$$

Now, FIND $\mathbf{y}(t)$, knowing (from the previous frame and the above data) that:

$$\mathbf{y}(t) = \begin{bmatrix} -10 & 10 \\ 10 & -10 \end{bmatrix} \mathbf{x} + \begin{bmatrix} 1 & 0 \\ 0 & 0 \end{bmatrix} \mathbf{u}$$

$$\mathbf{y} = \overset{\mathbf{C}}{\begin{bmatrix} -10 & 10 \\ \\ 10 & -10 \end{bmatrix}} \overset{\mathbf{x}}{\begin{bmatrix} -\dfrac{5}{4} + \dfrac{5}{2}t + \dfrac{5}{2}t^2 + \dfrac{5}{4}\epsilon^{-2t} \\ \\ \dfrac{5}{4} - \dfrac{5}{2}t + \dfrac{5}{2}t^2 - \dfrac{5}{4}\epsilon^{-2t} \end{bmatrix}} + \overset{\mathbf{D}}{\begin{bmatrix} 1 & 0 \\ \\ 0 & 0 \end{bmatrix}} \overset{\mathbf{u}}{\begin{bmatrix} 5t \\ \\ 0 \end{bmatrix}}$$

$$= \begin{bmatrix} 25 - 50t - 25\,\epsilon^{-2t} \\ \\ -25 + 50t + 25\,\epsilon^{-2t} \end{bmatrix} + \begin{bmatrix} 5t \\ \\ 0 \end{bmatrix}$$

$$= \begin{bmatrix} 25 - 45t - 25\,\epsilon^{-2t} \\ \\ -25 + 50t + 25\,\epsilon^{-2t} \end{bmatrix}$$

*Comment:*

Note again that finding **y**—a linear combination of **x** and **u**—is easy once **x** has been determined.

**16.8** To help visualize the relationship between the states **x**, and the outputs **y**, let's look at the S.F.G. corresponding to the present problem. Substituting the data of the previous frame into the state and output equations:

$$\dot{\mathbf{x}} = \begin{bmatrix} -1 & 1 \\ 1 & -1 \end{bmatrix} \mathbf{x} + \begin{bmatrix} 0.1 & 0 \\ 0 & 0.1 \end{bmatrix} \mathbf{u} \qquad \text{the state equation}$$

$$\text{and } \mathbf{y} = \begin{bmatrix} -10 & 10 \\ 10 & -10 \end{bmatrix} \mathbf{x} + \begin{bmatrix} 1 & 0 \\ 0 & 0 \end{bmatrix} \mathbf{u} \qquad \text{the output equation}$$

Mentally—or on scratch paper—take the Laplace transform of these equations, and then complete the S.F.G. below. *Hint:* Complete the graph corresponding to $\dot{\mathbf{x}} = \mathbf{Ax} + \mathbf{Bu}$ first, then add the output relationships.

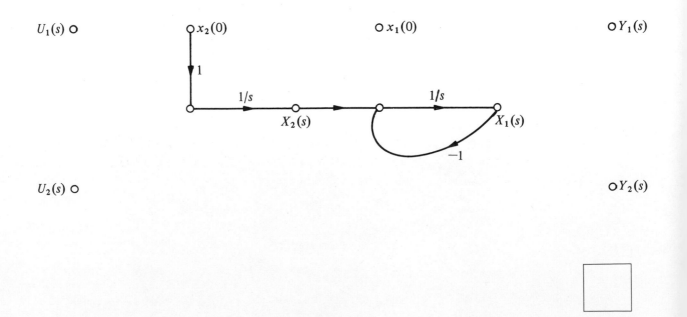

The next section will take you about an hour.

Transforming the state equation:

$$
\begin{bmatrix} sX_1(s) \\ sX_2(s) \end{bmatrix} = \begin{bmatrix} x_1(0) \\ x_2(0) \end{bmatrix} + \begin{bmatrix} -1 & 1 \\ 1 & -1 \end{bmatrix} \begin{bmatrix} X_1(s) \\ X_2(s) \end{bmatrix} + \begin{bmatrix} 0.1 & 0 \\ 0 & 0.1 \end{bmatrix} \begin{bmatrix} U_1(s) \\ U_2(s) \end{bmatrix}
$$

Transforming the output equation:

$$
\begin{bmatrix} Y_1(s) \\ Y_2(s) \end{bmatrix} = \begin{bmatrix} -10 & 10 \\ 10 & -10 \end{bmatrix} \begin{bmatrix} X_1(s) \\ X_2(s) \end{bmatrix} + \begin{bmatrix} 1 & 0 \\ 0 & 0 \end{bmatrix} \begin{bmatrix} U_1(s) \\ U_2(s) \end{bmatrix}
$$

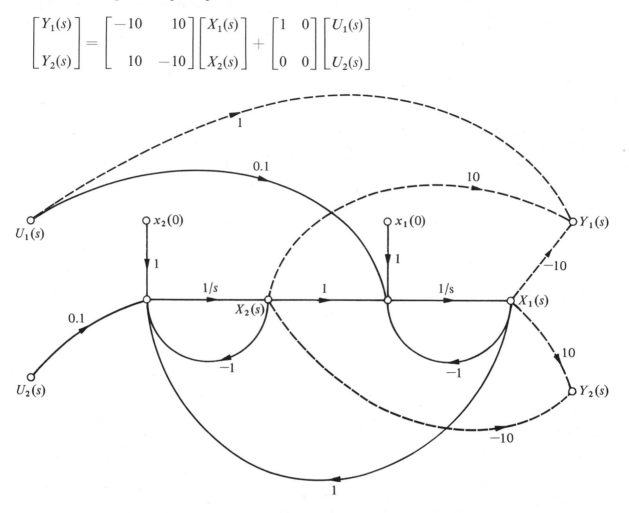

*Comment:*

Note that the problem is "solved" in terms of the state variables $\mathbf{X}(s)$. The outputs $\mathbf{Y}(s)$ are merely linear combinations of the states $\mathbf{X}(s)$ and the inputs $\mathbf{U}(s)$—shown with dashed branches in the S.F.G.

So far we have always described the system under investigation by an appropriate set of differential equations—which we have put in state form. However, sometimes we will have a system which is described by a transfer function.

**17.1**   For example:

$$H(s) = \frac{\Theta_F(s)}{R(s)} = \frac{10}{s^2 + 3s + 2}$$

where $\Theta_F(s)$ is the Laplace transform of the *forced* output due to the input $r(t)$. How might we obtain a state representation for this system? First, we see that:

$$(\underline{\hspace{3cm}})\Theta_F(s) = \underline{\hspace{1.5cm}}R(s)$$

---

**17.2**   This suggests that we should look at the differential equation:

$$\frac{d^2\theta}{dt^2} + 3\frac{d\theta}{dt} + 2\theta = 10r(t)$$

Transforming and rearranging:

$$(\underline{\hspace{3cm}})\Theta(s) = \underline{\hspace{4cm}}$$

---

**17.3**   Thus, setting the I.C.'s to zero, the last equation becomes:

$$(\underline{\hspace{3cm}})\Theta_F(s) = \underline{\hspace{1.5cm}}$$

which shows that the transfer function of frame **17.1** and the differential equation of frame **17.2** describe the same system.

---

Crossmultiplying:

$$(s^2 + 3s + 2)\Theta_F(s) = \underline{10R(s)}$$

---

$$s^2\Theta(s) - s\theta(0) - \dot{\theta}(0) + 3\{s\Theta(s) - \theta(0)\} + 2\Theta(s) = 10R(s)$$

Thus

$$\underline{(s^2 + 3s + 2)}\Theta(s) = \underline{10R(s) + \dot{\theta}(0) + \{s + 3\}\theta(0)}$$

---

$$\underline{(s^2 + 3s + 2)}\Theta_F(s) = \underline{10R(s)}$$

the *forced* output due to $R(s)$ alone, since the I.C.'s have been set to zero

---

**17.4**    Now, given that our system can be described by the equation:

$$\frac{d^2\theta}{dt^2} + 3\frac{d\theta}{dt} + 2\theta = 10r(t)$$

and defining $x_1 = \theta$, $x_2 = \dot{\theta}$, and $u_1 = r$,

$$\dot{x} = \left[\underline{\hspace{3cm}}\right] x + \left[\underline{\hspace{1cm}}\right] u_1$$

Thus we have obtained a state equation (in the state variables $x_1 = \theta$ and $x_2 = \dot{\theta}$) which corresponds to the original transfer function:

$$\frac{\Theta_F(s)}{R(s)} = \frac{10}{s^2 + 3s + 2}$$

$$\boxed{\phantom{xxx}}$$

---

**17.5**    Another example: Given

$$H(s) = \frac{P_F(s)}{Q(s)} = \frac{100}{s^3 + 5s^2 + 10}$$

The corresponding differential equation would be:

$$\underline{\hspace{6cm}} =$$

If we now choose $x_1 = p$, $x_2 = \dot{p}$, $x_3 = \ddot{p}$, and $u_1 = q$, we can represent the system by the state equation:

$$\dot{x} = \left[\underline{\hspace{3cm}}\right] x + \left[\underline{\hspace{1cm}}\right] u_1$$

$$\boxed{\phantom{xxx}}$$

$$\dot{\mathbf{x}} = \begin{bmatrix} 0 & 1 \\ -2 & -3 \end{bmatrix} \mathbf{x} + \begin{bmatrix} 0 \\ 10 \end{bmatrix} u_1$$

<hr />

it is legitimate to omit this term

$$\underline{\dddot{p} + 5\ddot{p} + 0\dot{p} + 10p = 100q}$$      (the variable is $p(t)$, *not* $p_F(t)$—see frame **17.2** and **17.3**)

Thus

$$\dot{\mathbf{x}} = \begin{bmatrix} 0 & 1 & 0 \\ 0 & 0 & 1 \\ -10 & 0 & -5 \end{bmatrix} \mathbf{x} + \begin{bmatrix} 0 \\ 0 \\ 100 \end{bmatrix} u_1$$

**17.6**  As a final example, let's consider:

$$\frac{\Theta_F(s)}{R(s)} = \frac{K}{s^n + a_n s^{n-1} + \cdots + a_2 s + a_1}$$

FIND a corresponding state variable representation:

First, the corresponding differential equation is:

$$\frac{d^n\theta}{dt^n} + a_n \frac{d^{n-1}\theta}{dt^{n-1}} + \cdots + a_2 \frac{d\theta}{dt} + a_1\theta = Kr(t)$$

Setting $x_1 = \theta$, $x_2 = \dot\theta, \cdots$, and $u_1 = r$,

$$\dot{\mathbf{x}} = \begin{bmatrix} 0 & 1 & 0 & 0 & . & . & . & . \\ 0 & 0 & 1 & 0 & 0 & . & . & . \\ . & . & . & . & . & . & . & . \\ 0 & 0 & . & . & . & . & . & 1 \\ -a_1 & -a_2 & . & . & . & . & . & -a_n \end{bmatrix} \mathbf{x} + \begin{bmatrix} 0 \\ 0 \\ . \\ . \\ K \end{bmatrix} u_1$$

*Comment:*

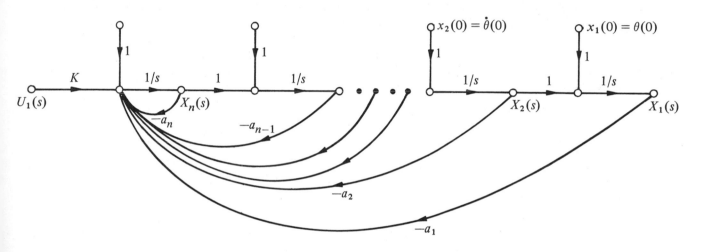

## TRANSFER FUNCTIONS WITH ZEROS

**17.7** Transfer functions often have a function of $s$ in the numerator as well as in the denominator. For example:

$$\frac{P_F(s)}{Q(s)} = \frac{10(s + 3)}{s^2 + 3s + 2}$$

There are several ways to obtain a state representation of such a system.† Here we will break the transfer function into two parts:

$$\frac{P_F(s)}{Q(s)} = \frac{10(s + 3)}{s^2 + 3s + 2} = \frac{10}{s^2 + 3s + 2} \cdot (s + 3)$$

We know that it is easy to find a state representation corresponding to the first factor, and we will show that the second factor corresponds to an output equation. For convenience we will define a new variable, $w(t)$ say, such that:

$$\frac{P_F(s)}{Q(s)} = \frac{10}{s^2 + 3s + 2} \cdot (s + 3) = \frac{W_F(s)}{Q(s)} \cdot \frac{P_F(s)}{W_F(s)}$$

Thus, comparing the two products:

$$\frac{W_F(s)}{Q(s)} = \underline{\hspace{6cm}}$$

---

**17.8** Corresponding to $\dfrac{W_F(s)}{Q(s)}$ is the state equation:

$$\dot{\mathbf{x}} = \left[\ \underline{\hspace{3cm}}\ \right] \mathbf{x} + \left[\ \underline{\hspace{1.5cm}}\ \right] u_1$$

---

$$\frac{W_F(s)}{Q(s)} = \frac{10}{s^2 + 3s + 2}$$

---

In the usual way, the differential equation is $\ddot{w} + 3\dot{w} + 2w = 10q(t)$. Setting $x_1 = w$, $x_2 = \dot{w}$, and $u_1 = q$:

$$\dot{\mathbf{x}} = \begin{bmatrix} 0 & 1 \\ -2 & -3 \end{bmatrix} \mathbf{x} + \begin{bmatrix} 0 \\ 10 \end{bmatrix} u_1$$

**17.9**   Now $\dfrac{P_F(s)}{W_F(s)} = $ _____ , from the previous page.

The corresponding differential equation is:

_____

☐

---

**17.10**   We have let $x_1 = w$ and $x_2 = \dot{w}$. Now, let $y_1 = p$, so that the above equation becomes:

$$y_1 = [\qquad]\mathbf{x}$$

☐

---

**17.11**   Recapitulating: we started with a transfer function (T.F.) which had a function of $s$ in its numerator. The procedure was:

1. to write the T.F. as a product, such that one term contained no numerator $s$'s,

2. to obtain a state representation of this term, yielding:

$$\dot{\mathbf{x}} = \mathbf{A}\mathbf{x} + \mathbf{B}u_1, \quad \text{and}$$

3. to show that the remaining term could be represented by an output equation:

$$y_1 = \mathbf{C}\mathbf{x}$$

That is, if a T.F. has numerator $s$'s, we can represent the system by a state equation *together with* an output equation.

*Note* that a T.F. relates a *single* output to a *single* input. These are now represented by $y_1$ and $u_1$ respectively.

☐

---

$$\frac{P_F(s)}{W_F(s)} = \underline{s + 3}$$

and the corresponding differential equation is:

$$\underline{\dot{w} + 3w = p(t)}$$

---

$$x_2 + 3x_1 = y_1$$

or, in matrix form:

$$y_1 = \underline{[3 \quad 1]}\mathbf{x} \qquad \xleftarrow{\hspace{2cm}} \mathbf{C}$$

**NOTE:**
Our system is described by the state equation (frame **17.8**) *together with* this output equation. $u_1 = q(t)$ is the input, and $y_1 = p(t)$ is the output corresponding to the transfer function $P_F(s)/Q(s)$.

---

**17.12** Let's try to get hold of this idea through another example:

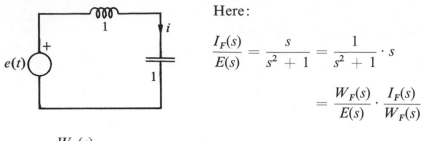

Here:

$$\frac{I_F(s)}{E(s)} = \frac{s}{s^2 + 1} = \frac{1}{s^2 + 1} \cdot s$$

$$= \frac{W_F(s)}{E(s)} \cdot \frac{I_F(s)}{W_F(s)}$$

That is, $\dfrac{W_F(s)}{E(s)} =$ _____ , corresponding to the differential equation:

_____

☐

---

**17.13** Thus $W_F(s)/E(s)$ may be represented by the state equation:

$$\dot{\mathbf{x}} = \begin{bmatrix} \ \ \\ \ \ \end{bmatrix} \mathbf{x} + \begin{bmatrix} \ \ \\ \ \ \end{bmatrix} u_1$$

☐

---

**17.14** Now:

$\dfrac{I_F(s)}{W_F(s)} =$ _____ , which corresponds to the differential equation: _____ .

☐

---

**17.15** If we let $y_1 = i$ (the system output), the output equation becomes: ·

$$y_1 = [\ \ \ \ \ \ ]\mathbf{x}$$

☐

$$\frac{W_F(s)}{E(s)} = \frac{1}{s^2 + 1} \quad \text{corresponds to } \underline{\ddot{w} + w = e(t).}$$

---

Setting $x_1 = w$, $x_2 = \dot{w}$, and $u_1 = e$ we have

$$\dot{\mathbf{x}} = \begin{bmatrix} 0 & 1 \\ -1 & 0 \end{bmatrix} \mathbf{x} + \begin{bmatrix} 0 \\ 1 \end{bmatrix} u_1$$

---

$$\frac{I_F(s)}{W_F(s)} = \underline{s} \text{ which corresponds to } \underline{\dot{w} = i}$$

---

Recalling that $x_1 = w$ and $x_2 = \dot{w}$,

$$y_1 = \underline{[0 \quad 1]\mathbf{x}}$$

*Comment:*
Again the state equation $\dot{\mathbf{x}} = \mathbf{Ax} + \mathbf{B}u_1$ *and* the output equation $y_1 = \mathbf{Cx}$ *together* represent the original T.F.

---

**197**

**17.16** A last example:

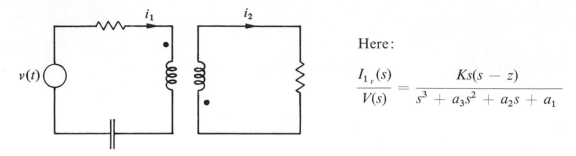

Here:

$$\frac{I_{1_F}(s)}{V(s)} = \frac{Ks(s-z)}{s^3 + a_3 s^2 + a_2 s + a_1}$$

The first step is to break the T.F. into two factors:

$$\frac{I_{1_F}(s)}{V(s)} = \underline{\hspace{4cm}}.$$

___

**17.17** Now FIND the corresponding state and output equations:

$$\frac{I_{1_F}(s)}{V(s)} = \frac{K}{s^3 + a_3 s^2 + a_2 s + a_1} \cdot s(s - z) \quad \text{or} \quad \frac{1}{s^3 + a_3 s^2 + a_2 s + a_1} \cdot Ks(s - z)$$

— no $s$'s in numerator

say $\quad \dfrac{W_F(s)}{V(s)} = \dfrac{K}{s^3 + a_3 s^2 + a_2 s + a_1}$

and $\quad \dfrac{I_{1_F}(s)}{W_F(s)} = s^2 - zs$

---

$$\ddot{w} + a_3 \ddot{w} + a_2 \dot{w} + a_1 w = Kv(t)$$

$$\dot{\mathbf{x}} = \begin{bmatrix} 0 & 1 & 0 \\ 0 & 0 & 1 \\ -a_1 & -a_2 & -a_3 \end{bmatrix} \mathbf{x} + \begin{bmatrix} 0 \\ 0 \\ K \end{bmatrix} u_1$$

$$\ddot{w} - z\dot{w} = i_1$$

or, $\mathbf{B} = \begin{bmatrix} 0 \\ 0 \\ 1 \end{bmatrix}$

$$y_1 = \begin{bmatrix} 0 & -z & 1 \end{bmatrix} \mathbf{x}$$

and $\mathbf{C} = \begin{bmatrix} 0 & -Kz & K \end{bmatrix}$
(corresponding to the
second alternative in the
previous frame)

**17.18**   COMPLETE the following S.F.G. corresponding to the equations of the previous frame:

$$\dot{\mathbf{x}} = \begin{bmatrix} 0 & 1 & 0 \\ 0 & 0 & 1 \\ -a_1 & -a_2 & -a_3 \end{bmatrix} \mathbf{x} + \begin{bmatrix} 0 \\ 0 \\ K \end{bmatrix} u_1$$

$$y_1 = \begin{bmatrix} 0 & -z & 1 \end{bmatrix} \mathbf{x}$$

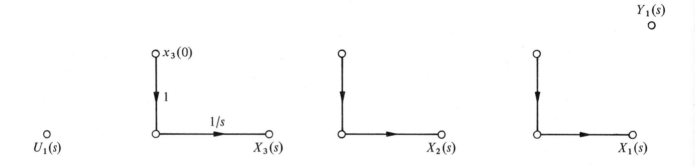

In the next section we will introduce another application of the output equation. Your time should be from 40–55 minutes.

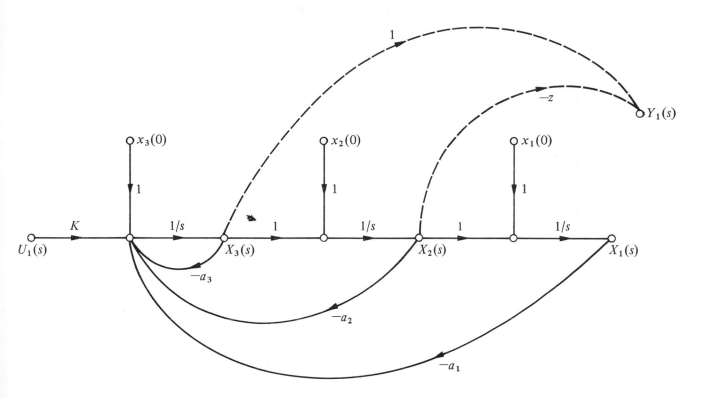

*Comments:*

1. $x_1(0)$, $x_2(0)$, and $x_3(0)$ are the initial values of the "dummy" variable $w(t)$ and may be determined as indicated in Appendix 2.

2. We have considered transfer functions where the numerator polynomial is of lower order than that of the denominator polynomial. Under these conditions $\mathbf{D} = \mathbf{0}$.

**18.1**

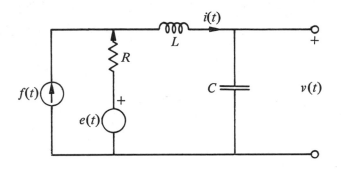

We considered this circuit earlier, once in terms of the states $v$ and $\frac{dv}{dt}$ (frame **3.7**), and again (in frame **3.8**) in terms of the states $v$ and $i$.

We will now take a slightly different point of view and get into trouble—deliberately. On the next page we will use an output equation to extricate ourselves.

From Kirchhoff's voltage law:

$$L\frac{di}{dt} + R\{i - f(t)\} + \frac{1}{C}\int_0^t i\,dt + v(0) = e(t)$$

Differentiating (to get rid of the integral) and rearranging,

$$\frac{d^2i}{dt^2} + \frac{R}{L}\frac{di}{dt} + \frac{1}{LC}i = \frac{R}{L}\frac{df(t)}{dt} + \frac{1}{L}\frac{de(t)}{dt}$$

If we were to proceed in the usual way:

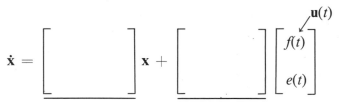

**18.2**   Derivatives in the **B**–matrix are undesirable. They imply input differentiation, which is difficult to simulate—particularly if the input has discontinuities where its derivative would become infinite.

On the following page we will investigate one way of dealing with this situation.

Setting $x_1 = i$ and $x_2 = di/dt$:

$$\dot{\mathbf{x}} = \begin{bmatrix} 0 & 1 \\ -\dfrac{1}{LC} & -\dfrac{R}{L} \end{bmatrix} \mathbf{x} + \begin{bmatrix} 0 & 0 \\ \dfrac{R}{L}\dfrac{d}{dt} & \dfrac{1}{L}\dfrac{d}{dt} \end{bmatrix} \begin{bmatrix} f(t) \\ e(t) \end{bmatrix}$$

**18.3**    Our circuit equation is:

$$\frac{d^2i}{dt^2} + \frac{R}{L}\frac{di}{dt} + \frac{1}{LC}i = \frac{R}{L}\frac{df(t)}{dt} + \frac{1}{L}\frac{de(t)}{dt}$$

We first consider the effect of the input $f(t)$ by setting the other input $e(t) = 0$, and therefore $de/dt = 0$. FIND the transfer function $I_F(s)/F(s)$:

*Hint:* Remember that to find a T.F., one sets the I.C.'s to zero.

**18.4**    Using the method of the previous section, OBTAIN the equivalent state and output equations:

**18.5**    This allows us to find the response—$I_F(s)$—due to the input $f(t)$  The other input and the I.C.'s of the original problem variables have been set equal to zero.

On the next page we will see how to obtain the response due to the other input, and Appendix 2 addresses itself to the consideration of the I.C.'s.

$$s^2 I(s) - si(0) - \left.\frac{di}{dt}\right|_0 + \frac{R}{L}\{sI(s) - i(0)\} + \frac{1}{LC} I(s) = \frac{R}{L}\{sF(s) - f(0)\}$$

Setting the I.C.'s to zero:

$$\frac{I_F(s)}{F(s)} = \frac{\dfrac{R}{L}s}{s^2 + \dfrac{R}{L}s + \dfrac{1}{LC}}$$

*Comment:*

On the next page we will find $I_F(s)/E(s)$, and hence the response due to the other input $e(t)$.

---

Letting $\dfrac{W_F(s)}{F(s)} = \dfrac{\dfrac{R}{L}}{s^2 + \dfrac{R}{L}s + \dfrac{1}{LC}}$, the state equation is:

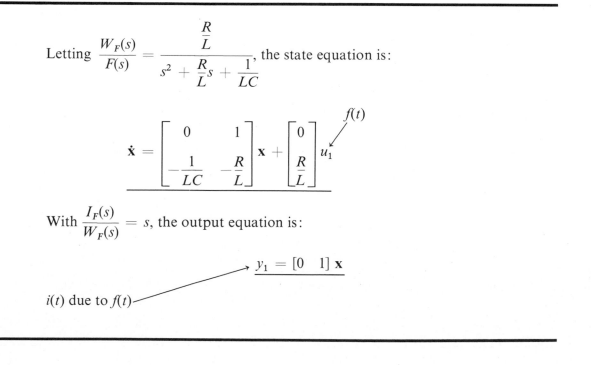

$$\dot{\mathbf{x}} = \begin{bmatrix} 0 & 1 \\ -\dfrac{1}{LC} & -\dfrac{R}{L} \end{bmatrix} \mathbf{x} + \begin{bmatrix} 0 \\ \dfrac{R}{L} \end{bmatrix} u_1$$

$f(t)$

With $\dfrac{I_F(s)}{W_F(s)} = s$, the output equation is:

$$y_1 = [0 \quad 1]\,\mathbf{x}$$

$i(t)$ due to $f(t)$

---

**18.6**     Given, again:

$$\frac{d^2i}{dt^2} + \frac{R}{L}\frac{di}{dt} + \frac{1}{LC}i = \frac{R}{L}\frac{df(t)}{dt} + \frac{1}{L}\frac{de(t)}{dt}$$

OBTAIN the transfer function $I_F(s)/E(s)$:

---

**18.7**     Now FIND the equivalent state and output equations:

---

**18.8**     Solving the equations of frame **18.4** would yield the response due to $f(t)$. Solving the equations above would lead to the response due to $e(t)$. If one were to add these two outputs as in the S.F.G. above opposite, one would obtain the response due to $e(t)$ and $f(t)$ acting together—by superposition.

The transfer function is:

$$\frac{I_F(s)}{E(s)} = \frac{\dfrac{1}{L}s}{s^2 + \dfrac{R}{L}s + \dfrac{1}{LC}}$$

(after setting $f(t)$, $\dfrac{df(t)}{dt}$, and the I.C.'s equal to zero)

*Comment:*

Once again we take the T.F. approach to avoid the derivative of the input, which would otherwise appear in the **B**–matrix.

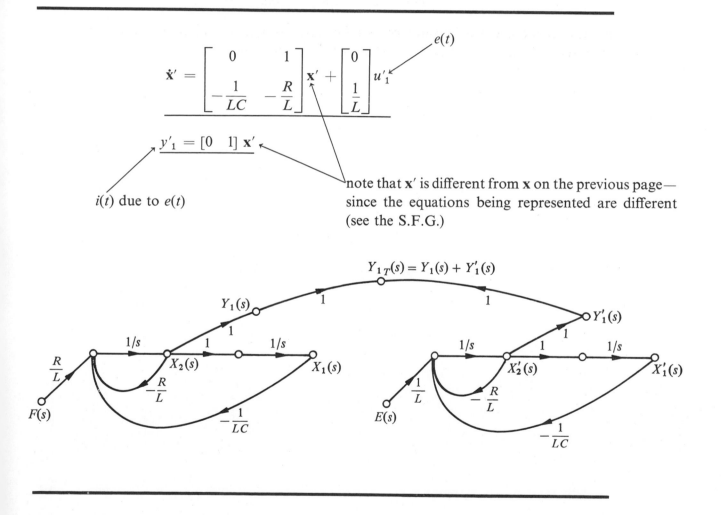

$$\dot{\mathbf{x}}' = \begin{bmatrix} 0 & 1 \\ -\dfrac{1}{LC} & -\dfrac{R}{L} \end{bmatrix} \mathbf{x}' + \begin{bmatrix} 0 \\ \dfrac{1}{L} \end{bmatrix} u'_1$$

$e(t)$

$$y'_1 = [0 \quad 1]\,\mathbf{x}'$$

$i(t)$ due to $e(t)$

note that $\mathbf{x}'$ is different from $\mathbf{x}$ on the previous page— since the equations being represented are different (see the S.F.G.)

$Y_{1T}(s) = Y_1(s) + Y'_1(s)$

207

## AUTOMOBILE TRANSMISSION

**18.9**

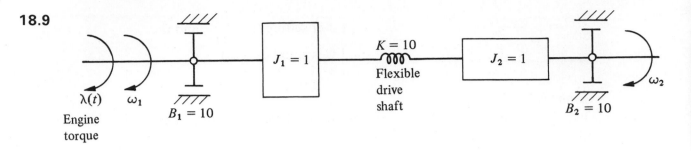

Engine
torque

Here the governing differential equations are:

$$\ddot{\omega}_1 + 10\dot{\omega}_1 + 10\omega_1 - 10\omega_2 = \dot{\lambda}(t)$$

$$-10\omega_1 + \ddot{\omega}_2 + 10\dot{\omega}_2 + 10\omega_2 = 0$$

Faced once more with a derivative of the input, and wishing to solve for $\omega_1$, we first transform (with zero I.C.'s), and FIND $\Omega_{1_r}(s)/\Lambda(s)$, using Cramer's rule:

Transforming with zero I.C.'s:

$$(s^2 + 10s + 10)\,\Omega_1(s) - 10\Omega_2(s) = s\Lambda(s)$$

$$-10\Omega_1(s) + (s^2 + 10s + 10)\,\Omega_2(s) = 0$$

Using Cramer's rule:

$$\Omega_{1_r}(s) = \cfrac{\begin{vmatrix} s\Lambda(s) & -10 \\ 0 & s^2 + 10s + 10 \end{vmatrix}}{\begin{vmatrix} s^2 + 10s + 10 & -10 \\ -10 & s^2 + 10s + 10 \end{vmatrix}}$$

$$\therefore \quad \frac{\Omega_{1_r}(s)}{\Lambda(s)} = \frac{s(s^2 + 10s + 10)}{s^4 + 20s^3 + 120s^2 + 200s} = \underline{\frac{s^2 + 10s + 10}{s^3 + 20s^2 + 120s + 200}}$$

**18.10**   We now have:

$$\frac{\Omega_{1_r}(s)}{\Lambda(s)} = \frac{s^2 + 10s + 10}{s^3 + 20s^2 + 120s + 200}$$

FIND the corresponding state and output equations:

---

**18.11**   Thus if a system's differential equation contains derivatives of the input, one approach is to determine the transfer function relating *one* output to *one* input, and then to find the corresponding state and output equations in the usual way. If there is more than one input, or if we require more than one output, the method must be repeated for each input–output pair.

---

The final review section will take you about an hour.

$$\dot{\mathbf{x}} = \begin{bmatrix} 0 & 1 & 0 \\ 0 & 0 & 1 \\ -200 & -120 & -20 \end{bmatrix} \mathbf{x} + \begin{bmatrix} 0 \\ 0 \\ 1 \end{bmatrix} u_1 \qquad \text{the state equation}$$

$$\underset{\omega_1}{\overset{}{\underline{y_1 = [10 \quad 10 \quad 1] \, \mathbf{x}}}} \qquad \text{the output equation}$$

*Comment:*

If you need more practice you might consider $\omega_2$ as the output. You will find:

$$\frac{\Omega_{2_F}(s)}{\Lambda(s)} = \frac{10}{s^3 + 20s^2 + 120s + 200}$$

Whence:

$$\dot{\mathbf{x}}' = \begin{bmatrix} 0 & 1 & 0 \\ 0 & 0 & 1 \\ -200 & -120 & -20 \end{bmatrix} \mathbf{x}' + \begin{bmatrix} 0 \\ 0 \\ 10 \end{bmatrix} u_1$$

and:

$$y'_1 = [1 \quad 0 \quad 0] \, \mathbf{x}' \quad \text{where } y'_1 \text{ is } \omega_2.$$

Note that in this case the output $\omega_2$ is one of the states $(x'_1)$.

**19.1**   The equation $\dot{\mathbf{x}}(t) = \mathbf{A}\mathbf{x}(t) + \mathbf{B}\mathbf{u}(t)$ has for its time domain solution:

$$\mathbf{x}(t) = \underline{\hspace{5cm}} \text{(see MASK)}$$

and at $t = T$:

$$\mathbf{x}(T) = \underline{\hspace{6cm}}$$

Now **B** is a matrix of constants and *if* $\mathbf{u}(t) = \mathbf{u}(0)$, a matrix of $\underline{\hspace{1.5cm}}$ in the interval $\underline{\hspace{2cm}} \leqslant t < \underline{\hspace{2cm}}$, then $\mathbf{B}\mathbf{u}(0)$ may be taken out of the integral. That is,

$$\mathbf{x}(T) = \underline{\hspace{6cm}}$$

$$= \underline{\hspace{2cm}} \mathbf{x}(0) + \underline{\hspace{2cm}} \mathbf{u}(0)$$

where $\boldsymbol{\varphi}(T) = \underline{\hspace{2cm}}$ and $\boldsymbol{\Delta}(T) = \underline{\hspace{5cm}}$

Next, if we let the initial time be $t_o$, rather than zero:

$$\mathbf{x}(\underline{\hspace{1.5cm}}) = \boldsymbol{\varphi}(T) \underline{\hspace{1.5cm}} + \underline{\hspace{3cm}},$$

and finally, if we let $t_o = kT$:

$$\mathbf{x}(\underline{\hspace{1.5cm}}) = \underline{\hspace{3.5cm}} \qquad kT \leqslant t < \overline{k + 1}T$$

$$\mathbf{x}(t) = \epsilon^{\mathbf{A}t}\mathbf{x}(0) + \epsilon^{\mathbf{A}t}\int_0^t \epsilon^{-\mathbf{A}\tau}\mathbf{B}\mathbf{u}d\tau$$

$$\mathbf{x}(T) = \epsilon^{\mathbf{A}T}\mathbf{x}(0) + \epsilon^{\mathbf{A}T}\int_0^T \epsilon^{-\mathbf{A}\tau}\mathbf{B}\mathbf{u}d\tau$$

$\mathbf{u}(t) = \mathbf{u}(0)$, a matrix of constants in the interval $0 \leqslant t < T$

$$\mathbf{x}(T) = \epsilon^{\mathbf{A}T}\mathbf{x}(0) + \left[ \epsilon^{\mathbf{A}T}\int_0^T \epsilon^{-\mathbf{A}\tau}d\tau\mathbf{B} \right]\mathbf{u}(0)$$

$$= \boldsymbol{\varphi}(T)\mathbf{x}(0) + \boldsymbol{\Delta}(T)\mathbf{u}(0)$$

where $\boldsymbol{\varphi}(T) = \epsilon^{\mathbf{A}T}$ and $\boldsymbol{\Delta}(T) = \epsilon^{\mathbf{A}T}\int_0^T \epsilon^{-\mathbf{A}\tau}d\tau\mathbf{B}$

$$\mathbf{x}(t_0 + T) = \boldsymbol{\varphi}(T)\mathbf{x}(t_0) + \boldsymbol{\Delta}(T)\mathbf{u}(t_0)$$

$$\mathbf{x}(\overline{k+1}T) = \boldsymbol{\varphi}(T)\mathbf{x}(kT) + \boldsymbol{\Delta}(T)\mathbf{u}(kT) \qquad kT \leqslant t < \overline{k+1}T$$

where (Notice!) $\mathbf{u}(t) = \mathbf{u}(kT)$ for $kT \leqslant t < \overline{k+1}T$

**19.2**   Before the computer can implement the calculation based on

$$\mathbf{x}(\overline{k+1}T) = \boldsymbol{\varphi}(T)\mathbf{x}(kT) + \boldsymbol{\Delta}(T)\mathbf{u}(kT),$$

the quantities $\boldsymbol{\varphi}(T)$ and $\boldsymbol{\Delta}(T)$ must be computed.  We know that:

$$\boldsymbol{\varphi}(T) = \epsilon^{\mathbf{A}T} = \underline{\hspace{2cm}} + \underline{\hspace{1.5cm}} + \underline{\hspace{1.5cm}} + \cdots$$

and $\boldsymbol{\Delta}(T) = \epsilon^{\mathbf{A}t} \displaystyle\int_0^T \epsilon^{-\mathbf{A}\tau} d\tau \mathbf{B} = \left[ \mathbf{I}T + \mathbf{A}\, \dfrac{T^2}{2!} + \underline{\hspace{1.5cm}} + \cdots \right] \underline{\hspace{1cm}}$

(the series for $\boldsymbol{\Delta}(T)$ was derived in frames **14.8–14.10**)

□

---

**19.3**   Looking at the above series *for* $\boldsymbol{\varphi}(T)$, you can see

that one multiplies the 1st  term by _____ to obtain the 2nd,

the 2nd term by _____ to obtain the 3rd,

the 3rd  term by _____ to obtain the 4th,

and the $L$th term by _____ to obtain the $L + 1$st.

□

---

**19.4**   From the above one can derive a procedure for the computation of $\boldsymbol{\varphi}(T)$. Use scratch paper and the flow chart of frame **14.7** to COMPUTE $\boldsymbol{\varphi}(0.1)$ corresponding to **A** below. You may terminate the calculation when the remaining terms in the series are all less than 0.01.

Given:

$$\mathbf{A} = \begin{bmatrix} -1 & 1 \\ 0 & -2 \end{bmatrix} \qquad \boldsymbol{\varphi}(0.1) = \begin{bmatrix} & \\ & \end{bmatrix}$$

□

---

$$\varphi(T) = \mathbf{I} + \mathbf{A}T + \mathbf{A}^2 \frac{T^2}{2!} + \cdots$$

$$\Delta(T) = \left[ \mathbf{I}T + \mathbf{A}\frac{T^2}{2!} + \mathbf{A}^2\frac{T^3}{3!} + \cdots \right] \mathbf{B}$$

---

1st term by $\mathbf{A}T$

2nd term by $\mathbf{A}\dfrac{T}{2}$

3rd term by $\mathbf{A}\dfrac{T}{3}$

$L$th term by $\mathbf{A}\dfrac{T}{L}$

---

$$\varphi_1(T) = \begin{bmatrix} 1 & 0 \\ 0 & 1 \end{bmatrix} \quad \text{and} \quad \varphi'_1(T) = \begin{bmatrix} 1 & 0 \\ 0 & 1 \end{bmatrix} \qquad (T = 0.1)$$

$$\varphi_2(T) = \begin{bmatrix} 1 & 0 \\ 0 & 1 \end{bmatrix} + \begin{bmatrix} -0.1 & 0.1 \\ 0 & -0.2 \end{bmatrix} = \begin{bmatrix} 0.9 & 0.1 \\ 0 & 0.8 \end{bmatrix}$$

$$\varphi_3(T) = \begin{bmatrix} 0.9 & 0.1 \\ 0 & 0.8 \end{bmatrix} + \begin{bmatrix} 0.005 & -0.015 \\ 0 & 0.020 \end{bmatrix} = \begin{bmatrix} 0.905 & 0.085 \\ 0 & 0.820 \end{bmatrix}$$

---

**19.5** Similarly, as in frames **14.10** and **14.11**, one can obtain a flow chart for the calculation of $\Delta(T)$. If you feel you want more practice, COMPUTE $\Delta(0.1)$ using the flow chart in frame **14.11**.

Given:

$$\mathbf{A} = \begin{bmatrix} -1 & 1 \\ 0 & -2 \end{bmatrix} \quad \text{and} \quad \mathbf{B} = \begin{bmatrix} 0 \\ 1 \end{bmatrix}, \quad \Delta(0.1) = \begin{bmatrix} \phantom{xxxxx} \end{bmatrix}$$

---

**19.6** Now, use the result $\mathbf{x}(\overline{k+1}T) = \boldsymbol{\varphi}(T)\mathbf{x}(kT) + \Delta(T)\mathbf{u}(kT)$ to COMPUTE $\mathbf{x}(0.1)$ and $\mathbf{x}(0.2)$.

Given: $\boldsymbol{\varphi}(0.1) = \begin{bmatrix} 0.905 & 0.085 \\ 0 & 0.820 \end{bmatrix} \qquad \mathbf{x}(0) = \begin{bmatrix} 0 \\ -2 \end{bmatrix}$

$\Delta(0.1) = \begin{bmatrix} 0.005 \\ 0.090 \end{bmatrix}$

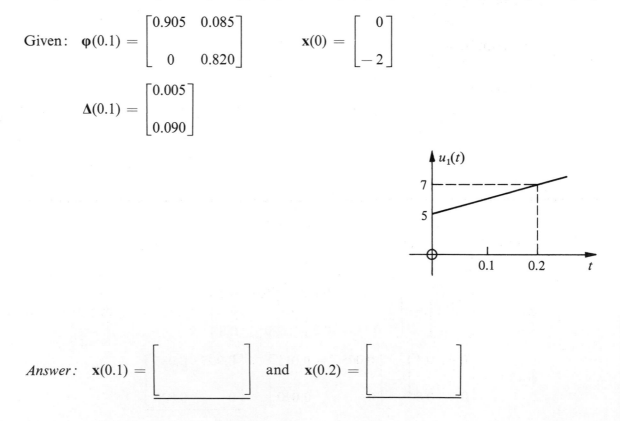

*Answer:* $\mathbf{x}(0.1) = \begin{bmatrix} \phantom{xxxx} \end{bmatrix}$ and $\mathbf{x}(0.2) = \begin{bmatrix} \phantom{xxxx} \end{bmatrix}$

$$\Delta(0.1) \doteq \begin{bmatrix} 0.005 \\ 0.090 \end{bmatrix}$$

$$\mathbf{x}(0.1) = \begin{bmatrix} 0.905 & 0.085 \\ 0 & 0.820 \end{bmatrix} \begin{bmatrix} 0 \\ -2 \end{bmatrix} + \begin{bmatrix} 0.005 \\ 0.090 \end{bmatrix} 5 \overset{u_1(0)}{\longleftarrow}$$

$$= \begin{bmatrix} -0.170 \\ -1.640 \end{bmatrix} + \begin{bmatrix} 0.025 \\ 0.450 \end{bmatrix} = \begin{bmatrix} -0.145 \\ -1.190 \end{bmatrix}$$

$$\mathbf{x}(0.2) = \begin{bmatrix} 0.905 & 0.085 \\ 0 & 0.820 \end{bmatrix} \overset{\mathbf{x}(0.1)}{\begin{bmatrix} -0.145 \\ -1.190 \end{bmatrix}} + \begin{bmatrix} 0.005 \\ 0.090 \end{bmatrix} 6 \overset{u_1(0.1)}{\longleftarrow}$$

$$= \begin{bmatrix} -0.232 \\ -0.976 \end{bmatrix} + \begin{bmatrix} 0.030 \\ 0.540 \end{bmatrix} = \begin{bmatrix} -0.202 \\ -0.436 \end{bmatrix}$$

*Comment:*
You might like to review the computer flow chart implementing this procedure in frame
**13.24**.

**19.7**

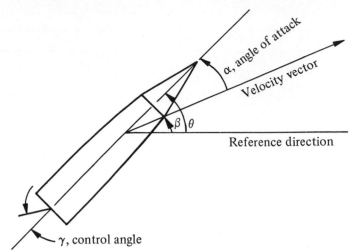

α, angle of attack

Velocity vector

β θ

Reference direction

γ, control angle

The equations governing the steering of a ship on the ocean, or of a missile through the atmosphere, can often be simplified into the following form, where $\gamma(t)$ is the input:

$$\dot{\alpha} - \dot{\theta} + k_1\alpha = k_2\gamma(t) \quad \ldots \quad (1)$$

$$\ddot{\theta} + k_3\dot{\theta} + k_4\alpha = k_5\gamma(t) \quad \ldots \quad (2)$$

If you were to put these equations into state variable form, you would choose ____, ____, and $\alpha$ as the state variables.

☐

---

**19.8**  In state form:

$$\dot{\mathbf{x}} = \left[ \quad\quad\quad\quad \right] \mathbf{x} + \left[ \quad \right] \mathbf{u}$$

☐

---

**19.9**  If we want as outputs the quantities:

$$y_1 = \theta, \quad y_2 = \alpha, \quad y_3 = \beta, \quad \text{and} \quad y_4 = \dot{\beta} = \dot{\theta} - \dot{\alpha}$$

then:

$$\mathbf{y} = \left[ \quad\quad\quad\quad \right] \mathbf{x} + \left[ \quad\quad \right] \mathbf{u}$$

*Hint:* To find $y_4$, rearrange equation (1) in frame **19.7**.

☐

$$\begin{array}{c}\text{or}\quad \omega\\[-4pt]\nearrow\end{array}$$

$\theta$, $\dot{\theta}$ and $\alpha$ would be obvious choices for the states. In the next frame we will use $x_1 = \theta$, $x_2 = \dot{\theta}$, and $x_3 = \alpha$.

---

$$\mathbf{A} = \begin{bmatrix} 0 & 1 & 0 \\ 0 & -k_3 & -k_4 \\ 0 & 1 & -k_1 \end{bmatrix} \quad \text{and} \quad \mathbf{B} = \begin{bmatrix} 0 \\ k_5 \\ k_2 \end{bmatrix}$$

---

$y_1 = \theta = x_1$

$y_2 = \alpha = x_3$

$y_3 = \beta = \theta - \alpha = x_1 - x_3$

$y_4 = \dot{\beta} = \dot{\theta} - \dot{\alpha} = k_1\alpha - k_2\gamma(t) = k_1 x_3 - k_2 u_1$

$$\therefore \quad \mathbf{C} = \begin{bmatrix} 1 & 0 & 0 \\ 0 & 0 & 1 \\ 1 & 0 & -1 \\ 0 & 0 & k_1 \end{bmatrix} \quad \text{and} \quad \mathbf{D} = \begin{bmatrix} 0 \\ 0 \\ 0 \\ -k_2 \end{bmatrix}$$

---

**19.10** Suppose we have solved the state equations and hence know that at time $t = 5$,

$$\mathbf{x}(5) = \begin{bmatrix} 1 \\ -2 \\ 3 \end{bmatrix} \text{ and } \mathbf{u}(5) = 4.$$

Given also the result of the last frame,

$$\mathbf{y} = \begin{bmatrix} 1 & 0 & 0 \\ 0 & 0 & 1 \\ 1 & 0 & -1 \\ 0 & 0 & k_1 \end{bmatrix} \mathbf{x} + \begin{bmatrix} 0 \\ 0 \\ 0 \\ -k_2 \end{bmatrix} \mathbf{u}$$

FIND $\mathbf{y}$ (5):

**19.11** The following S.F.G. represents the state equation of frame **19.8**. ADD and LABEL the branches corresponding to the output equation given in the previous frame:

$$\mathbf{y}(5) = \begin{bmatrix} 1 & 0 & 0 \\ 0 & 0 & 1 \\ 1 & 0 & -1 \\ 0 & 0 & k_1 \end{bmatrix} \begin{bmatrix} 1 \\ -2 \\ 3 \end{bmatrix} + \begin{bmatrix} 0 \\ 0 \\ 0 \\ -k_2 \end{bmatrix} 4$$

$$= \begin{bmatrix} 1 \\ 3 \\ -2 \\ 3k_1 - 4k_2 \end{bmatrix}$$

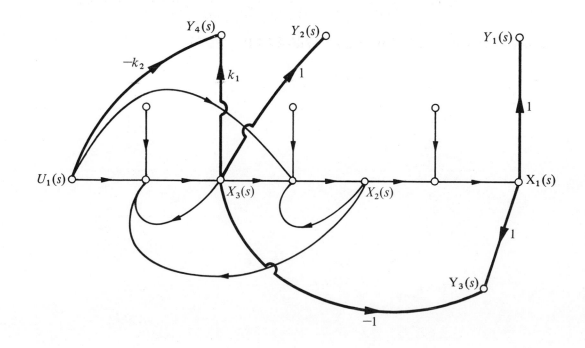

**19.12**    Let's change the subject.

Given a transfer function $H(s) = \dfrac{K_F(s)}{R(s)} = \dfrac{50}{(s+1)(s^2+2s+3)}$,

FIND the corresponding state representation:

*Hint:* What is the differential equation corresponding to this T.F.?

---

**19.13**    Now, OBTAIN the state representation corresponding to:

$$G(s) = \frac{M_F(s)}{N(s)} = \frac{50\,(s+2)}{(s+1)\,(s^2+2s+3)} = \underline{\hspace{3cm}} \cdot (\qquad)$$

(if you need help, REVIEW frames **17.7–17.11**)

---

$$H(s) = \frac{K_F(s)}{R(s)} = \frac{50}{s^3 + 3s^2 + 5s + 3} \quad \text{corresponds to:}$$

$$\dddot{k} + 3\ddot{k} + 5\dot{k} + 3k = 50r(t)$$

$$\dot{\mathbf{x}} = \begin{bmatrix} 0 & 1 & 0 \\ 0 & 0 & 1 \\ -3 & -5 & -3 \end{bmatrix} \mathbf{x} + \begin{bmatrix} 0 \\ 0 \\ 50 \end{bmatrix} u_1$$

where:

$$\mathbf{x} = \begin{bmatrix} k \\ \dot{k} \\ \ddot{k} \end{bmatrix} \quad \text{and} \quad u_1 = r(t)$$

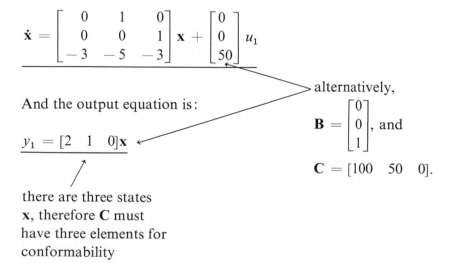

$$\frac{M_F(s)}{N(s)} = \frac{W_F(s)}{N(s)} \cdot \frac{M_F(s)}{W_F(s)} = \frac{50}{s^3 + 3s^2 + 5s + 3} \cdot (s + 2)$$

As above:

$$\dot{\mathbf{x}} = \begin{bmatrix} 0 & 1 & 0 \\ 0 & 0 & 1 \\ -3 & -5 & -3 \end{bmatrix} \mathbf{x} + \begin{bmatrix} 0 \\ 0 \\ 50 \end{bmatrix} u_1$$

And the output equation is:

$$y_1 = [2 \quad 1 \quad 0]\mathbf{x}$$

there are three states
$\mathbf{x}$, therefore $\mathbf{C}$ must
have three elements for
conformability

alternatively,

$$\mathbf{B} = \begin{bmatrix} 0 \\ 0 \\ 1 \end{bmatrix}, \text{ and}$$

$$\mathbf{C} = [100 \quad 50 \quad 0].$$

**19.14**   Given the differential equation:

$\ddot{\theta} + k_1\ddot{\theta} + k_2\dot{\theta} = k_3\dot{\lambda}(t) + k_4\lambda(t)$ where $\lambda(t)$ is the input, OBTAIN the state variable representation:

Apart from "computer time," the next short section—the last—should not take more than 20–30 minutes.

Setting the I.C.'s to zero:

$$\{s^3 + k_1 s^2 + k_2 s\} \, \Theta_F(s) = \{k_3 s + k_4\} \, \Lambda(s)$$

Letting:

$$\frac{\Theta_F(s)}{\Lambda(s)} = \frac{W_F(s)}{\Lambda(s)} \cdot \frac{\Theta_F(s)}{W_F(s)} = \frac{1}{s^3 + k_1 s^2 + k_2 s} \cdot (k_3 s + k_4)$$

Then:

$$\dot{\mathbf{x}} = \begin{bmatrix} 0 & 1 & 0 \\ 0 & 0 & 1 \\ 0 & -k_2 & -k_1 \end{bmatrix} \mathbf{x} + \begin{bmatrix} 0 \\ 0 \\ 1 \end{bmatrix} u_1$$

and:

alternatively,

$$y_1 = [k_4 \quad k_3 \quad 0] \, \mathbf{x}$$

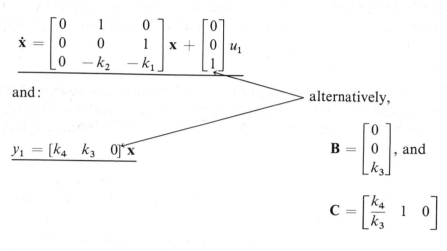

$$\mathbf{B} = \begin{bmatrix} 0 \\ 0 \\ k_3 \end{bmatrix}, \text{ and}$$

$$\mathbf{C} = \begin{bmatrix} \dfrac{k_4}{k_3} & 1 & 0 \end{bmatrix}$$

Earlier, we used the computer to calculate the states, $\mathbf{x}(t)$, of the state equation $\dot{\mathbf{x}} = \mathbf{Ax} + \mathbf{Bu}$. Now we will extend the use of the computer program to the evaluation of the outputs, $y = \mathbf{Cx} + \mathbf{Du}$, as well.

SUBROUTINE FIDEL, as listed in Appendix 3, will perform this additional task if it is provided with the necessary data—NY (the number of outputs) and the elements of $\mathbf{C}$ and $\mathbf{D}$. The data format is described in the comment cards at the start of the subroutine:

```
      SUBROUTINE FIDEL
      DIMENSION A(8,8),B(8,8),X0(8),XK(8),PHI(8,8),PHITRM(8,8),
     1DEL(8,8),DELTRM(8,8),UK(8),AT(8,8),XKPLS1(8),P(8),Q(8),YK(8),
     2C(8,8),D(8,8)
C
C
C          READ N (= SYSTEM ORDER), M (= NUMBER OF INPUTS), AND
C                  NY (= NUMBER OF ELEMENTS IN THE OUTPUT MATRIX, Y)
C                  FROM THE FIRST THREE COLUMNS OF THE FIRST DATA CARD.
C                  (THE THIRD COLUMN SHOULD BE BLANK IF THE OUTPUT
C                  MATRIX, Y, IS NOT TO BE CALCULATED.)
C          READ A-MATRIX FROM NEXT DATA CARD(S) -- 15 COLUMNS FOR EACH
C                  ELEMENT, INCLUDING DECIMAL POINT.
C          READ B-MATRIX FROM NEXT DATA CARD(S) -- AS FOR A-MATRIX.
C          READ THE C-MATRIX -- IF NY IS NOT ZERO (OR BLANK).
C          READ THE D-MATRIX -- IF NY IS NOT ZERO (OR BLANK).
C          READ X0-MATRIX (INITIAL CONDITIONS) FROM NEXT CARD(S).
C          READ T (= TIME INCREMENT), KMAX (= NUMBER OF TIME INCREMENTS),
C                  AND NUMBT (= NUMBER OF TERMS IN SERIES) FROM NEXT
C                  CARD. 15 COLUMNS, WITH DECIMAL POINT, FOR T
C                  NEXT 4 COLUMNS FOR KMAX (E.G. 0050)
C                  NEXT 2 COLUMNS FOR NUMBT (E.G. 05)
```

**WARNING**—SEE NOTE OPPOSITE

## NOTE ON THE EVALUATION OF $\varphi(T)$ AND $\Delta(T)$:

Although the series for $\varphi(T)$ and $\Delta(T)$ will always converge, in theory, the calculation of $A^2T^2$, $A^3T^3$, ... may result in the generation of numbers larger than can be accepted by your computer. This will happen if the elements of $AT$ are much greater than one. The note at the end of Appendix 1 describes how one may recognize and avoid this difficulty.

**20.1**　As a simple example, reviewing the computation of **x** and introducing the computation of **y**, let's consider the missile in frame **19.7**. If we put $k_1 = 2$, $k_2 = -10$, $k_3 = 4$, $k_4 = 17$, and $k_5 = 10$, then:

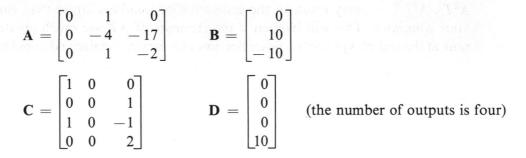

$$\mathbf{A} = \begin{bmatrix} 0 & 1 & 0 \\ 0 & -4 & -17 \\ 0 & 1 & -2 \end{bmatrix} \qquad \mathbf{B} = \begin{bmatrix} 0 \\ 10 \\ -10 \end{bmatrix}$$

$$\mathbf{C} = \begin{bmatrix} 1 & 0 & 0 \\ 0 & 0 & 1 \\ 1 & 0 & -1 \\ 0 & 0 & 2 \end{bmatrix} \qquad \mathbf{D} = \begin{bmatrix} 0 \\ 0 \\ 0 \\ 10 \end{bmatrix} \qquad \text{(the number of outputs is four)}$$

Use the computer to EVALUATE $\mathbf{x}(t)$ and $\mathbf{y}(t)$ up to $t = 1.5$ seconds using a time increment of $T = 0.1$ second. Also given are:

$$\mathbf{u}(t) = u_1 = 0.1 \quad \text{and} \quad \mathbf{x}(0) = \begin{bmatrix} 1 \\ 0 \\ 0.2 \end{bmatrix}$$

We must put KMAX = 15 in order to calculate forward from $t = 0$ to $t = 1.5$ in 15 steps of $T = 0.1$. The choice of NUMBT, the number of terms in the $\varphi$ and $\Delta$ series, should ensure that $\varphi(T)$ and $\Delta(T)$ converge to an accurate value before the series are terminated. We chose NUMBT = 10 which was *very* safe. A value of 5 would probably be adequate.

Our calculation (which may not agree exactly with yours, unless you also used NUMBT = 10) yielded:

$$\varphi(0.1) = \begin{bmatrix} 1.000 & 0.080 & -0.069 \\ 0.000 & 0.610 & -1.226 \\ 0.000 & 0.072 & 0.754 \end{bmatrix} \text{ and } \Delta(0.1) = \begin{bmatrix} 0.068 \\ 1.491 \\ -0.843 \end{bmatrix}$$

$$\mathbf{x}(0) = \begin{bmatrix} 1.0 \\ 0.0 \\ 0.2 \end{bmatrix} \qquad \mathbf{y}(0) = \begin{bmatrix} 1.0 \\ 0.2 \\ 0.8 \\ 1.4 \end{bmatrix}$$

$$\mathbf{x}(1.5) = \begin{bmatrix} 1.864 \\ 0.756 \\ -0.116 \end{bmatrix} \qquad \mathbf{y}(1.5) = \begin{bmatrix} 1.864 \\ -0.116 \\ 1.981 \\ 0.768 \end{bmatrix}$$

**20.2** Given that a current in a circuit is related to a source voltage by the transfer function:

$$\frac{I_F(s)}{V(s)} = \frac{10s(s + 1)}{s^3 + 4s^2 + 6s + 4}$$

use the computer to FIND the *forced* response (I.C.'s equal to zero) when $v(t) = 2 \sin 0.1t$. It is sufficient if you continue your solution to $t = 10$ seconds.

$$\frac{I_F(s)}{V(s)} = \frac{W_F(s)}{V(s)} \cdot \frac{I_F(s)}{W_F(s)}$$

$$= \frac{10}{s^3 + 4s^2 + 6s + 4} \cdot (s^2 + s)$$

Hence,

$$\mathbf{A} = \begin{bmatrix} 0 & 1 & 0 \\ 0 & 0 & 1 \\ -4 & -6 & -4 \end{bmatrix} \quad \mathbf{B} = \begin{bmatrix} 0 \\ 0 \\ 10 \end{bmatrix} \quad \mathbf{C} = \begin{bmatrix} 0 & 1 & 1 \end{bmatrix} \text{ and } \mathbf{D} = \mathbf{0}.$$

A reasonable choice for $T$ is 0.5 second, for KMAX, 20, and for NUMBT, 10.

(You should consider for a moment why we chose these values!)

In SUBROUTINE INPUT you should have:
$UK(1) = 2.* \text{SIN} (0.1 * \text{TIME})$

Our results:

$$\boldsymbol{\varphi}(0.5) = \begin{bmatrix} 0.949 & 0.417 & 0.063 \\ -0.253 & 0.570 & 0.164 \\ -0.658 & -1.240 & -0.087 \end{bmatrix} \text{ and } \boldsymbol{\Delta}(0.5) = \begin{bmatrix} 0.126 \\ 0.632 \\ 1.644 \end{bmatrix}$$

$$\mathbf{x}(10) = \begin{bmatrix} 3.67 \\ 0.34 \\ -0.06 \end{bmatrix} \text{ and } \mathbf{y}(10) = y_1(10) = 0.28$$

(at $t = 0$, $\mathbf{x}(0) = \mathbf{0}$ and $y(0) = 0$)

**20.3**  (Optional extra problem)

Repeat the previous problem, given the (different) T.F.:

$$\frac{I_F(s)}{V(s)} = \frac{10s(s + 2)}{s^3 + 4s^2 + 6s + 4}$$

**Note:** You can solve this in two ways:

1. Straightforwardly, and

2. Realizing that $(s + 2)$ cancels in the T.F.

You might like to try both—to see if your answers check.

1.
$$
A = \begin{bmatrix} 0 & 1 & 0 \\ 0 & 0 & 1 \\ -4 & -6 & -4 \end{bmatrix}, \quad B = \begin{bmatrix} 0 \\ 0 \\ 10 \end{bmatrix}, \quad C = [0 \quad 2 \quad 1], \text{ and } D = 0
$$

2.

$$
\frac{I_F(s)}{V(s)} = \frac{10s(s+2)}{(s^2 + 2s + 2)(s+2)} = \frac{10s}{s^2 + 2s + 2}
$$

$$
\therefore \quad A = \begin{bmatrix} 0 & 1 \\ -2 & -2 \end{bmatrix}, \quad B = \begin{bmatrix} 0 \\ 10 \end{bmatrix}, \quad C = [0 \quad 1], \text{ and } D = 0
$$

*Solution 1:*

$$
\varphi(0.5) = \begin{bmatrix} 0.949 & 0.417 & 0.063 \\ -0.253 & 0.570 & 0.164 \\ -0.658 & -1.240 & -0.087 \end{bmatrix} \text{ and } \Delta(0.5) = \begin{bmatrix} 0.126 \\ 0.632 \\ 1.644 \end{bmatrix}
$$

(these are the same as in the previous problem, since A and B are the same)

$$
x(10) = \begin{bmatrix} 3.67 \\ 0.34 \\ -0.06 \end{bmatrix} \text{ and } y(10) = 0.62
$$

*Solution 2:*

$$
\varphi(0.5) = \begin{bmatrix} 0.823 & 0.291 \\ -0.582 & 0.241 \end{bmatrix} \text{ and } \Delta(0.5) = \begin{bmatrix} 0.885 \\ 2.908 \end{bmatrix}
$$

$$
x(10) = \begin{bmatrix} 7.67 \\ 0.62 \end{bmatrix} \text{ and } y(10) = 0.62
$$

(the output $y$, is identical in the two methods of solution; *but*, note that the states $x$ are quite different)

YOU WILL NO LONGER NEED THE MASK AS AN ANSWER SHIELD. FOR REFERENCE, THE DATA ON THE MASK ARE REPEATED INSIDE THE BACK COVER.

## SOME FINAL COMMENTS

You should now be skilled in the basic techniques of state variable analysis, which you will find are becoming widely used for the study of linear (and nonlinear) systems.

In particular, you know how:

1. to put a system's differential equations into state variable form, even when input derivatives appear in the equations;

2. to find a system's output equation, when the output variables are given;

3. to obtain a system's state (and output) equations, when only a transfer function is specified;

4. to solve the state equation:
   a. using the S.F.G. method,
   b. using the matrix method, and
   c. using the time domain method; and

5. to compute the solution in the time domain, using a digital computer.

You have *not* learned how to write a system's equations directly in state variable form. Your instructor will discuss this topic with you, or you may refer to Appendix 3, and references 7 and 8.

If now or later you wish to review the subject matter, the TABLE OF CONTENTS will be a useful guide. Sections 12, 15, and 19 will be especially helpful in this regard.

*If you are to make the best use of this program, you should work the following exam. Doing so will provide you with additional review and practice, and give you a measure of your mastery over the material.*

Before you start, however, take a break of a day or so, and then REVIEW the material, just as you would for any other exam—see the last paragraph, opposite.

Then choose a time when you have *two hours* available, and work the exam in this alloted time. Do *not* refer to anything except the data inside the back cover (or on the MASK) unless asked to do otherwise in a specific problem.

To help you allocate your time, estimated working times have been noted next to each question. These add up to 120 minutes. Each question is worth as many points as the given working time. The highest score is thus 120.

**1.** Put the following equation in state variable form:

(4 min)

$$\frac{d^3v}{dt^3} + k_3 \frac{d^2v}{dt^2} + k_2 \frac{dv}{dt} + k_1 v = Kf(t)$$

---

**2.** Given:

(8 min)

$$3\frac{d^2p}{dt^2} + 2\frac{dp}{dt} + p - 2q = 5f(t) - 7g(t)$$

$$2\frac{d^2q}{dt^2} - 3\frac{dq}{dt} + 5p = 3g(t)$$

FIND **A** and **B**:

**3.**

(10 min)

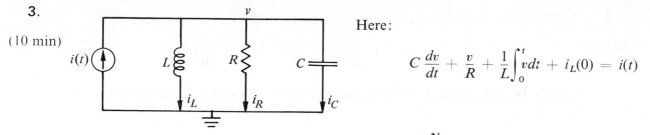

Here:

$$C\frac{dv}{dt} + \frac{v}{R} + \frac{1}{L}\int_0^t v\,dt + i_L(0) = i(t)$$

The desired outputs are $i_R = \frac{v}{R}$ and $i_C = i(t) - \frac{v}{R} - \frac{1}{L}\int_0^t v\,dt - i_L(0)$. Defining the states and inputs as:

$$x_1 = \int_0^t v\,dt, \; x_2 = v, \; u_1 = i(t), \text{ and } u_2 = i_L(0),$$

OBTAIN the state and output equations:

*Answer:*

$$\dot{\mathbf{x}} = \begin{bmatrix} \phantom{xxxx} \end{bmatrix}\mathbf{x} + \begin{bmatrix} \phantom{xxxx} \end{bmatrix}\mathbf{u}; \; \mathbf{y} = \begin{bmatrix} i_R \\ i_C \end{bmatrix} = \begin{bmatrix} \phantom{xxxx} \end{bmatrix}\mathbf{x} + \begin{bmatrix} \phantom{xxxx} \end{bmatrix}\mathbf{u}$$

**4.** Given:

(10 min)

$$C\frac{d^2v}{dt^2} + \frac{1}{R}\frac{dv}{dt} + \frac{1}{L}v = \frac{di(t)}{dt}$$

FIND the state and output equations relating the output $v$ to the input $i(t)$:
(10 min)

---

**5.** OBTAIN a state equation to represent the system described by:

(4 min)

$$\frac{P_F(s)}{Q(s)} = \frac{5}{s(s+1)(s+2)}$$

---

**6.** OBTAIN a state and an output equation to represent the system described by:

(8 min)

$$\frac{\Theta_F(s)}{R(s)} = \frac{K(s^2 - 1)}{s^4 + 3s^2 - 7s - 5}$$

---

**7.** Given:

(7 min) $\dot{x} = Ax + Bu$, SHOW that $X(s) = (sI - A)^{-1}x(0) + (sI - A)^{-1}BU(s)$.

**8.**

(12 min)

Given:

$$\dot{\mathbf{x}} = \begin{bmatrix} -1 & 0 \\ 0 & -2 \end{bmatrix} \mathbf{x} + \begin{bmatrix} 1 \\ 1 \end{bmatrix} \mathbf{u}, \quad \mathbf{x}(0) = \begin{bmatrix} -2 \\ 3 \end{bmatrix}, \quad \text{and} \quad \mathbf{u} = u_1 = 5,$$

FIND $\mathbf{x}(t)$, *using the result of the previous problem:*

---

**9.** FIND $\mathbf{\Phi}(s)$, and hence $\boldsymbol{\varphi}(t)$, for the system of the previous problem:

(3 min)

---

**10.** Given:

(15 min)

$$\dot{\mathbf{x}} = \begin{bmatrix} -0.2 & 1.44 \\ -1 & -2.8 \end{bmatrix} \mathbf{x} + \begin{bmatrix} 0 \\ 1 \end{bmatrix} \mathbf{u}, \text{ DRAW the corresponding S.F.G.:}$$

Then, FIND $x_1(t)$, given $\mathbf{u} = u_1 = 2$, and $\mathbf{x}(0) = \begin{bmatrix} 0 \\ 3 \end{bmatrix}$:

$$\left[ \text{As a check, you should find that the graph determinant } \mathbf{\Delta} = \frac{(s + 1)(s + 2)}{s^2}. \right]$$

**11.** Go back to frames **15.12–15.14** and REVIEW the derivation of the time domain solution:

(15 min)

$$\mathbf{x}(t) = \epsilon^{\mathbf{A}t}\mathbf{x}(0) + \epsilon^{\mathbf{A}t}\int_0^t \epsilon^{-\mathbf{A}\tau}\mathbf{B}\mathbf{u}(\tau)d\tau$$

*Use this result* to FIND $\mathbf{x}(0.1)$, given the state equation:

$$\dot{\mathbf{x}} = \begin{bmatrix} 0 & 1 \\ -1 & 0 \end{bmatrix}\mathbf{x} + \begin{bmatrix} 0 \\ 1 \end{bmatrix}\mathbf{u}, \text{ with } \mathbf{x}(0) = \begin{bmatrix} 1 \\ 2 \end{bmatrix}, \text{ and } \mathbf{u} = u_1 = 10^3 t$$

**12.**    Knowing that the solution of $\dot{\mathbf{x}} = \mathbf{Ax} + \mathbf{Bu}$ is:

(8 min)

$$\mathbf{x}(t) = \epsilon^{\mathbf{A}t}\mathbf{x}(0) + \epsilon^{\mathbf{A}t}\int_0^t \epsilon^{-\mathbf{A}\tau}\mathbf{Bu}(\tau)d\tau$$

SHOW that if $\mathbf{u}(t) = \mathbf{u}(0)$ for $0 \leqslant t < T$, then:

$$\mathbf{x}(T) = \boldsymbol{\varphi}(T)\mathbf{x}(0) + \Delta(T)\mathbf{u}(0),$$

and OBTAIN expressions for $\boldsymbol{\varphi}(T)$ and $\Delta(T)$:

---

**13.**    Now, by shifting the origin first to $t_o$ and then to $kT$, SHOW that if $\mathbf{u}(t) = \mathbf{u}(kT)$ for $kT \leqslant$
$t < \overline{k+1}T$, then:

(6 min)

$$\mathbf{x}(\overline{k+1}T) = \boldsymbol{\varphi}(T)\mathbf{x}(kT) + \Delta(T)\mathbf{u}(kT):$$

---

**14.** Go back to frames **14.4–14.11** and REVIEW the procedure for computing $\varphi(T)$ and $\Delta(T)$.

(10 min) Given:

$$\varphi(1) = \begin{bmatrix} 1 & 1 \\ 0 & 1 \end{bmatrix}, \ \Delta(1) = \begin{bmatrix} 0.5 \\ 1 \end{bmatrix}, \ x(0) = \begin{bmatrix} 0 \\ -1 \end{bmatrix}, \text{ and } u_1(t) \text{ as shown:}$$

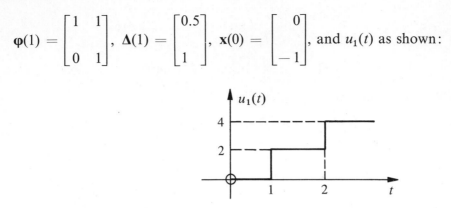

CALCULATE $x(1)$ and $x(2)$ *using the result of the previous problem:*

The test solution follows. You can grade yourself if you wish, making some estimate of partial credit where you have erred.

| # | Value | Score |
|---|---|---|
| 1 | 4 | |
| 2 | 8 | |
| 3 | 10 | |
| 4 | 10 | |
| 5 | 4 | |
| 6 | 8 | |
| 7 | 7 | |
| 8 | 12 | |
| 9 | 3 | |
| 10 | 15 | |
| 11 | 15 | |
| 12 | 8 | |
| 13 | 6 | |
| 14 | 10 | |
| Total | 120 | |

**1.**

$$\dot{\mathbf{x}} = \begin{bmatrix} 0 & 1 & 0 \\ 0 & 0 & 1 \\ -k_1 & -k_2 & -k_3 \end{bmatrix} \mathbf{x} + \begin{bmatrix} 0 \\ 0 \\ K \end{bmatrix} u_1 \quad \text{or } \mathbf{u}$$

[here $x_1 = v$, $x_2 = \dot{v}$, $x_3 = \ddot{v}$, and $u_1 = f(t)$]

**2.** Choosing $x_1 = p$, $x_2 = \dot{p}$, $x_3 = q$, $x_4 = \dot{q}$, $u_1 = f(t)$, and $u_2 = g(t,)$:

$$\dot{\mathbf{x}} = \underbrace{\begin{bmatrix} 0 & 1 & 0 & 0 \\ -\dfrac{1}{3} & -\dfrac{2}{3} & \dfrac{2}{3} & 0 \\ 0 & 0 & 0 & 1 \\ -\dfrac{5}{2} & 0 & 0 & \dfrac{3}{2} \end{bmatrix}}_{\mathbf{A}} \mathbf{x} + \underbrace{\begin{bmatrix} 0 & 0 \\ \dfrac{5}{3} & -\dfrac{7}{3} \\ 0 & 0 \\ 0 & \dfrac{3}{2} \end{bmatrix}}_{\mathbf{B}} \mathbf{u}$$

(if you choose your variables differently, your **A** and **B** matrices will differ accordingly)

**3.**

$$\mathbf{A} = \begin{bmatrix} 0 & 1 \\ -\dfrac{1}{LC} & -\dfrac{1}{RC} \end{bmatrix}, \mathbf{B} = \begin{bmatrix} 0 & 0 \\ \dfrac{1}{C} & -\dfrac{1}{C} \end{bmatrix},$$

$$\mathbf{C} = \begin{bmatrix} 0 & \dfrac{1}{R} \\[2mm] -\dfrac{1}{L} & -\dfrac{1}{R} \end{bmatrix}, \quad \mathbf{D} = \begin{bmatrix} 0 & 0 \\ 1 & -1 \end{bmatrix}$$

**4.** The appropriate T.F. is $\dfrac{V_F(s)}{I(s)} = \dfrac{\dfrac{1}{C}s}{s^2 + \dfrac{1}{RC}s + \dfrac{1}{LC}}$

$$\therefore \; \dot{\mathbf{x}} = \begin{bmatrix} 0 & 1 \\[2mm] -\dfrac{1}{LC} & -\dfrac{1}{RC} \end{bmatrix} \mathbf{x} + \begin{bmatrix} 0 \\[2mm] \dfrac{1}{C} \end{bmatrix} u_1 \qquad \text{represents} \quad \dfrac{\dfrac{1}{C}}{s^2 + \dfrac{1}{RC}s + \dfrac{1}{LC}}$$

and $y_1 = [0 \quad 1] \, \mathbf{x}$     represents $s$

**5.**
$$\dot{\mathbf{x}} = \begin{bmatrix} 0 & 1 & 0 \\ 0 & 0 & 1 \\ 0 & -2 & -3 \end{bmatrix} \mathbf{x} + \begin{bmatrix} 0 \\ 0 \\ 5 \end{bmatrix} \mathbf{u} \quad \longleftarrow \text{or } u_1$$

**6.**
$$\dot{\mathbf{x}} = \begin{bmatrix} 0 & 1 & 0 & 0 \\ 0 & 0 & 1 & 0 \\ 0 & 0 & 0 & 1 \\ 5 & 7 & -3 & 0 \end{bmatrix} \mathbf{x} + \begin{bmatrix} 0 \\ 0 \\ 0 \\ K \end{bmatrix} \mathbf{u}$$

$y_1 = [-1 \quad 0 \quad 1 \quad 0] \, \mathbf{x}$

**7.** See frames **7.8** and **7.9**.

**8.**
$$(s\mathbf{I} - \mathbf{A})^{-1} = \begin{bmatrix} \dfrac{1}{s+1} & 0 \\[3mm] 0 & \dfrac{1}{s+2} \end{bmatrix}$$

$$\mathbf{X}(s) = \begin{bmatrix} \dfrac{-2}{s+1} \\[4mm] \dfrac{3}{s+2} \end{bmatrix} + \begin{bmatrix} \dfrac{5}{s(s+1)} \\[4mm] \dfrac{5}{s(s+2)} \end{bmatrix}$$

$$\mathbf{x}(t) = \begin{bmatrix} -2\,\epsilon^{-t} \\[4mm] 3\,\epsilon^{-2t} \end{bmatrix} + \begin{bmatrix} 5(1 - \epsilon^{-t}) \\[4mm] \dfrac{5}{2}(1 - \epsilon^{-2t}) \end{bmatrix}$$

**9.**    $\boldsymbol{\Phi}(s) = (s\mathbf{I} - \mathbf{A})^{-1}$

$$\therefore\ \boldsymbol{\varphi}(t) = \begin{bmatrix} \epsilon^{-t} & 0 \\[2mm] 0 & \epsilon^{-2t} \end{bmatrix}$$

**10.**

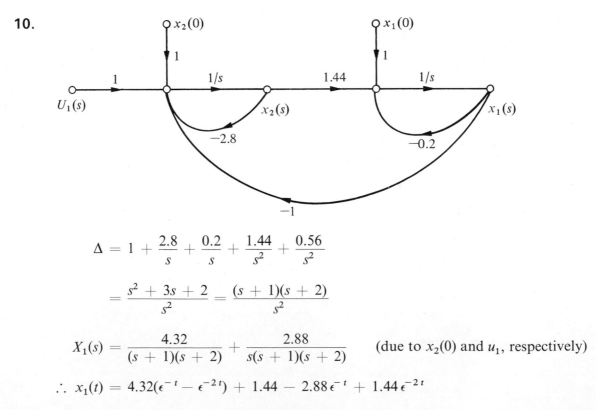

$$\Delta = 1 + \frac{2.8}{s} + \frac{0.2}{s} + \frac{1.44}{s^2} + \frac{0.56}{s^2}$$

$$= \frac{s^2 + 3s + 2}{s^2} = \frac{(s+1)(s+2)}{s^2}$$

$$X_1(s) = \frac{4.32}{(s+1)(s+2)} + \frac{2.88}{s(s+1)(s+2)} \qquad \text{(due to } x_2(0) \text{ and } u_1, \text{ respectively)}$$

$$\therefore\ x_1(t) = 4.32(\epsilon^{-t} - \epsilon^{-2t}) + 1.44 - 2.88\,\epsilon^{-t} + 1.44\,\epsilon^{-2t}$$

**11.**

$$\epsilon^{A(0.1)} = \begin{bmatrix} 1 & 0 \\ 0 & 1 \end{bmatrix} + \begin{bmatrix} 0 & 1 \\ -1 & 0 \end{bmatrix}(0.1) + \begin{bmatrix} -1 & 0 \\ 0 & -1 \end{bmatrix}\frac{(0.1)}{2} + \cdots$$

$$\doteq \begin{bmatrix} 1 & 0.1 \\ -0.1 & 1 \end{bmatrix}$$

$$\therefore \; \mathbf{x}_{\text{I.C.}}(0.1) \doteq \begin{bmatrix} 1 & 0.1 \\ -0.1 & 1 \end{bmatrix} \begin{bmatrix} 1 \\ 2 \end{bmatrix} \doteq \begin{bmatrix} 1.2 \\ 1.9 \end{bmatrix}$$

$$\mathbf{x}_F(0.1) \doteq \begin{bmatrix} 1 & 0.1 \\ -0.1 & 1 \end{bmatrix} \int_0^{0.1} \begin{bmatrix} 1 & -\tau \\ \tau & 1 \end{bmatrix} \begin{bmatrix} 0 \\ 1 \end{bmatrix} 10^3 \tau \, d\tau = \begin{bmatrix} 0.167 \\ 5.033 \end{bmatrix}$$

$$\mathbf{x}(0.1) \doteq \begin{bmatrix} 1.37 \\ 6.93 \end{bmatrix}$$

**12.** See frame **14.17**.

**13.** See frame **14.17**.

**14.** $\mathbf{x}(1) = \begin{bmatrix} -1 \\ -1 \end{bmatrix}$ and $\mathbf{x}(2) = \begin{bmatrix} -1 \\ 1 \end{bmatrix}$

The following computer program was designed* to parallel the mathematical development in Sections 13 and 14. It was not intended to be computationally efficient or elegant. It has been run on an IBM System 360/67 using FORTRAN IVG, and may require minor modifications for other FORTRANs.

To simplify the mechanics of running the program, SUBROUTINE FIDEL and its supporting subroutines can be placed on your computer system's FORTRAN library file, and you will then require only the short input program, SUBROUTINE INPUT, and the data, punched on cards. These are described on page 149.

## SUBROUTINE FIDEL†

```
      SUBROUTINE FIDEL
      DIMENSION A(8,8),B(8,8),X0(8),XK(8),PHI(8,8),PHITRM(8,8),
     1DEL(8,8),DELTRM(8,8),UK(8),AT(8,8),XKPLS1(8),P(8),Q(8),YK(8),
     2C(8,8),D(8,8)
C
C           READ N (= SYSTEM ORDER), M (= NUMBER OF INPUTS), AND
C                 NY (= NUMBER OF ELEMENTS IN THE OUTPUT MATRIX, Y)
C                 FROM THE FIRST THREE COLUMNS OF THE FIRST DATA CARD.
C                 (THE THIRD COLUMN SHOULD BE BLANK IF THE OUTPUT
C                 MATRIX, Y, IS NOT TO BE CALCULATED.)
C           READ A-MATRIX FROM NEXT DATA CARD(S) -- 15 COLUMNS FOR EACH
C                 ELEMENT, INCLUDING DECIMAL POINT.
C           READ B-MATRIX FROM NEXT DATA CARD(S) -- AS FOR A-MATRIX.
C           READ THE C-MATRIX -- IF NY IS NOT ZERO (OR BLANK).
C           READ THE D-MATRIX -- IF NY IS NOT ZERO (OR BLANK).
C           READ X0-MATRIX (INITIAL CONDITIONS) FROM NEXT CARD(S).
C           READ T (= TIME INCREMENT), KMAX (= NUMBER OF TIME INCREMENTS),
C                 AND NUMBT (= NUMBER OF TERMS IN SERIES) FROM NEXT
C                 CARD. 15 COLUMNS, WITH DECIMAL POINT, FOR T
C                 NEXT 4 COLUMNS FOR KMAX (E.G. 0050)
C                 NEXT 2 COLUMNS FOR NUMBT (E.G. 05)
C
      READ(5,100) N,M,NY
  100 FORMAT(3I1)
      READ (5,101) ((A(I,J),J=1,N),I=1,N)
  101 FORMAT(5F15.5)
      READ (5,101) ((B(I,J),J=1,M),I=1,N)
      IF(NY.EQ.0)GO TO 1
      READ(5,101) ((C(I,J),J=1,N),I=1,NY)
      READ(5,101) ((D(I,J),J=1,M),I=1,NY)
    1 READ(5,101) (X0(I),I=1,N)
      READ(5,102) T,KMAX,NUMBT
  102 FORMAT(F15.5,I4,I2)
```

---

\* Thanks are due to D. G. Williams, Director of the Computer Facility at the Naval Postgraduate School, for this program.

† When first using the program you should ignore all reference to the **Y**, **C**, and **D** matrices, and to NY.

```
C
C
C           PRINT THE INPUT DATA
C
      WRITE(6,110) N,M
  110 FORMAT( '1FIDEL SOLUTION OF STATE EQUATIONS',//,' INPUT DATA --',
     1       //,' SYSTEM ORDER, N = ',I1,'   NUMBER OF INPUTS, M = ',I1)
      IF(NY.EQ.0)GO TO 2
      WRITE(6,122) NY
  122 FORMAT(' NUMBER OF OUTPUTS, NY = ',I1)
    2 WRITE(6,123)
  123 FORMAT(/,' A-MATRIX --')
      CALL PRINTM (A,N,N)
      WRITE(6,111)
  111 FORMAT(/,' B-MATRIX -- ')
      CALL PRINTM (B,N,M)
      IF(NY.EQ.0)GO TO 3
      WRITE(6,124)
  124 FORMAT(/,' C-MATRIX --')
      CALL PRINTM(C,NY,N)
      WRITE(6,125)
  125 FORMAT(/,' D-MATRIX --')
      CALL PRINTM(D,NY,M)
    3 WRITE(6,112)
  112 FORMAT(/, ' I.C. MATRIX, X0 --')
      CALL PRINTV (X0,N)
      WRITE(6,113) T,KMAX,NUMBT
  113 FORMAT(/,' TIME INCREMENT, T =',F8.5,'  NUMBER OF INCREMENTS, KMAX
     1 =' ,I4,/, ' NUMBER OF TERMS IN SERIES, NUMBT =',I2,/,'1')
C
C
C           INITIALIZE
C
      CALL SETUNI(PHI,N)
      CALL SETUNI(PHITRM,N)
      CALL SMULT(T,B,DEL,N,M)
      CALL COPYM(DEL,DELTRM,N,M)
      CALL SMULT(T,A,AT,N,N)
      L = 1
C
C
C           SUM THE SERIES FOR PHI AND DEL TO NUMBT TERMS
C
   10 XL=L
      RPL=1./XL
      RPLP1=1./(XL+1.)
      CALL MMULT(PHITRM,AT,PHITRM,N,N,N)
      CALL SMULT(RPL,PHITRM,PHITRM,N,N)
      CALL MADD(PHI,PHITRM,PHI,N,N)
      CALL MMULT(AT,DELTRM,DELTRM,N,N,M)
      CALL SMULT(RPLP1,DELTRM,DELTRM,N,M)
      CALL MADD(DEL,DELTRM,DEL,N,M)
      L = L + 1
      IF(L-NUMBT)10,11,11
C
C
C           PRINT THE PHI AND DEL MATRICES AND THE LAST TERM IN THE
C                    SERIES -- AS AN INDICATION OF TRUNCATION ERRORS.
C
   11 CONTINUE
      WRITE(6,114)
  114 FORMAT(' PHI-MATRIX --')
      CALL PRINTM (PHI,N,N)
      WRITE(6,115)
  115 FORMAT(/, ' LAST TERM IN THE SERIES FOR PHI --')
      CALL PRINTM (PHITRM,N,N)
      WRITE(6,116)
  116 FORMAT(///, ' DEL-MATRIX --')
      CALL PRINTM(DEL,N,M)
      WRITE(6,117)
  117 FORMAT(/, ' LAST TERM IN THE SERIES FOR DEL --')
      CALL PRINTM (DELTRM,N,M)
```

```
C
C           INITIALIZE LOOP
C
      K=0
      CALL CPYVEC(X0,XK,N)
      WRITE(6,118)
  118 FORMAT('1SYSTEM INPUT AND RESPONSE --')
C
C             START THE LOOP TO PRINT THE X(KT), Y(KT), AND U(KT) MATRICES,
C                  WHERE  Y(KT) = C * X(KT) + D * U(KT),  AND TO
C                  CALCULATE   X(KT + T) = PHI * X(KT) + DEL * U(KT).
   20 FK=K
      TIME=FK*T
C
C        CALL SUBROUTINE INPUT TO GET THE UK'S
C
      CALL INPUT(M,T,K,TIME,XK,UK)
      WRITE(6,119) K,TIME
  119 FORMAT(//,' K =',I3, '    TIME =', F10.5,//,' INPUT MATRIX, U(K) --
     1 ')
      CALL PRINTV (UK,M)
      WRITE(6,120)
  120 FORMAT(/, ' RESPONSE MATRIX, X(K) --')
      CALL PRINTV (XK,N)
      IF(NY.EQ.0)GO TO 4
      CALL MVMULT(C,XK,P,NY,N)
      CALL MVMULT(D,UK,Q,NY,M)
      CALL ADDVEC(P,Q,YK,NY)
      WRITE (6,121)
  121 FORMAT(/, ' OUTPUT MATRIX, Y(K) --')
      CALL PRINTV (YK,NY)
    4 IF(K-KMAX)300,301,301
C
C          CALCULATE X(KT+T) = PHI * XK(T) + DEL * U(KT)
C
  300 CALL MVMULT(PHI,XK,P,N,N)
      CALL MVMULT(DEL,UK,Q,N,M)
      CALL ADDVEC(P,Q,XKPLS1,N)
      CALL CPYVEC(XKPLS1,XK,N)
      K=K+1
      GO TO 20
  301 CONTINUE
      RETURN
C
C      STOP IS IN THE MAIN PROGRAM
C
      END
```

## THE SUPPORTING SUBROUTINES

```
      SUBROUTINE COPYM(A,B,L,M)
      DIMENSION A(8,8),B(8,8)
      DO 1 I=1,L
      DO 1 J=1,M
    1 B(I,J)=A(I,J)
      RETURN
      END


      SUBROUTINE CPYVEC(X,Y,L)
      DIMENSION X(8),Y(8)
      DO 1 I=1,L
    1 Y(I)=X(I)
      RETURN
      END
```

```
      SUBROUTINE SETUNI(A,L)
      DIMENSION A(8,8)
      DO 1 I=1,L
      DO 1 J=1,L
      IF(I.EQ.J)GO TO 2
      A(I,J)=0.
      GO TO 1
    2 A(I,I)=1.
    1 CONTINUE
      RETURN
      END


      SUBROUTINE MMULT(A,B,C,L,M,N)
      DIMENSION A(8,8),B(8,8),C(8,8),D(8,8)
      DO 1 I=1,L
      DO 1 K=1,N
      SUM=0.
      DO 2 J=1,M
    2 SUM=SUM+A(I,J)*B(J,K)
    1 D(I,K) = SUM
      CALL COPYM(D,C,L,N)
      RETURN
      END


      SUBROUTINE SMULT(SCALAR,A,B,L,M)
      DIMENSION A(8,8),B(8,8)
      DO 1 I=1,L
      DO 1 J=1,M
    1 B(I,J)=SCALAR*A(I,J)
      RETURN
      END


      SUBROUTINE MVMULT(A,X,Y,L,M)
      DIMENSION A(8,8),X(8),Y(8)
      DO 2 I=1,L
      SUM=0.
      DO 1 J=1,M
    1 SUM=SUM+A(I,J)*X(J)
    2 Y(I)=SUM
      RETURN
      END


      SUBROUTINE MADD(A,B,C,L,M)
      DIMENSION A(8,8),B(8,8),C(8,8)
      DO 1 I=1,L
      DO 1 J=1,M
    1 C(I,J)=A(I,J)+B(I,J)
      RETURN
      END


      SUBROUTINE ADDVEC(X,Y,Z,L)
      DIMENSION X(8),Y(8),Z(8)
      DO 1 I=1,L
    1 Z(I)=X(I)+Y(I)
      RETURN
      END
```

```
      SUBROUTINE MSUBT(A,B,C,L,M)
      DIMENSION A(8,8),B(8,8),C(8,8)
      DO 1 I=1,L
      DO 1 J=1,M
    1 C(I,J)=A(I,J)-B(I,J)
      RETURN
      END


      SUBROUTINE PRINTM (A,L,M)
      DIMENSION A(8,8)
      DO 1 I=1,L
      WRITE(6,200) (A(I,J),J=1,M)
  200 FORMAT(' ',8F15.5)
    1 CONTINUE
      RETURN
      END


      SUBROUTINE PRINTV (A,N)
      DIMENSION A(8)
      WRITE (6,200) (A(I),I=1,N)
  200 FORMAT (1X,F15.5)
      RETURN
      END
```

## CHOICE OF VALUES FOR *T* AND NUMBT

The proper choice of value for $T$ (time increment) and NUMBT (number of terms in the $\varphi$ and $\Delta$ series) is not obvious.[*][†] As a first try, one should probably try to choose $T$ so that $1 < \| \mathbf{A} \| T < 10$, where $\| \mathbf{A} \|$ is defined to be the sum of all the $|a_{ij}|$, that is, $\| \mathbf{A} \| = \sum_{i,j=0}^{n} |a_{ij}|$. However, this may lead to a value of $T$ which is very small compared with the total time for which a solution is required (resulting in KMAX > 100, say). In such a case it will be necessary to magnitude-scale your equations,[*] as is commonly necessary when using an analog computer.[‡]

When choosing $T$, it is also necessary to bear in mind that each input is represented in the computation by a piecewise constant function of periodicity $T$. This may suggest the need for a smaller value of $T$ if one or more inputs are varying rapidly.

When a value for $T$ has been selected, a trial value for NUMBT can be chosen as the greater of 2 and $2 \| \mathbf{A} \| T$.

The last term retained in both the $\varphi$ and $\Delta$ series is printed out by the program. Inspection of these two matrices should indicate whether adequate accuracy has been achieved. If it has not, either $T$ should be reduced or NUMBT increased—or the equations rescaled.

To check the accuracy of your computations, the simplest procedure is to rerun the problem with (say) half the value of $T$. There should not be any significant discrepancy between the two solutions.

[*] M. L. Liou, "A Novel Method of Evaluating Transient Response," *Proc. IEEE*, January, 1966.

[†] W. Everling and M. L. Liou, "On the Evaluation of $\epsilon^{AT}$ by Power Series," *Proc. IEEE*, March, 1967.

[‡] See, for example, Clarence L. Johnson, *Analog Computer Techniques* (New York: McGraw-Hill Book Company, 1956).

We suppose that we are given:

$$\frac{\Theta_F(s)}{R(s)} = \frac{K(s^m + c_m s^{m-1} + \cdots + c_2 s + c_1)}{s^n + a_n s^{n-1} + \cdots + a_2 s + a_1} \qquad m < n$$

In order to solve for $\theta(t)$, we must be given the I.C.'s $\theta(0)$, $\dot{\theta}(0)$, $\ldots$, $\theta^{(n-1)}(0)$, and also

$r(0)$, $\dot{r}(0)$, $\ldots$, $r^{(m-1)}(0)$.

Corresponding to the T.F., we have:

$$\dot{\mathbf{x}} = \begin{bmatrix} 0 & 1 & 0 & 0 & \cdots & \cdot \\ 0 & 0 & 1 & 0 & \cdots & \cdot \\ \cdot & \cdot & \cdot & \cdot & \cdots & \cdot \\ -a_1 & -a_2 & -a_3 & -a_4 & \cdots & -a_n \end{bmatrix} \mathbf{x} + \begin{bmatrix} 0 \\ 0 \\ \vdots \\ K \end{bmatrix} u_1$$

and $y_1 = [c_1 \quad c_2 \quad c_3 \quad \cdots \quad c_m \quad 1 \quad 0 \quad 0 \quad \cdots] \mathbf{x}$, where $y_1(t) = \theta(t)$, and $u_1(t) = r(t)$.

In order to solve for $\mathbf{x}$, and hence for $y_1$, we must know $\mathbf{x}(0)$. We will now show—by example—how $\mathbf{x}(0)$ can be obtained from the given data.

*Example:*

Given:

$$\frac{\Theta_F(s)}{R(s)} = \frac{K(s - z)}{s^2 + a_2 s + a_1} \quad \text{and } \theta(0), \dot{\theta}(0), \text{ and } r(0).$$

The state equation is:

$$\dot{\mathbf{x}} = \begin{bmatrix} 0 & 1 \\ -a_1 & -a_2 \end{bmatrix} \mathbf{x} + \begin{bmatrix} 0 \\ K \end{bmatrix} u_1$$

and the output equation is:

$$y_1 = [-z \quad 1]\mathbf{x}$$

From the output equation,

$$y_1(0) = \theta(0) = -z x_1(0) + x_2(0) \tag{1}$$

Next, differentiating the output equation,

$$\dot{y}_1 = \dot{\theta} = -z\dot{x}_1 + \dot{x}_2$$

Substituting $\dot{x}_1 = x_2$, and $\dot{x}_2 = -a_1x_1 - a_2x_2 + Ku_1$,

$$\dot{y}_1(0) = \dot{\theta}(0) = -a_1x_1(0) + (-z - a_2)x_2(0) + Ku_1(0) \tag{2}$$

Finally, equations (1) and (2) can be solved for $x_1(0)$ and $x_2(0)$ in terms of the (given) $\theta(0)$, $\dot{\theta}(0)$, and $u_1(0)$.

$$\underset{r(0)}{\uparrow}$$

There are several possible approaches to the writing of a system's state equations. Here we will introduce, concisely, a simple and relatively systematic technique.

Assuming that the system may be described in terms of interactions between a finite number of lumped elements, the first step is necessarily to define the elements.

## IDEAL, PASSIVE, TWO-TERMINAL ELEMENTS

Resistance: $v_1 \xrightarrow{i} \overset{R}{\wedge\wedge\wedge} v_2$     $i = \dfrac{1}{R}(v_1 - v_2) \triangleq \dfrac{1}{R}v_{12}$*

Inductance: $v_1 \xrightarrow{i} \underset{L}{\text{⌒⌒⌒}} v_2$     $v_{12} = L\dfrac{di}{dt}$

Capacitance: $v_1 \xrightarrow{i} \overset{}{|}\underset{C}{|} v_2$     $i = C\dfrac{dv_{12}}{dt}$

Dashpot: $v_1 \xrightarrow{\mathscr{F}} \underset{B}{\boxminus} v_2$     $\mathscr{F} = B(v_1 - v_2) \triangleq Bv_{12}$

Spring: $v_1 \xrightarrow{\mathscr{F}} \underset{K}{\text{⌒⌒⌒}} v_2$     $v_{12} = \dfrac{1}{K}\dfrac{d\mathscr{F}}{dt}$†

Mass: $v_1 \xrightarrow{\mathscr{F}} \boxed{M}\text{---} v_2$     $\mathscr{F} = M\dfrac{dv_{12}}{dt}$    ($v_2$ is the constant or zero velocity of an inertial reference)

and so on, for rotational, pneumatic, hydraulic, chemical . . . elements. (see BIBLIOGRAPHY, reference 8)

---

* $\triangleq$ means "equal, by definition."

† More usually, $\mathscr{F} = K(x_1 - x_2) \triangleq Kx_{12}$, but we will find it convenient to differentiate this equation, as indicated.

These relations can be conveniently tabulated as follows:

| ELEMENT TYPE | ELECTRICAL SYSTEM | MECHANICAL TRANSLATION | MECHANICAL ROTATION | FLUID SYSTEM |
|---|---|---|---|---|
| DISSIPATION | $i = \dfrac{1}{R} v_{12}$ | $\mathscr{F} = B v_{12}$ | $\lambda = B_r \omega_{12}$ | $q = \dfrac{1}{R_f} p_{12}$ |
| THROUGH   VARIABLE | $v_{12} = L\dfrac{di}{dt}$ | $v_{12} = \dfrac{1}{K}\dfrac{d\mathscr{F}}{dt}$ | $\omega_{12} = \dfrac{1}{K}\dfrac{d\lambda}{dt}$ | $p_{12} = M\dfrac{dq}{dt}$ |
| ACROSS   VARIABLE | $i = C\dfrac{dv_{12}}{dt}$ | $\mathscr{F} = M\dfrac{dv_{12}}{dt}$ | $\lambda = J\dfrac{d\omega_{12}}{dt}$ | $q = C_f\dfrac{dp_{12}}{dt}$ |

Realizing that our objective is an equation of the form $\dot{\mathbf{x}} = \mathbf{A}\mathbf{x} + \mathbf{B}\mathbf{u}$, we write only the derivative forms of each element's equation. We will not need, for example, the fact that

$$i = \frac{1}{L}\int_0^t v_{12}\,dt + i(0)$$ for an inductor.

## THROUGH AND ACROSS VARIABLES

In the above table we have implicitly defined "through" variables as those which have the same value *throughout* an element and "across" variables as those which depend upon a difference *across* an element. Thus current, force, and flow rate are through variables, while voltage, velocity, and pressure are across variables.

We can then identify "through-type elements" as those whose through variable is differentiated in the defining equation, "across-type elements" as those whose across variable is differentiated, and "dissipation-type elements" as those whose across and through variables are related algebraically.

In general, we may represent a dissipation-type element by:

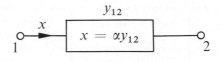

or, more neatly, by the "linear graph segment":

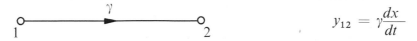

$$x = \alpha y_{12}$$

Similarly, the general across-type element becomes:

$$x = \beta \frac{dy_{12}}{dt}$$

And the general through-type element is:

$$y_{12} = \gamma \frac{dx}{dt}$$

The purpose of this taxonomy is to establish a structure which can be applied to any kind of system—mechanical, electrical, thermal . . . .

## IDEAL, PASSIVE, *N*-PORT ELEMENTS

The elements previously discussed are often called "one-port" elements, in that they have only one entry point. Often, however, we will have to deal with "two-port" or even "*n*-port" elements.

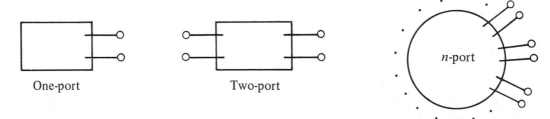

One-port          Two-port          *n*-port

We will limit our discussion to two-ports, and more particularly to two ideal passive elements. First, there is the ideal transformer, which may be represented as follows:

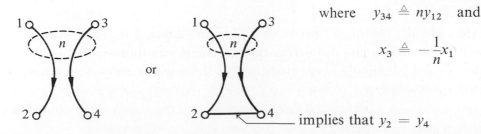

where $y_{34} \triangleq n y_{12}$ and

$$x_3 \triangleq -\frac{1}{n} x_1$$

or

implies that $y_2 = y_4$

The constant $n$ is called the transformation ratio, $x_1$ is the through variable entering terminal 1, and $x_3$ enters terminal 3. As examples we have the lever, the gearbox, and the electrical (ideal) transformer:

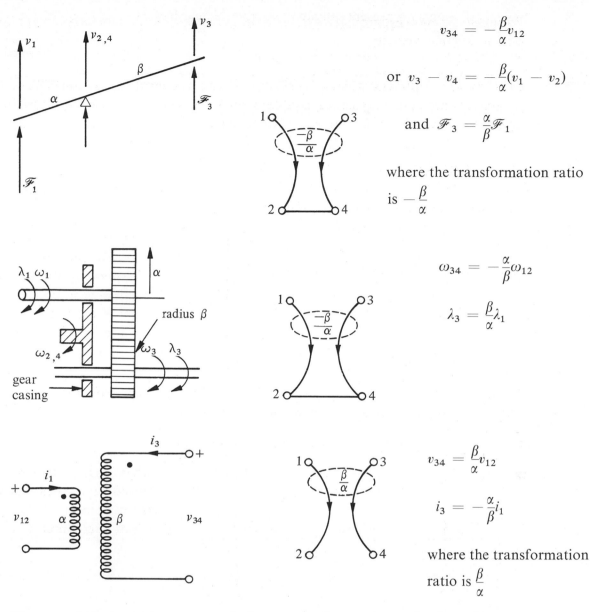

$$v_{34} = -\frac{\beta}{\alpha} v_{12}$$

$$\text{or } v_3 - v_4 = -\frac{\beta}{\alpha}(v_1 - v_2)$$

$$\text{and } \mathscr{F}_3 = \frac{\alpha}{\beta} \mathscr{F}_1$$

where the transformation ratio is $-\frac{\beta}{\alpha}$

$$\omega_{34} = -\frac{\alpha}{\beta} \omega_{12}$$

$$\lambda_3 = \frac{\beta}{\alpha} \lambda_1$$

$$v_{34} = \frac{\beta}{\alpha} v_{12}$$

$$i_3 = -\frac{\alpha}{\beta} i_1$$

where the transformation ratio is $\frac{\beta}{\alpha}$

The second ideal, passive two-port is the gyrator. Its representation is as shown:

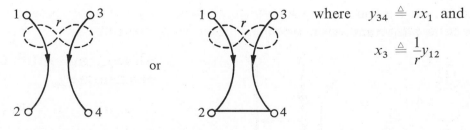

or

where $\quad y_{34} \triangleq r x_1$ and

$$x_3 \triangleq \frac{1}{r} y_{12}$$

The constant $r$ is called the gyration ratio. Notice that the gyrator transforms a through variable into an across variable and vice versa, whereas the transformer transforms magnitudes only—it does not "gyrate."

The most common example of a gyrator is the gyroscope which transforms an applied torque into an angular velocity.

Other more complicated multi–port elements could be considered, as could elements whose parameters are time-varying, or nonlinear, or ones which give rise to partial differential equations. We will not discuss any of these here.

## IDEAL SOURCES

An independent *across source* is represented by:

where $y_{12}(t) \triangleq y(t)$, the *given* source function; $x_s$, the corresponding through variable, will depend upon the remainder of the system to which the source is connected

Examples would be a voltage source in an electrical circuit, an applied velocity in a mechanical system, or a pressure difference in a fluid system.

Similarly, an independent *through source* is represented by:

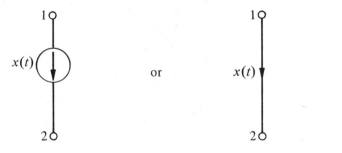

where $x(t)$ is the *given* source function; $y_{12}$ will depend upon the remainder of the system to which the source is connected

For example: an electrical current source, an applied force or torque, or an applied flow-rate.

Next, one has the *dependent* across source:

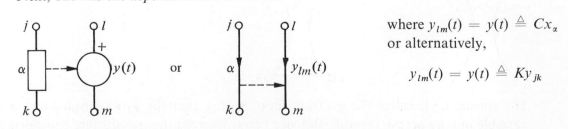

where $y_{lm}(t) = y(t) \triangleq Cx_\alpha$ or alternatively,

$$y_{lm}(t) = y(t) \triangleq Ky_{jk}$$

Notice that the source may be dependent on *either* a through *or* an across variable.

Finally, there is the *dependent* through source:

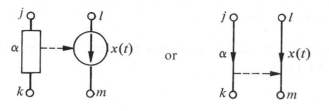

where $x(t) \triangleq Cx_\alpha$
or alternatively,
$$x(t) \triangleq Ky_{jk}$$

## THE GENERALIZED KIRCHHOFF LAWS

Now that we have a framework for considering the component elements of a system, we must obviously proceed to the connected system itself. For example:

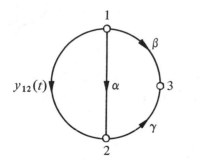

here $y_{12}(t)$ is an across source, and $\alpha$, $\beta$, and $\gamma$ are two-terminal elements; this representation is called a "linear graph"

We now postulate that at any node (or vertex), the incident *through* variables sum algebraically (or vectorially) to zero:

$$\sum_{\text{vertex}} x = 0$$

We will call this "Kirchhoff's through law."

In the above example at node 1:

$$x_s + x_\alpha + x_\beta = 0$$

where $x_s$ is the through variable in the source, and $x_\alpha$ and $x_\beta$ are the through variables in the elements $\alpha$ and $\beta$.

Similarly, equations could be written at the other two nodes.

We can also postulate that the *across* variables around any loop must sum to zero:

$$\sum_{\text{loop}} y_{ij} = 0 \qquad \text{called "Kirchhoff's across law"}$$

Referring to the same example above:

$$y_{12} + y_{23} + y_{31} = 0 \qquad \text{around the loop 1–2–3–1}$$

One may also write:

$$y_{12} + y_{21} = 0 \qquad \text{around the loop } 1\text{–}2\text{–}1$$

It is well known that these postulates are valid in an electrical circuit, and they will also be found to apply in many other situations.

*Example 1*

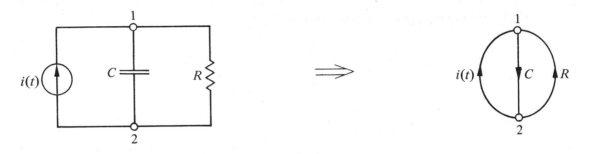

Here the source $i(t)$ is given, as is its reference direction. *However*, the reference directions in the other elements can be chosen arbitrarily. From Kirchhoff's through law at node 1 (or 2):

$$\sum_{\text{node}} i = 0 \qquad \text{or} \qquad i(t) - i_C + i_R = 0$$

But, $i_C = C\dfrac{dv_{12}}{dt}$ and $i_R = \dfrac{1}{R}v_{21} = -\dfrac{1}{R}v_{12}$

Therefore:

$$\dfrac{dv_{12}}{dt} = -\dfrac{1}{RC}v_{12} + \dfrac{1}{C}i(t) \text{ which is the state equation for this simple circuit.}$$

*Example 2*

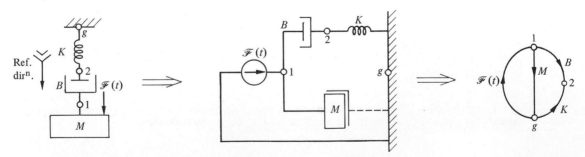

Notice again that the reference direction of the source is given: that is, since $\mathscr{F}(t)$ is shown to be in the same direction as the physical reference direction, $\mathscr{F}(t)$ must be shown *entering* node 1 in the graph. The choice of the other directions is arbitrary.

From Kirchhoff's through law at nodes 1 and 2:

$$\mathscr{F}(t) - \mathscr{F}_B - \mathscr{F}_M = 0 \quad \text{and} \quad \mathscr{F}_B + \mathscr{F}_K = 0$$

And from Kirchhoff's across law around the path 1–g–2–1:

$$v_{1g} + v_{g2} + v_{21} = 0$$

Also, $\quad \mathscr{F}_B = Bv_{12}, \mathscr{F}_M = M\dfrac{dv_{1g}}{dt}$, and $v_{g2} = \dfrac{1}{K}\dfrac{d\mathscr{F}_K}{dt}$

If, guided by the fact that $v_{1g}$ and $\mathscr{F}_K$ are differentiated in the last two equations, we choose $v_{1g}$ and $\mathscr{F}_K$ as states, we can use the other four equations to substitute for $\mathscr{F}_m$ and $v_{g2}$ in terms of the states $v_{1g}$ and $\mathscr{F}_K$ and the input $\mathscr{F}(t)$:

$$\frac{dv_{1g}}{dt} = \frac{1}{M}\mathscr{F}_m = \frac{1}{M}\{\mathscr{F}(t) - \mathscr{F}_B\} = \frac{1}{M}\mathscr{F}_K + \frac{1}{M}\mathscr{F}(t)$$

$$\frac{d\mathscr{F}_K}{dt} = Kv_{g2} = K(-v_{1g} - v_{21}) = K(-v_{1g} + v_{12})$$

$$= K\left(-v_{1g} + \frac{\mathscr{F}_B}{B}\right) = -Kv_{1g} - \frac{K}{B}\mathscr{F}_K$$

Thus we now have a set of state equations for this system in terms of the (physical) state variables $v_{1g}$ and $\mathscr{F}_K$, and the input $\mathscr{F}(t)$. That is:

$$\dot{\mathbf{x}} = \begin{bmatrix} 0 & \dfrac{1}{M} \\ -K & -\dfrac{K}{B} \end{bmatrix}\mathbf{x} + \begin{bmatrix} \dfrac{1}{M} \\ 0 \end{bmatrix}u_1$$

where $\quad \mathbf{x} = \begin{bmatrix} x_1 \\ x_2 \end{bmatrix} = \begin{bmatrix} v_{1g} \\ \mathscr{F}_K \end{bmatrix} \quad$ and $\quad \mathbf{u} = u_1 = \mathscr{F}(t)$

## SYSTEMATIC FORMULATION OF THE STATE EQUATIONS

The choice of states is not always as obvious as in the preceding example. Here we will present—without proof—an algorithm for obtaining a set of state equations in terms of physical variables.

First, we define a "tree" of a linear graph as a subset of the graph elements such that *all* nodes are touched and such that there are *no* closed paths.

For our purposes we choose a special tree,† which

1. includes *all across* sources,
2. includes *no through* sources,

---

† There may be more than one tree satisfying these requirements.

3. includes as *many across* elements as possible, and

4. includes as *few through* elements as possible.

Next we write the terminal equations for all the *across* elements *which are in the tree*, and for all the *through* elements *which are not in the tree*. These equations will define the states as in the previous example. Then one may substitute for all other variables in terms of the states and the inputs. The result will be the state equation.

*Example 3*

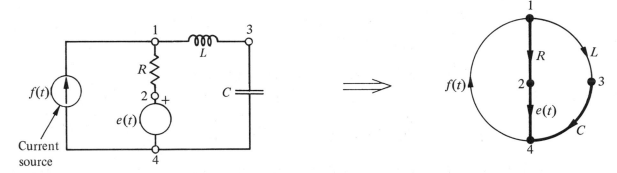

The graph tree has been indicated in heavy lines. It is easy to see that it is the *only* choice of a tree which satisfies the four requirements listed above.†

The terminal equations for across element(s) in the tree, and for through element(s) *not* in the tree, are:

$$\frac{dv_{34}}{dt} = \frac{1}{C} i_C \quad \text{and} \quad \frac{di_L}{dt} = \frac{1}{L} v_{13}$$

$v_{34}$ and $i_L$ will be the states, and it remains to substitute for $i_C$ and $v_{13}$ in terms of $v_{34}$, $i_L$, $f(t)$, and $e(t)$.

Thus:

$$i_C = i_L \qquad \qquad \text{(Kirchhoff's through law at node 3)}$$

and:

$$v_{13} = -v_{34} + v_{24} + v_{12} \qquad \qquad \text{(Kirchhoff's across law)}$$

$$= -v_{34} + e(t) + R\{f(t) - i_L\}$$

$$\therefore \quad \begin{bmatrix} \dfrac{dv_{34}}{dt} \\[2ex] \dfrac{di_L}{dt} \end{bmatrix} = \begin{bmatrix} 0 & \dfrac{1}{C} \\[2ex] -\dfrac{1}{L} & -\dfrac{R}{L} \end{bmatrix} \begin{bmatrix} v_{34} \\[2ex] i_L \end{bmatrix} + \begin{bmatrix} 0 & 0 \\[2ex] \dfrac{R}{L} & \dfrac{1}{L} \end{bmatrix} \begin{bmatrix} f(t) \\[2ex] e(t) \end{bmatrix}$$

(this was the state equation we found in frame **3.8**)

---

† In such cases it is not really necessary to draw the graph. With a little experience the choice of states will be obvious.

**266**

*Example 4*

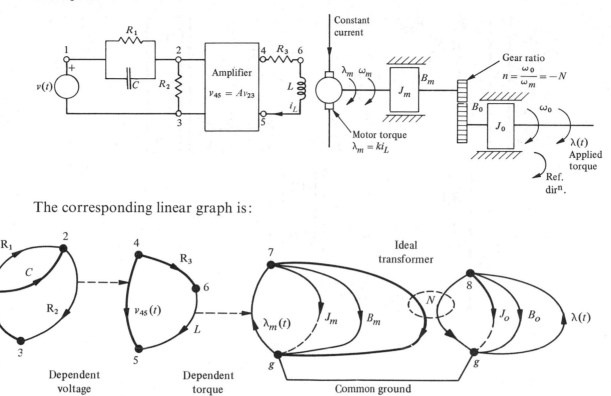

The corresponding linear graph is:

**Note:** When selecting the trees, one side of an ideal transformer *must* be treated as an across source, the other as a through source. The particular choice is arbitrary.

The terminal equations for the across elements in each tree, and for the through elements not in either tree, are:

$$\frac{dv_{12}}{dt} = \frac{1}{C} \, i_C; \quad \frac{di_L}{dt} = \frac{1}{L} \, v_{65}; \quad \frac{d\omega_{8g}}{dt} = \frac{1}{J_0} \, \lambda_{J_0}$$

There are thus three states, $v_{12}$, $i_L$, and $\omega_{8g}$. It remains to substitute for $i_C$, $v_{65}$, and $\lambda_{J_0}$ in terms of the states and the given inputs. It is not hard to find:

$$i_c = -\frac{R_1 + R_2}{R_1 R_2} \, v_{12} + \frac{1}{R_2} \, v(t)$$

$$v_{65} = -A v_{12} - R_3 i_L + A v(t)$$

$$\lambda_{J_0} = -\frac{J_0(B_0 + B_m/N^2)}{J_0 + J_m/N^2} \, \omega_{8g} - \frac{k J_0/N}{J_0 + J_m/N^2} \, i_L - \frac{J_0}{J_0 + J_m/N^2} \, \lambda(t)$$

Whence:

$$
\begin{bmatrix} \dot{v}_{12} \\ \dot{i}_L \\ \dot{\omega}_{8g} \end{bmatrix} = \begin{bmatrix} -\dfrac{R_1 + R_2}{R_1 R_2 C} & 0 & 0 \\ -\dfrac{A}{L} & -\dfrac{R_3}{L} & 0 \\ 0 & -\dfrac{k/N}{J_0 + J_m/N^2} & -\dfrac{B_0 + B_m/N^2}{J_0 + J_m/N^2} \end{bmatrix} \begin{bmatrix} v_{12} \\ i_L \\ \omega_{8g} \end{bmatrix}
$$

$$
+ \begin{bmatrix} \dfrac{1}{R_2 C} & 0 \\ \dfrac{A}{L} & 0 \\ 0 & -\dfrac{1}{J_0 + J_m/N^2} \end{bmatrix} \begin{bmatrix} v(t) \\ \lambda(t) \end{bmatrix}
$$

## BIBLIOGRAPHY

If you want to see more examples and applications, or if you wish to investigate some of the more advanced aspects of state variable analysis, the following references will be helpful:

1. Zadeh, L. A., and C. A. Desoer, *Linear System Theory*. New York: McGraw-Hill Book Company, 1963.

   This should be regarded as the original text on state variable analysis—an advanced graduate text.

2. DeRusso, P. M., R. J. Roy, and C. M. Close, *State Variables for Engineers*. New York: John Wiley & Sons, Inc., 1965.

3. Elgerd, O. I., *Control Systems Theory*. New York: McGraw-Hill Book Company, 1967.

4. Ogata, K., *State Space Analysis of Control Systems*. Englewood Cliffs, N. J.: Prentice-Hall, Inc., 1967.

5. Schultz, D. G., and J. L. Melsa, *State Functions and Linear Control Systems*. New York: McGraw-Hill Book Company, 1967.

6. Timothy, L. K., and B. E. Bona, *State Space Analysis*. New York: McGraw-Hill Book Company, 1968.

These five texts provide the background needed for an advanced study of linear and non-linear systems, sampled-data systems, and optimal control theory. They delve more deeply than does the program into state variable and matrix analysis. The topics considered include the Lagrangian formulation of state equations for physical systems, Lyapunov stability, controllability and observability, and optimal control.

∗ 7. Roe, P. H. O'N., *Networks and Systems*. Reading, Mass.: Addison-Wesley Publishing Co., Inc., 1966.

∗ 8. Shearer, J. L., A. T. Murphy, and H. H. Richardson, *Introduction to System Dynamics*. Reading, Mass.: Addison-Wesley Publishing Co., Inc., 1967.

A more detailed treatment of the material in Appendix 3—on the formulation of a system's state equations—is presented in these two texts.

9. Strum, R. D., and J. R. Ward, *Laplace Transform Solution of Differential Equations*. Englewood Cliffs, N. J.: Prentice-Hall, Inc., 1968.

10. Ward, J. R., and R. D. Strum, *The Signal Flow Graph in Linear Systems Analysis*. Englewood Cliffs, N. J.: Prentice-Hall, Inc., 1968.

These two programmed texts provide an introduction to the Laplace transform and to Signal Flow Graphs—prerequisites to the present program.

11. Rohrer, R. A., *Circuit Theory: An Introduction to the State Variable Approach*. New York: McGraw-Hill Book Company, 1970.

12. Kirk, D. E., *Optimal Control Theory: An Introduction*. Englewood Cliffs, N. J.: Prentice-Hall, Inc., to be published in 1971.

These two recent texts are based on the matrix methods of state variable analysis.

# NOTES

**NOTES**

## LAPLACE TRANSFORM

| $f(t)$     $t \geqslant 0$ | $\mathscr{L}[f(t)] = F(s)$ |
|---|---|
| $A$ | $A/s$ |
| $A\epsilon^{at}$ | $A/(s - a)$ |
| $At^n$ | $An!/s^{n+1}$ |
| $A \cos \omega t$ | $As/(s^2 + \omega^2)$ |
| $A\delta(t)$ | $A$ |
| $2M\epsilon^{\alpha t} \cos(\omega t + \theta)$ | $\dfrac{M\epsilon^{j\theta}}{s - \alpha - j\omega} + \dfrac{M\epsilon^{-j\theta}}{s - \alpha + j\omega}$ |

$$\mathscr{L}\left[\frac{df(t)}{dt}\right] = sF(s) - f(0)$$

$$\mathscr{L}\left[\frac{d^n f}{dt^n}\right] = s^n F(s) - s^{n-1}f(0) - s^{n-2}df/dt\big|_0 - \cdots$$

$$\cdots - sd^{n-2}f/dt^{n-2}\big|_0 - d^{n-1}f/dt^{n-1}\big|_0$$

$$\mathscr{L}\left[\int_0^t f(t)\, dt\right] = F(s)/s$$

## INVERSE OF MATRIX

If $\quad \mathbf{M} = \begin{bmatrix} m_{11} & m_{12} & \cdots & \\ m_{21} & m_{22} & \cdots & \\ & & \cdots & \\ m_{n1} & m_{n2} & \cdots & m_{nn} \end{bmatrix}$

then $\quad \mathbf{M}^{-1} = $ inverse of $\mathbf{M} = \dfrac{\text{adj}\,\mathbf{M}}{\det \mathbf{M}} = \dfrac{\mathbf{C}^T}{|\mathbf{M}|}$

where $\quad |\mathbf{M}| \;=\;$ determinant of $\mathbf{M}$
$\qquad\quad \mathbf{C} \;=\;$ matrix of cofactors of $\mathbf{M}$
$\qquad\quad \mathbf{C}^T \;=\;$ transpose of $\mathbf{C}$

$$c_{ij} = (-1)^{i+j} \begin{vmatrix} m_{11} & m_{12} & \cdots & \cdot \\ m_{21} & m_{22} & \cdots & \cdot \\ & & \cdots & \cdot \\ m_{n1} & & \cdots & \cdot\, m_{nn} \end{vmatrix}$$

strike out the $i$th row and $j$th column

## MASON GAIN RULE

$$\boxed{T = \frac{\sum P_k \Delta_k}{\Delta}}$$

where   $T \;=\;$ actual transmission gain from *an input node* to *an output node*.

$\quad \Delta \;=\;$ graph determinant, formed by striking out terms containing *products* of touching loops from the expression:

$$(1 - L_1)(1 - L_2)(1 - L_3) \ldots (1 - L_j) \ldots$$
$$= 1 - \sum \text{ loop gains}$$
$$+ \sum \text{ products of the loop gains two at a time}$$
$$- \sum \text{ products of the loop gains three at a time, and so on.}$$

$\quad L_j \;=\;$ gain around the $j$th loop
$\quad P_k \;=\;$ gain of the $k$th direct path from input to output
$\quad \Delta_k \;=\;$ cofactor of the $k$th path, formed by striking out from $\Delta$ all terms containing $L$'s which are touched by the $k$th path.